Bullshit
R. P. Blackmur (bum?)
A Critic's Job of Work

NOVELS AND ARGUMENTS

NOVELS AND ARGUMENTS

INVENTING RHETORICAL CRITICISM

Zahava Karl McKeon

THE UNIVERSITY OF CHICAGO PRESS

CHICAGO AND LONDON

ZAHAVA KARL McKEON
is associate professor of English
at DePaul University.

The University of Chicago Press, Chicago 60637
The University of Chicago Press, Ltd., London
©1982 by The University of Chicago
All rights reserved. Published 1982
Printed in the United States of America
89 88 87 86 85 84 83 82   5 4 3 2 1

Library of Congress Cataloging in Publication Data

McKeon, Zahava Karl.
   Novels and arguments.

   Bibliography: p.
   Includes index.
   1. Fiction—Technique.   2. Criticism.   I. Title.
PN3335.M38   808.3   82–2677
ISBN 0–226–56034–1   AACR2

For Richard McKeon

CONTENTS

ACKNOWLEDGMENTS

It gives me great pleasure to be able to thank those who have helped to make this book possible. I am greatly indebted to published criticism, and I have acknowledged that debt in the notes; but I want to mention here Kenneth Burke, whose works initiated my long love affair with literary criticism. I am grateful, too, to Bruce Bashford for his perceptive understanding of what I was trying to do, and for his constructive suggestions. To Wayne Booth, who read the manuscript in an earlier stage and in its final form, I owe special thanks; *The Rhetoric of Fiction* made me see what I wanted to do, while its author offered encouragement and support in the doing. I thank Michael Arnold for proofreading the manuscript and Helen Montgomery for her invaluable help with page proofs and in compiling the index. Finally, I am glad to be able to acknowledge here my intellectual debt to my husband, Richard McKeon, the companion and teacher whose profound learning and broad scholarship have been a never failing resource through the long period of thought and labor that produced this book.

PART ONE

THE FORM OF RHETORICAL CRITICISM

Modes of Discourse—Kinds of Rhetoric

ONE

INTRODUCTION

Literary critics in the twentieth century have turned their attention increasingly to the serious study of prose fiction. The emergence of the novel as the dominant literary genre since the eighteenth century accounts, to a large extent, for this critical interest in it, as do the experiments with form and technique that have characterized the novel's development throughout the twentieth century. While it is probably the case that, to critics, radical technical innovation is intrinsically interesting, it is certainly the case that some twentieth-century novels require considerable skill and effort of any reader if he is to read them through at all, much less with genuine appreciation. Whatever explanations are offered to account for the many experiments with technique, it is not surprising that, for example, *Ulysses* and *Orlando*, or the novels of Gertrude Stein, or those of Robbe-Grillet, Samuel Beckett, and John Hawkes, or Donald Barthelme and Joyce Carol Oates more recently, should engage, indeed demand special critical attention. Distortions in sequence—logical, chronological, and syntactic—experiments with narrative point of view and with language itself, have been a challenge to critics of the novel for the past half century.

However, there have been still other curious developments in the novel. It might have been said, for example, of the early experiments of James Joyce and Virginia Woolf that they represented in some sense the ultimate fruition of naturalism, and were thus recognizable moments in a continuing tradition.[1] The novels of Günter Grass, however, pose a different kind of problem. His technique—in the most general sense—is quite conventional beside that of *Ulysses;* but the tale told by the hero of *The Tin Drum* is both "realistic" and literally fantastic. John Barth writes allegory (it would seem to be that, at least) in *Giles Goat-Boy* and an elaborate parody of an eighteenth-century novel in *The Sot-Weed Factor*. John Fowles has produced a Victorian novel with two alternative endings in *The French Lieutenant's Woman,* and in Muriel Spark's *Memento Mori* death uses the telephone to inform his victims of their imminent departure.

The merging of the "real" and the "fantastic," in the events of a novel

3

as well as in the possibly distorted consciousness of its characters, has become quite common in serious fiction since 1950, and poses its own complex critical problems. On the other hand, the novel has evolved mergings with what we have ordinarily thought of as "fact" in contrast to fiction: thus Truman Capote's "novel" *In Cold Blood,* or Norman Mailer's *Armies of the Night*—an account of the march on the Pentagon—the two parts of which he calls "the novel as history" and "history as a novel."

Finally, there are the novels which do not fuse realism and fantasy, fact and fiction, and do not present technical innovations radical enough to disconcert the experienced reader. Yet even many of these are experienced as problematic in a way that seems to distinguish them from the novels of the eighteenth and nineteenth centuries. Perhaps a single, simple example will help to indicate the kind of ambiguity I have in mind.

Saul Bellow's short novel *Seize the Day,*[2] is a straightforward account of the activities, thoughts, recollections, and feelings during a single day of a man separated from his wife, suffering serious financial difficulties, and desperately seeking a way out of his dilemma. He is a failure according to the conventional criteria he himself shares, and when his fairly wealthy father refuses to help him, he permits a casual acquaintance to speculate on the stock market with the last of his money, and loses it all. At the end of the novel he has wandered into the funeral of a total stranger beside whose coffin he stands weeping hysterically: "The flowers and lights fused ecstatically in Wilhelm's blind, wet eyes; the heavy sea-like music came up to his ears. It poured into him where he had hidden himself in the center of a crowd by the great and happy oblivion of tears. He heard it and sank deeper than sorrow, through torn sobs and cries toward the consummation of his heart's ultimate need." (p. 118).

What does the ending mean? That may seem a simpleminded question, but unless we can appreciate the significance of that ending— which is an ending of the novel, not a resolution or even an implied resolution of the complex and subtle problems that beset Wilhelm—we have not appreciated the novel at all insofar as it is something more than a *picture in words.* This is not to ask what is the "moral" of the story; nor is it to imply that Bellow should have made his meaning clear. It is to say that the concluding paragraph itself implies some kind of insight or illumination which reveals significance in and imparts significance to the sad, banal, and sordid events that precede it. This lack of clarity—the need to interpret not because there is an unmistakable multiplicity of meaning in a work, but because until we interpret in some way we cannot determine whether or not there are multiple meanings—this kind of ambiguity seems pervasive in the twentieth-century novel and will be found in technically traditional novels as well as in those which are highly innovative.[3]

These developments in the novel have produced as their inevitable corollary a variety of critical approaches; but they have also altered radically the critical perspective on novels of an earlier day. It is in contrast with the practice of most eighteenth- and nineteenth-century novelists that Wayne Booth's concept of the unreliable narrator takes on its meaning (*Rhetoric of Fiction,* part 3). He has also noted the current tendency to impute irony to works originally read "straight" (ibid., pp. 367–74). An interesting example of this can be seen in modern discussions of *Moll Flanders.* Critical readers agree that in telling her story Moll quite "unconsciously" exposes the deficiency of her moral consciousness. The question is whether Defoe intended her to do so or simply shared her debased moral standards. If the first alternative is correct, the novel is a masterpiece of irony; if the second, this delightful novel is delightful to us quite accidentally! Agreeing that Defoe probably did not intend the irony, Ian Watt chooses the second alternative: "The accidents of history, then, treated Defoe fortunately," he says.[4] Dorothy Van Ghent, however, cannot concede that great art might be an accident of historical change, in this instance a change in the moral perspective of readers, and she resolves the conflict by suggesting that "a great book could not be written by an impoverished soul, and . . . imponderable traits of moral sensitivity and prophetic intuition might lie in an author and realize themselves in his book without his recognition of them."[5] She grants that this is a guess, but her judgment of the book forces her to assume that it is a good guess. Watt himself is not altogether content with accident, but calls the novel "a masterpiece not of irony but of impersonation" (p. 126), thus rescuing it in another way for its place among literary "classics." Implicit in this issue is the central problem of the critical task of judgment, and both the task and the problem have altered with time.

I have tried to sketch briefly some of the difficulties presented by the novel in the twentieth century, both in itself and in the altered perspective it has engendered with respect to the novel as a whole. If we turn now to criticism to examine in some detail the response to these developments in the novel, we will discover that whereas the widespread concern with prose fiction is a relatively new phase in the long history of criticism, some of the theoretical controversies among critics of the novel are part of a traditional conflict between a view of literature that focuses on the effects produced by a literary work and the means that produce them and on the personality and psychology of the artist, and a view that considers the work as an object, a whole made up of interrelated parts to be studied as a thing in itself regardless of the quality of mind of the artist or of any response the work may or may not evoke in an audience.

Although Plato and Aristotle do not engage in any interchange on the subject, this theoretical opposition appears as early as their treatments of poetry and can be seen in Plato's exclusion of poets from his ideal state on the basis of what poetry *does* because of what it is[6] and, on the other hand, in Aristotle's treatment of the artificial object in terms of criteria which render irrelevant considerations of effect, moral or otherwise.[7] However, we need not rehearse the history of criticism to adduce evidence of this controversy, since twentieth-century criticism offers many examples more immediately relevant to prose fiction.

The terms of the controversy are and have always been ambiguous. The term "poetics" is not uncommon in current criticism of the novel; but I shall try to demonstrate that, despite explicit references to Aristotle as the source of the term, no contemporary criticism of the novel is poetic in the Aristotelian sense. Aristotle's *Poetics* is a treatise on productive science, the science of the artificial object, the made object which comes into existence not because of any internal necessity of its nature but because a poet makes it. Aristotle establishes the natural origin of works of art by observing that men take pleasure both in imitating and in looking at imitations,[8] but the science of poetic is concerned not with the nature of men but with the artificial object; consequently, the psyches of poet and audience are not relevant to poetic. These are investigated in other treatises and in the *Rhetoric*, which is not a science pertinent to a specific subject matter, as the artificial object is the subject matter of poetic, but is an art of inventing the best available means of persuasion in particular circumstances.[9]

Nature, whether the actions of men or natural things, is certainly the object of imitations; but clearly the form imitated is not naturally implicated with the material that embodies it. For example, wood and chlorophyl are not material components of the identifiable tree in a painting as they are in nature. Thus literary works are distinguished from the other fine arts by their means of imitation, which is language.[10] Finally, it is important to note that poetic is, for Aristotle, a science of existing artificial objects, not an investigation of poetry as an abstract concept. He is concerned with form which is, together with structure, an ubiquitous term in contemporary criticism, but it is the form of individual poems, not the form of poetry.

There is currently a lively interest in a poetics of the novel; the critics attempting to develop it are committed to a formal study and are not directly concerned with novelists or audiences. Nevertheless, their conception of poetic departs in three important respects from what I shall call the intrinsic approach of the *Poetics*. First, with regard to the exis-

6

tential status of the object of structural analysis, there is Tzvetan Todorov's account of poetic theory:

> In other words, structural analysis coincides (in its basic
> tenets) with theory, with poetics of literature. Its object is the
> literary discourse rather than works of literature, literature
> that is virtual rather than real. Such analysis seeks no longer
> to articulate a paraphrase, a rational resume of the concrete
> work, but... to present a spectrum of literary possibilities,
> in such a manner that the existing works of literature appear
> as particular instances that have been realized.... It would
> be unable to state the individual specificity of each work.[11]

This approach, quite similar to that of Northrop Frye,[12] in rejecting the
concrete work in its uniqueness as the primary focus of inquiry, must
inevitably assimilate its poetics of fiction to a poetics of literature.[13]

The second departure stems from a radical change, in much current
criticism, in the *conception of language* which is, for Aristotle, the material cause or matter of the literary work.[14] Thus, David Lodge argues
against what he calls "neo-Aristotelianism" from a standpoint which
holds that language is primary:

> I am certainly skeptical of the possibilities of formulating a
> poetics of the novel analogous to that which Aristotle for-
> mulated for the tragic drama of his time... because so many
> of the philosophical assumptions underlying Aristotle's de-
> scriptive apparatus have been undermined.... I am far from
> claiming that the fundamental axiom that novels are verbal
> constructs yields any foolproof or exclusive prescriptions for
> critical procedure. I do believe, however, that if... we try to
> define the novel as a genre by reference to its distinguishing
> characteristics, we shall find its way of using language the
> most promising area for inquiry.[15]

The trend in criticism represented by Lodge is inspired, he has said,[16]
by methods developed by the "New Criticism" for the study of poetry;
its relevance to this discussion arises not only from the prominence of
structure and form in its vocabulary but also from its focus on the
artificial object as verbal construct, a linguistic approach frequently
and, I am convinced, erroneously assumed to be necessarily rhetorical.

Malcolm Bradbury sees the "verbal construct" critics as analyzing
literary works as if they were "a rhetoric independent of writers and
readers."[17] Moreover, leading critics of this school would seem to agree.
Wimsatt and Brooks explain that they use the term "form" "to refer to
all those elements of a verbal composition—rhythm, metrics, structure,
coherence, emphasis, diction, images—which can more or less readily
be discussed as if they were not a part of the poem's 'content,' message

or doctrine. . . . It is all that the old rhetorical theory might call either 'disposition' or 'elocution.' . . . Nevertheless . . . the poetic dimension is just that dramatically unified meaning which is coterminous with form."[18] This is a conception of rhetoric divorced from persuasion, from reference outward to audience; in effect, it makes the study of rhetoric synonymous with the analysis of linguistic devices exclusive of meaning (except insofar as the totality of devices is in itself meaning). I shall try to show later that such a drastic shrinking of the range of the concept of rhetoric must seriously impoverish the criticism of prose fiction. However, I want to stress the point here that this conception of rhetoric is not only a mistaken notion of what rhetoric is; it is also a mistaken notion of what "language" critics like Lodge are doing.

Lodge, as we have seen, believes that it may be impossible to construct a poetics of the novel through language.[19] Linguistic analysis, however, can be as intrinsic or structural as poetic. When Aristotle treats diction poetically, he analyzes it relative to the ends appropriate to artistic production.[20] Not only are sound, rhythm, style, and imagery important, but also the function of the language in establishing necessity and probability, and its appropriateness in relating the thought of a character to his actions. Criteria for judging the various uses of language distinguish the language of poetry from that of rhetoric and the practical and theoretic sciences. The language of rhetoric is closer to that of ordinary speech so that certain words and images and stylistic devices will differentiate between rhetorical and poetic uses; but the element of thought is referred to the *Rhetoric* for discussion since thought is defined as saying what is appropriate to the occasion, and the analysis in the *Rhetoric* will be applicable to the speeches of tragedy (which are imitative of an occasion in which thought would be expressed) with respect to that criterion of appropriateness.

Aristotle's treatment of diction is based on a conception of language as a conventional symbol system, natural in origin, which functions as a rational instrument and varies according to the ends it serves. In this kind of analysis, considerations prior to language are always constitutive. Literary works are not primarily linguistic artifacts but are artificial objects that imitate the actions of men by means of language. The qualities achieved in the work of art determine the criteria for the poetic use of language. The criteria to be applied to rhetorical diction are found "in appropriateness to the effect intended to be produced in an audience."[21]

When language is primary, and the critic intends an intrinsic analysis of a literary whole, let us say a novel, the whole that emerges will not be rhetorical because rhetorical analysis depends on a prior conception of the novel and its parts as in some sense functional for producing an effect. The critic may concede, and usually does, that the novel will

8

produce an effect; however, effect will have no bearing on what it is in itself. Nor will the whole be poetic; there can be no distinction of parts like plot, action, and character since those have no reality outside of the language itself. The resulting structure is grammatical. Linguistic analysis reveals neither the *argument* of rhetoric nor the *plot* of poetic but the *pattern* of a self-contained and self-defining linguistic structure, and this is a grammar.

Meaning in rhetoric depends on the relation of what is said to the end of persuasion, in poetic on the object of imitation. That is, in rhetoric what is said is determined by what one wishes to persuade an audience of; in poetic, thought expressed must make sense as the expression of the kind of character which leads to a given kind of action. In both cases something other than language determines what the words will be. Aristotle can refer in the *Poetics* to the *Rhetoric* for the treatment of thought because, in both persuasion and depiction of action, human character and ideas furnish the criteria for appropriate language. In the grammatical approach to criticism the linguistic pattern itself becomes synonymous with meaning.

Grammatical analysis of imagery, syntax, rhythm, and vocabulary reveals patterns that may perhaps be called "character," "event," "situation," or "attitude." This structure, however, is additive. The "whole" that is the novel is constructed by discerning and putting together the smaller and larger patterns. If one of these seems more persistent than the rest, it may be interpreted as a theme unifying the novel. The patterns give coherence to the structure; the additive method does not seem well adapted for revealing any single unifying principle except by a calculative determination of frequency for a given symbol or pattern of imagery.

The grammatical critic, then, sees himself as opposed not to rhetoric but to poetic. The third departure from poetic occurs in critics who are commited to "poetic" and take Aristotle—in greater or lesser degree—as their model. R. S. Crane, for example, adapted the *Poetics* for dealing with prose fiction. But his discussion of the plot of *Tom Jones*[22] is of a structure of effect-producing parts. The action, character, thought, diction, and narration (the latter replaces spectacle as the manner of imitation in works not presented on a stage), as they are related to one another in temporal succession from beginning through middle to end, are described and analyzed as devices producing a series of expectations, desires, emotions, and satisfactions in the reader.

What is more important, however, is the way in which Aristotle's six parts of tragedy have altered in function. If one were to use Aristotle's method, one would indeed begin with object, means, and manner from which Aristotle derives his six parts of tragedy. However, the subsequent inductive examination of novels or a single novel might yield something other than the six parts Aristotle discovered in the tragedies he examined. Instead of using this method, Crane takes the five parts (omitting melody) and uses them *topically* to discover the structure of *Tom Jones*. Topics are the empty commonplaces of rhetoric; they are variables which take on meaning only when they are given particularity in application. Plot becomes the synthesizing principle for Crane, but whether this principle is in action—as it is for Aristotle—in character, or in thought depends on the particular novel. Plot has lost its univocal meaning of action and become a rhetorical commonplace. The resulting analysis is certainly structural, and the renewed interest in the *Poetics* has been very fruitful for twentieth-century criticism.[23] But it has not produced a poetics of fiction or a productive science of the artificial object.[24]

However, since rhetoric seems to color so many efforts in poetic, is it true to say that rhetoric is an important approach in the current criticism of prose fiction? Let me try to answer that, first of all, by introducing a qualification: if we mean rhetorical in a strictly adjectival sense, it is true. There are rhetorical criteria involved wherever criticism focuses on the relation of the novel to the artist who made it or to the audience which experiences it. If we speak of the intellectual or emotional effects of a novel or parts of a novel on readers, our criticism is to that extent rhetorical. Ian Watt's *The Rise of the Novel* is, it seems to me, primarily sociological criticism. But to the extent to which he tries to determine the effect on eighteenth-century English society of Richardson's novels, he is within the purview of rhetoric. On the other hand, if we ask whether anyone is attempting to develop rhetorics of fiction comparable in scope to the efforts devoted to poetics of the novel, the answer would be decidedly negative.

The lack of critical interest in such an enterprise may seem quite paradoxical in light of the ubiquity of the rhetorical in contemporary critical theory. Yet I think the reason for that lack is, after all, not too difficult to discern. We might try to get at it by examining the one recent example of criticism in which rhetoric seems not an intrusion into or an aspect of an approach basically nonrhetorical but, rather, the focus of the investigation.

In *The Rhetoric of Fiction* Wayne Booth examines fiction as "the art of communicating with readers—the rhetorical resources available to the writer of epic, novel, or short story as he tries, consciously or unconsciously, to impose his fictional world upon the reader" (preface). Surely this is the rhetoric of fiction? But indeed it is not, because the rhetorical resources examined are those of narrative technique; *The Rhetoric of Fiction* is an exhaustive study of point of view in narration, in the telling of a story. As such, it is a brilliant and valuable critical document and has been justly influential. But as rhetoric of fiction it is, like the "intrusions" I have noted, only a partial treatment. However, it provides valuable insight into the question of why there are no full-scale inquiries into the rhetoric of fiction, and it does so in two ways: first of all, although there have been instances in criticism of the traditional rhetorical emphasis on tropes and style, of the general rhetorical considerations of "effect," and of the use as commonplaces of terms borrowed from the *Poetics,* this is the first critical study to use Aristotle's rhetorical concept of the ethical proof, the persuasive function of the orator's character as it is projected in the speech; for clearly, that is precisely what Booth's implied author is. Second, the book opens up a host of interesting problems. As the analysis progresses, it becomes increasingly obvious that point of view, narrative technique, is not the only means by which the author controls the reader's responses. Every fresh example of point of view threatens to exceed its limit and implicate every other aspect of the novel. It is as if, until one analyzes the rhetoric of point of view exhaustively, one cannot recognize that the rhetoric of point of view does not exhaust the rhetoric of fiction.

However, this is not the only problem. When a speech is analyzed in rhetoric, it is taken for granted that the speech is meant, as a whole, to convey an idea and to convince an audience, at the very least, of the correctness, the truth, or the value of it. From the perspective of circumstantial particularity, rhetorical analysis can disclose what the speech (or essay, etc.) was designed to achieve as persuasion and diagnose the causes of its success or failure or probable success or failure in view of circumstances. We can judge the soundness of the premises, whether the speech relies on rational argument or emotional trickery, and whatever our final judgment of the speech and its content, it is always a judgment relative to the end of persuasion in the circumstances envisioned. Thus it is possible to realize that an argument was valid under a set of circumstances that no longer obtains, that it has lost its force for the present circumstances, and to grant that it may perhaps regain its persuasive force in the future. Sometimes the reverse occurs, and the poor rhetoric of yesterday becomes persuasive today.

Poetic, dealing with an artificial object, has no circumstantial criteria. The plot of *Oedipus Rex* is what it is regardless of the philosophic and religious beliefs of the twentieth century. If we say that it is a great play because, despite our different beliefs about fate, responsibility, and justice, it contains human values that are permanent and transcend the temporal circumstances incorporated in its composition, we are making a rhetorical judgment relative to the circumstances of contemporary audiences. In poetic it is great because, to put it one way, of the formal actualization of the potentiality of its parts.

Let me return to *The Rhetoric of Fiction* after what may have seemed a digression. The problem that led to it, however, is one that accounts for much of the critical opposition to the book and may shed some light on the consequences of partial rhetorical analysis as well as on the reasons for its remaining partial. The problem arises from Booth's criticism of objective points of view which leave ambiguous the moral norms of the novel, i.e., leave uncertain the ethical position the reader is meant to adopt. The difficulty is compounded because Booth is himself embarrassed by the ethical criteria he has obviously felt impelled to introduce (p. 372). There are, perhaps, a number of possible explanations for both the criteria and the embarrassment, and more than one may be accurate. But I should like to suggest one that bears directly upon the conflict between rhetoric and poetic which I have been discussing.

If the end of rhetoric is persuasion, it is entirely proper to ask what an audience is being persuaded to do or to believe in a given rhetorical document. Let us consider Booth's example of Robbe-Grillet's novel, *The Voyeur*. Here is his comment:

> The book is a brilliant culmination of more than a hundred years of experimentation with inside views and the sympathetic identification they can yield. It does, indeed, lead us to experience intensely the sensations and emotions of a homicidal maniac. But is this really what we go to literature for? Quite aside from the question of how such a book might affect readers who already have homicidal tendencies, is there no limit to what we will praise, provided it is done with skill? (p. 384)

The comment is about effect, but with respect to what action advocated, what belief? A rhetorical analysis is incomplete unless emotion or feeling evoked is related to the entire argument. Are we meant to learn how it feels to be mad so that we may become more sympathetic with madmen? Are we meant to learn that no one can be sure of the distinction between reality and illusion? Unless we know how Booth construes the argument of the novel, we cannot judge whether or not the skill was exercised on a worthy object.

His judgment is a rhetorical judgment improperly rendered; consequently it is embarrassing as are the other similar judgments in the book. Moreover, not only is it a rhetorically faulty judgment, it is *poetically* inappropriate altogether, and it is precisely in terms of poetic criteria that Booth's analysis is conceived. His treatment of point of view unfolds in a context of plot analysis; his concept of the novel is of a whole made up of interrelated parts. One takes the kind of whole as given and judges whether or not it is fully realized in the interrelation of parts. To ask whether one artificial object is intrinsically more worthy than another is to ask a question which the poetic apparatus is not equipped to answer.[25] The interpenetration of rhetoric and poetic in

12

The Rhetoric of Fiction is responsible for the apparent insolubility of some of the problems it raises.

Why, then, should anyone interested in treating fiction as rhetoric—and that would seem to be what Booth wants to do—choose to do so in the conceptual vocabulary of poetic? Let me try to suggest a possible answer. The several devices of fiction—agents, events, ideas, narration, the resources of language—each of these, whether we make a longer or shorter list, takes on its full significance in the context of the others, their interrelatedness and the work of fiction as whole. Critics who examine that whole, who argue, quite rightly, that to give significance to one part in isolation is to distort its significance, tend to assume that rhetoric and poetic, and especially poetic, must be taken as substantive—that novels may be rhetorical insofar as they do communicate to readers, but that in their essence they are made objects and are the one thing which their makers intend them to be. Therefore, they must be treated poetically; subsequently, we can consider the effects of the whole and the parts poetically determined and poetically significant.

This is to assume that a literary work has one, unambiguous meaning, or identity. It is also to assume that the only kind of wholeness or integral coherence is that of the artificial object of poetic. Neither assumption is true. In the first place a novel is at least four objects: it is an *artificial object,* and as such its structure is a function of the relation of parts to whole, the meaning of "part" and "whole" determined by the object's qualification as an imitation. If the artificial object is treated poetically, one focuses on the action depicted, on the agents who act and their character and thought which move them to act; this focus suggests an analysis of the complications of action and their resolution which reveals, in turn, the relation of parts to whole or the structure of the work, a structure we call *plot* in the poetic critical mode. The artificial object, so treated, is atemporal, static with respect to time, and therefore is unchanged in the history of the criticism of it. There is, of course, time within the plot, which gives the artificial object its static form.

But a novel need not be perceived as an artificial object only. It is also a *natural* object, and, indeed, it may be difficult in an age of experimental science, organ transplants, and "found object" art to conceive of a useful distinction between the natural and the artificial. As a product of human activity and human language the novel is unquestionably a natural object constructed from the natural elements that compose human circumstance. These elements may be the experienced emotions that are crucial to the early critical work of I. A. Richards,[26] the range of feeling denoted and connoted by words; or they may be the elements of language itself that figure as primary in the work of David Lodge. But when the elements composing the novel as natural object are carefully constructed into a whole, the structure of which may be characterized by a linguistic *pattern*, the object has been treated grammatically.

Both as artificial object and as natural object, and whether or not treated poetically or grammatically, the novel is seen as object, independent of its maker or its readers. Nevertheless, the literary work, like the speech, comes into being by means of an author or speaker; and the very existence of literary criticism presupposes reader or audience. If the novel as artificial or natural object remains a thing in itself, the novel is also, inevitably, an *expressive object*; as such it may be seen as not essentially, but only accidentally, to borrow Aristotle's term, an imitation of action or a natural or a verbal construct. Rather it is an expression of the artist's personality and circumstances. It may be analyzed in Freudian terms, as Ernest Jones did *Hamlet*.[27] It may be analyzed as Kenneth Burke does,[28] to disclose a structure of motivation which he calls, in its wholeness, a "strategy for encompassing a situation," a "symbolic action."

Both kinds of analysis are grammatical, a construction of a pattern of meaning from elements purported to constitute human personality and determine human motives. Jones stresses the unconscious and the primal family nexus, Burke a combination of unconscious imperatives shared by all men, and unique personal history, artistic intention and immediate situation. It is this perceived rootedness in the grammatical together with its characteristic emphasis on the primacy of language that has led, it seems to me, to Burke's being taken as part of the "New Criticism" despite his emphasis on biography, so inimical to the New Critics.

For both the Freudians and Burke the artist disclosed by the symbolic action is central, and although the "symbolic" structure remains static, too, it will be articulated as a different whole, and its parts will differ from those of the same work as natural or artificial object. Then, the expressive object may be seen as expressive of the artist's milieu rather than his biography in purely psychological terms. The result may be a sociological criticism like the Marxist criticism of Arnold Kettle.[29] Ian Watt combines sociological, biographical, and rhetorical approaches.[30] But to the extent that these modes are mixed they depart from intrinsic criticism, since a coherent structural analysis of a single work requires a coherent structure of critical terms.

It is also the case that the expressive object is often treated dialectically. As I have noted earlier, for both Todorov and Frye its structure is assimilated to the structure of literature as a whole and can no longer be said to express a particular author, however his personality and creative gift may be understood. But the dialectically determined structure of a work is almost always the structure of an object seen as in some sense expressive because the object is always only an embodiment or reflection of a more comprehensive archetypal whole which it may be said to express.

Finally, the novel is a *communicative object;* aside from its poetic structure, its grammatical structure, and its dialectical structure, it has a communicative rhetorical structure which differs from the others as audience does from art object and both do from author or source. Now if the use of the term rhetoric in this formulation seems unfamiliar, it is not at all surprising. Our conceptions of rhetoric are derived initially from experience in the classroom, and we all know that it has to do with the most skillful use of language, including appropriate embellishments, to convey ones ideas to an audience, in words calculated to evoke the response of a particular audience: thus the injunctions to students to decide *to whom* their essays are addressed. To this end is devoted the study of "composition," used as synonymous with rhetoric, recalled fondly or otherwise from one's freshman year at college. Certainly it is a legitimate sense of the term, and I shall return to it in chapter 2. But it does not by any means encompass the meaning of rhetoric.

However, even in Aristotle's day there was a tendency to treat rhetoric as merely a way of effectively conveying ideas or, to put it as clearly and as bluntly as I can, a way of couching my ideas or opinions in the kind of language most likely to persuade my audience (or readers) to agree with me. Aristotle complained that such an approach omitted the heart of rhetoric:

> Now hitherto the authors of "Arts of Speaking" have built up but a small portion of the art of Rhetoric truly considered; for this art consists of proofs alone—all else is but accessory. . . . [They] are concerned in the main with matters external to the direct issue. Thus the arousing of prejudice, of pity, of anger, and the like feelings in the soul, does not concern the facts, but has regard to those who decide.[31]

Rhetoric "truly considered" has to do with "proofs," structured argument which can move *minds* to belief, rather than simply with the devices—in effect of diction—which arouse particular *emotions* in particular persons. It is with this sense of rhetoric as a structure of argument, of meaning, that I shall be concerned.

Rhetorical analysis of a novel as *communicative object,* then, does not reveal a pattern, a plot, or an archetype (or myth); it reveals an *argument,* and alone of the four, the communicative structure is dynamic. As circumstances and audiences change with time, the rhetoric of the novel changes with time; consequently, the novel as communicative object does not have one structure, but potentially many because effect varies with audience. However, the structures of argument that may be predicated of any novel will be finite in number, and the rhetorical critic must produce an argument that meets the same tests of cogency, the same requirements of evidence that he applies to the arguments he analyzes.

Thus, a novel may be said to be more than one kind of whole depending upon the perspective from which it is contemplated, and rhetoric and poetic, grammar and dialectic are methods or arts by means of which these structural aspects may be examined. The recognition of multiple structures removes the necessity for doing poetic in order to preserve the integrity of a work when the questions relevant to any inquiry are not poetic.

However, a curious paradox remains unresolved. In rhetoric, criteria must be found in reference to audience; how, then, is structural rhetorical criticism possible, since structure is intrinsic to a literary work while rhetoric would seem to be extrinsic, viewing the work in light of criteria located outside the work, in audience? The paradox is not real, but only apparent, and results from a misunderstanding of how audience functions as the source of criteria in rhetoric.

Audience is an extrinsic factor if we think of an orator (or a novelist) deciding to address a particular audience, investigating its background, preferences, beliefs, prejudices, etc., then, on the basis of this information, constructing a speech calculated to appeal to such a group. If we consider the converse of that, the absurdity of the notion should emerge. We might conceive of the critic taking a careful, scientific survey of an audience, calculating the effects of the speech noted (exhaustively, of course—during, immediately following, perhaps a month later—and by means of computer) then examining the speech (or novel) for the elements which produced the effects. The second alternative is obviously absurd, hardly more feasible in the case of an identifiable audience than in the case of the indeterminate readers of a novel. The first alternative is equally absurd; the factors influencing particular human responses are too complex and too uncertain.

Audience as a criterion does not mean that the characteristics of a particular or a general audience are the elements from which a speaker makes his speech. It does mean that the kind of judgment the orator wishes to elicit determines the kind of speech he will make. In book 1 of the *Rhetoric* Aristotle differentiates three kinds of rhetoric by means of three kinds of audience: if the audience required is one that will choose between alternative courses of civic action, the orator frames a speech that will induce it to make that kind of decision, and we have political oratory. If the audience required must judge the guilt or innocence of someone accused of a crime, the speech evokes that kind of judgment and we have forensic oratory. If the orator wishes to have an audience that will admire and applaud his skill as an orator, he makes a speech that elicits praise for itself, and we have epideictic or display oratory.[32] We can broaden these three kinds of rhetoric so that they extend to all deliberation, not only political—to critical judgments beyond the law court, to skillful displays of the way things are, both positive and negative—and the history of rhetoric is, indeed, a history of this extension of its range and significance.[33] What should be understood here is that the orator *makes* his audience; he constitutes it through his speech as the appropriate audience for his purpose.

In book 2 of the *Rhetoric* Aristotle refers to audience a second time, and in this case the emotions of the audience enter into the analysis.[34] Here again, however, the emotions are not those of particular audiences but, rather, the kinds of emotions natural to men. These the orator must use to *constitute* his audience as disposed to be persuaded to decide or judge as he wishes them to. Potentially, all men can be moved to anger, joy, fear, hope, etc. In using the devices that will evoke emotions appropriate to his purposes, the orator makes his audience.

Because the orator makes the audience through the speech, a structural rhetorical analysis is not in fact a contradiction in terms. The orator "makes" the audience by persuading it about something such that the audience, feeling, believing, and therefore judging as a result of persuasion, will *act*—to release a defendant, to award damages, to pass a law or reject it, and so on. The structure of a speech is a structure of emotion and belief. We need, however, to examine that a little more closely.

The structure of a speech considered rhetorically as a mode of persuasion, unlike a scientific demonstration considered relative to its principles and subject matter, cannot be analyzed in itself. The argument must be considered relative to orator and audience. These are the three "modes" or moments of proof that Aristotle distinguishes: the character of the orator (which gives the argument plausibility and authority), the enthymemes and examples (in which the argument is expressed), and the emotions and opinions of the audience (which the argument produces or makes). Since emotions and belief, arising from the feelings of the audience and the thought of the orator, are manifested (in the enthymemes, etc.) as the argument that is the speech, rhetorical analysis, properly conceived, is as intrinsic with respect to a work as are grammar and poetic.

However, it may be objected that a novel is not a call to action as a speech is. Let us accept this objection as valid for the purposes of this argument, setting aside the influence to action that some nineteenth-century novels were meant to have.[35] If we recall Aristotle's comment on epideictic (note 32), we will see that the call to action characterizes two kinds of rhetoric—forensic and political—but not the third. That is, the structure of emotion and belief in forensic and political speeches is made by the orator with respect to what he is *talking about*. The audience feels and believes and judges what it must do about someone's guilt or innocence or the expedience of a political act. In epideictic the audience is not judge but onlooker, and the structure of feeling comes into play with respect to the speech itself. If the audience judges, it judges the speech qua speech, the skill of the orator in other words. Thus, just as Booth could analyze the implied author in all his manifestations without introducing biographical information, it is equally feasible to discover the kind of audience and the kinds of effects a novelist is trying to "make" without resorting to information outside the novel.[36]

What, then, would be the advantage of confronting the problems of the novel rhetorically? I noted earlier that twentieth-century novels have represented a variety of difficulties. Northrop Frye has complained that "novel" is no longer adequate to designate all long prose fictions.[37] The neo-Aristotelians, following Crane (see note 24), distinguished initially between mimetic and didactic literary works. Sheldon Sacks has added another term and postulates three kinds of fictions—apologues, satires, and represented actions.[38] It seems to me not insignificant that he derives an additional term by distinguishing two modes of didactic. I would suspect that an increasing number of novels would be placed in the didactic category by neo-Aristotelian critics precisely because it is difficult to render these novels intelligible and meaningful through poetic analysis as they understand it.

If we approach novels in terms of static categories, they simply defy classification, and the categories begin to multiply, producing still another arena for critical controversy. However, as I have tried to indicate, there is no reason to assume that a novel must be classified as one sort of entity and treated accordingly. All novels are, whatever else they may be, communicative structures. As such they are rhetorical structures, and they all have arguments. Moreover, many of the persistent question elicited by twentieth-century novels are clearly rhetorical insofar as they involve the idea and thought of the whole. What is conveyed by distortions of syntax and sequence? Why do novelists write "eighteenth-century" and "nineteenth-century" novels in the 1960s? In other words, what do such apparent anachronisms communicate or seem to be meant to communicate? What does a novelist mean by giving equal status to the apparently fantastic elements existing side by side with the realistic in a novel? In what sense is a novel history and history a novel?

Questions of this kind have been answered by a host of critics with the blanket assertion that the novels which provoke them reflect a culture of conflicting values, of rapid and often frightening technological advances, and so on. Thus, Scholes and Kellogg can say that "the authoritarian monism of the fully omniscient mode of narration has become less and less tenable in modern times."[39] It seems to me that this rests on the unexamined assumption that eras of the past—specifically the two great centuries of the novel, the eighteenth and the nineteenth—were periods of serene cultural consensus. However, even if we accept the circumstances of the twentieth century as an explanation of the trends in the novel which are under discussion, this kind of explanation evades the critical responsibility of explicating the individual work. Moreover, it fails to account for the rich variety of responses to the alleged common cultural condition; and where the critical answer to some of these questions is not an evasion, it tends to rely not on a fully articulated critical method but on critical insight. Finally, only rhetorical analysis, which allows for mulitple communicative structures or arguments in a single novel, can deal directly and critically with the phenomenon of the change in what a novel communicates that is correlative with change in the circumstances of readers. Critics have never denied the phenomenon itself (although they often seem to find it deplorable); thus commitment to a single approach, yielding a static structure, frequently leads to embarrassment. Either we deny the collective experience of *Moll Flanders*, or we must struggle to find reasons for it. From the perspective of the novel as *expressive* object, there should be no dilemma. We are in trouble only when that analysis must account for the novel's effect two hundred years later. Rhetorical analysis permits a distinction between what is expressed and what that expression communicates, and can deal critically and cogently with the latter.

We need something more, then, than partial examinations of rhetoric variously incorporated in other critical approaches to the novel. Rather, we can and should devise means of dealing with the structure of prose works as communicative objects; that is, we should explore the rhetoric of the novel. Let us consider how this can be done.

First of all, it seems to me that the discussion thus far reveals a twofold problem, one aspect of which concerns the novel itself, while the other involves critical method. I have suggested that, in effect, many of the difficulties that critics encounter in dealing with the novel stem from a confusion of the two—that, for example, the idea of the novel as artificial or natural object or verbal construct leads critics to deny the legitimacy of treating it as communicating meaning (see note 24). However, poetic is not what a novel "is" but a way of treating it as a made object, just as grammar and dialectic treat it as a linguistic or natural or expressive artifact, and rhetoric as an artifact which communicates. These are methods common to literary criticism. There are, of course, many others, a few of which I have already noted.[40]

Theoretically, any discourse may be analyzed and interpreted by means of any method. Newton's *Principia,* for example, is as much an artificial object, a natural object, an expressive object, and a communicative object as is *War and Peace;* in practice, however, poetic has been confined to the examination of belles lettres, plays and poems and stories, whereas rhetoric, oriented outward as it is from the discursive object to communication of meaning, is widely employed, in one form or another in many other fields. Consequently, when we engage in rhetorical analysis, the status of the object of analysis cannot be taken for granted. To put it another way: suppose that, having recognized that there are many critical approaches to the novel, all of which may be illuminating and valuable, we choose to examine it rhetorically since that seems the best way to answer questions of meaning that seem especially germane for the twentieth-century novel. Because we have chosen a method much broader in its practical application than the field of "imaginative literature," we must consider whether the method will function differently with respect to the novel. Thus the notion of "the novel" itself emerges as the second aspect of the problem.

Let me try to clarify it by examining the work of two critics who do use rhetorical methods. I noted earlier that Kenneth Burke treats literary works as expressive objects, i.e., symbolic actions which are the strategies of their authors "for encompassing a situation." I want to call special attention here to the symbolic action or literary work as pointing to an underlying structure of motivation; for Burke, we understand that literary work only when we grasp the underlying motive which produces it. In effect, then, Burke uses rhetorical commonplaces, pairs of contraries or contradictories, to disclose the motivational structure or strategy he is seeking. But his concern with underlying motives, the careful construction of them through statistical analysis of the elements into patterns of imagery,[41] is clearly grammatical; thus he gives us a mixture of grammar and rhetoric analogous to R. S. Crane's mixture of poetic and rhetoric. Furthermore, all of the structures men make are strategies: philosophic systems, constitutions, scientific theories, etc., as well as works of art. We would expect, then, that independent of the rhetorical method Burke would be primarily concerned with motive. We would also expect it to be of secondary importance whether the symbolic action were what we call a novel, a poem, or a play, and this is indeed the case in his criticism.[42]

Wayne Booth, on the other hand, limits his discussion to prose fiction and, in fact, to the novel. Yet, curiously enough, his conception of the novel has in common with Burke's a locus that finally attenuates the significance of genre distinction. He does not see the novel as a motivational structure, and is not concerned with the author's psyche. The novel is rather an embodiment of values, and the value system of a

novel is its real meaning and its fundamental being.[43] Indeed, embodiment is again the "reflection" of dialectical criticism. For Frye the
work embodies myths which are timeless, therefore unchanging and
prior to and clearly transcending an individual, historically placed
work; for Booth it embodies values which share these same characteristics of timelessness. Thus we get a mixture of dialectical with rhetorical
criticism in Booth's work as well as the admixture of poetic which we
discussed earlier. Most important, however: despite their absence in
the discussion, a philosophical essay and a treatise on politics can also
be said to embody a system of values.

It is instructive to see how the rhetorical method functions for both
Burke and Booth. Since Burke recognizes that men share a common
underlying nature, he can focus on the literary object as expressive on
the assumption that what we share in common with the artist guarantees communication. The critic's job is to explicate the motivational
factors unique to the artist, so that rhetoric as a means of discovery is
central. For Booth, the object as communicative is the central critical
focus since the communication of values cannot be taken for granted as
either phenomenally self-evident or naturally guaranteed. But in both
cases the conception of the novel as embodying values or motives is
such that novels are not distinguishable, with any precision, from other
linguistic artifacts. Because Booth focuses on communication, his position is peculiarly difficult. The rhetorical method, universally applicable
to any subject matter in theory and, as it happens, in practice as well,
does not of itself distinguish novels from speeches; it discriminates
perspectives rather than making substantive distinctions. Thus Booth
seems inevitably to demand the same mode of communicating meaning, the same kind of unequivocal clarity from the novel that one ex-
pects in a treatise: "Any story will be unintelligible unless it includes,
however subtly, the amount of *telling* necessary . . . to make us aware of
the value system which gives it its meaning."[44] Finally, one might
argue that whatever a man projects as his vision of the way things are,
such projections are made from inevitably limited and consequently
distorted perspectives. In that case, philosophies and novels are equally
fictions; and, indeed, existentialists have written their philosophies in
novels, plays, and treatises.[45] There would seem to be little reason,
then, for treating the rhetoric of the novel as different from the rhetoric
of anything else.

It seems to me that the positions I have touched on have considerable
merit, and throw light on the complexities of human discourse in their
several ways. Nevertheless, I am convinced that from these positions
we cannot deal adequately with the problems posed by the novel in the
twentieth century. And these problems, generated initially by the
("novel") techniques and subject matters of novels written in the twen-

tieth century, have radically altered our way of looking at novels written earlier. Thus we are concerned with the novel itself, whatever that may mean, because from the standpoint of the twentieth-century reader all the novels he reads are twentieth-century novels, and our conclusions must be applicable to any works said to be novels, regardless of when they were written.

Let me suggest finally that despite the theoretical cogency of a position which collapses the distinction between the novel and other modes of discourse, we almost always *know experientially* the difference between a novel and a treatise, and we cannot deal adequately with the rhetoric of the novel without intellectually validating that distinction.

Recognizing, then, that a novel is not a forensic or political speech, yet is like an epideictic speech in which an onlooker or observer judges the speech itself, and that a novel conveys a meaning through a structure of argument in sequential and consequential discourse, in the following inquiry I shall use traditional conceptual resources of rhetoric to discover the kinds of arguments that characterize novels, and to find a way of distinguishing novels from other discursive wholes, as well as distinguishing the genres of the novel. Finally, since the communicative structure alters with circumstance, I will try to discover in the light of new circumstances aspects of the novel thus far unrecognized.

TWO

ABOUT FICTIVE ARGUMENT

It would seem to be useful at this point to gather together the strands of the inquiry that have been separated thus far. We have seen that all critics have a conception of *what* a novel is, and that this conception conditions the critic's treatment of novels. The novel may be seen as an object or product, a whole unifying parts; it may be seen as an object reflecting an underlying nature, a symbolic construction from parts; it may be seen as an embodiment or synthesis of values (indeed, the myths or archetypes of some critics are usually interpreted as narrative expressions of value); finally, it may be seen as an object of formative intention, an expression of intent which is, in turn, experienced by others because the intention is objectified.

We have also seen that critics use arts, and since the art a critic chooses needn't be determined by what he takes a novel to be, there is always complex interaction between *what* he looks at in a novel and *how* he looks at it. Such complexity leads to a richly rewarding diversity among critics, and our appreciation of literature would be poorer without it. However, I am concerned here with rhetorical criticism, which seems always to be practiced only in conjunction with other arts or disciplines regardless of what the novel is seen to be fundamentally.

In one sense, of course, "mixtures" of method are quite understandable; they are evidence of a critic's perception that every novel is not only the object he believes it is but also the objects all other critics believe it to be as well. Thus, for example, as I pointed out earlier, Kenneth Burke constructs a pattern grammatically, but rhetorical commonplaces discover the elements that will compose the pattern, and Wayne Booth treats a unified whole poetically to find the parts and their interrelation in which an image of values is dialectically discerned and the way the values are transmitted is rhetorically determined. This sort of thing occurs because all novels are products of art, expressing human nature and values and the intentions of the particular persons who made them, and all critics know that they are and must account for them as such in their critical interpretations.

They do that in one of two ways, or both: they risk a certain loss of cogency by using two or more methods simultaneously, as I have just indicated, or they postulate the relevance for criticism of only *one* aspect of the novel. Aristotle discussed values, nature, and psychology in other treatises, devoting *Poetics* to the made, artificial object itself. Today, Tzvetan Todorov frankly begs off from saying anything about a particular work, and David Lodge says that criticism can be concerned only with language because there is nothing else in a novel. R. S. Crane used poetic and rhetoric, but considered questions of meaning with respect to the whole of a novel illegitimate, and when such questions became importunate, he termed the works which inspired them "didactic." Kenneth Burke can ignore audience because the artist's underlying nature is like that of his audience. The mixtures of method risk incoherence; the arbitrary limitation of subject risks aridity and sometimes triviality.

There is, however, considerable advantage in using rhetoric alone, without admixture of the others, as a critical method. First of all, whereas poetic, grammar, and dialectic tend to deal with a work of literature as primarily artificial, natural, or expressive object, rhetoric points to it as communicative object. This means that aspects of the work seen as external to it by other methods can be found in the work itself as a fictive or made argument. That is, the author who is irrelevant to a poetic or grammatical analysis of an independent, self-contained object becomes the ethical proof in rhetoric and thus part of the argument of a work analyzed rhetorically. The audience, external and irrelevant to poetic and grammar, and also to dialectic which treats an embodiment of unchanging myths or values, is source of proof in rhetoric through its emotions and thus also part of the argument of a literary work. The meaning of the argument itself, the thought of the speech as "whole," is irrelevant for poetic, but it is the structure of a work analyzed rhetorically.

What, then, is an argument? From the perspective of communication, rhetorically, anything we experience, anything we see or hear, do or read, or think about, or say, can be interpreted in a great many ways, each one of which is an argument; that is, a structure of communication is an argument, and it is arguments that convey meaning. All attempts to render meaningful, i.e., to interpret, the chaotic incidents of experience by means of structure are arguments, and, consequently, all arguments are fictive. They are made just as the arguments of works we call novels are made. This is true not only of arguments like modes of literary criticism, for example, that interpret discourse. Railroad tracks and buildings, paved roads and street signs, supermarkets, their aisles and shelves arranged in special patterns—all are fictive arguments, which make particulars by relating variables such that they take on meaning by being made manifest as a connected flow.

24

Railroad tracks by their simple presence impose meaning on a stretch of space; they constitute it as part of a continuum between a "somewhere" and a "somewhere else." Paved roads and street signs perform similarly, while supermarkets make a myriad of objects into particulars of a certain kind in complex interrelation with other objects so constituted. These are arguments which make discrete experiences possible for us; without fictive arguments we would perhaps experience signals, but we would be unable to make sense of them, to identify particulars as such and such. It is difficult to find ways of illustrating because in fact we ourselves make fictive arguments all the time, even when we do not come upon the road signs and supermarkets which, subsequently, we interpret in order to make sense of them, too. One might say that experience without fictive argument would be like listening to an unknown foreign language. One cannot even affirm that the sounds are a language, but one is experiencing sounds. The analogy is not, however, apposite because we interpret the situation and make sense, if not of the sounds, then of our plight in listening thus helplessly to them.

What is important is that the fictive arguments, whether street signs or histories, are not "about" experience. Rather, any one of them will constitute *an* experience; fictive arguments invent not only statements but also all that is involved in statements: their subject matters, their authors and audiences, the ideas they express, and the things they present.

So, too, the structures of behavior in individual lives, and the lives of communities of men and women, are fictive arguments, like the arguments of philosophical, psychological, or political theories, or novels, which give coherence to human experience; just as the arguments by which we read those same works of discourse as we experience them are fictive arguments that render them coherent and therefore communicative structures. Finally, verbal discourse, insofar as it can be said to convey meaning, does so because it is *consequential*. As a first step, then, in investigating fictive argument, we must explore the ways in which discourse is rendered consequential.

Of course we will hope to find more than one way since we have assumed that rhetoric, seeking communicative structure, takes its departure from audience, and audiences change with time; thus rhetoric always postulates more than one communicative structure for any discursive whole. And, of course, our hope is well founded since to start us off in our inquiry we have an old tradition which holds that discourse is divided into four parts—exposition, description, narration, and argument. Modern textbook anthologies for the teaching of rhetoric are organized in a variety of ways, but this four-part distinction of modes emerges at some point in most of them, and a great many are arranged in accordance with it. In a discursive sequence we can explain something, tell what something is like in terms of our perception of it, give an account of a series of events or occurrences of some sort, or make out a case for one position as preferable to another. In these very general terms, that would seem to exhaust the function of extended written discourse.

However, after the modes of discourse have been distinguished from one another and characterized, some difficulties arise. To get at these, let us consider the treatment of some authors and editors of rhetoric anthologies and handbooks who give prominence to the four modes of discourse. Jerome W. Archer and Joseph Schwartz devote sections 2–5 of a seven-part division to exposition, argument, description, and narration:

> The organization of this anthology of readings remains tra-
> ditional in that the bulk of the book is concerned with an
> examination of the major forms of discourse—exposition, ar-
> gument, description and narration.[1]

Cleanth Brooks and Robert Penn Warren, who combine an anthology with a grammar, composition, and mechanics handbook, devote a special section to the four modes of discourse, reserving the readings to a separate section organized in terms of ad hoc genres. After explaining the four modes and the fact that they are never "pure," they go on to say:

> At this point the student may well ask: "What becomes of the
> notion of a kind of discourse as the main intention if the
> kinds are so mixed up in ordinary practice?" This is a rea-
> sonable question, and the answer to it is fundamental. *In a
> good piece of writing the mixing of the kinds of discourse is never
> irresponsible. There is always a main intention, a fundamental
> purpose*. . . . But always, in any piece of writing, the writer
> should know what his main intention is, whether he wants
> chiefly to explain, persuade, describe, or narrate.[2]

Robert W. Daniel, in a combined grammar, composition, rhetoric text similar to that of Brooks and Warren, offers five very brief selections, which he then uses illustratively throughout the text:

> If you assume that a given piece of writing belongs to one of
> the modes and to no other—that a mixture of the modes is
> exceptional—you will be quite mistaken. . . . When we say
> that a work belongs to a certain mode, we mean that mode
> *predominates* in it. Calling "The Blue Hotel" a narrative is
> equivalent to saying that its most important aspect is its
> narration—and, for purposes of classification, never mind its
> descriptive passages. For this reason, the terms themselves

26

are sometimes combined; you may call a work "descriptive exposition," for instance, if you mean that it is predominantly expository, with description also figuring in it.[3]

The texts I have just cited are typical of those that treat of the four modes of discourse to any considerable extent. Authors of such texts agree that the four modes of discourse are, in fact, always mixed; they agree that it is nonetheless possible to find relatively pure examples for systematic analysis. Above all, they seem to agree that classification and analysis according to the four modes are possible and useful because, while the modes are always mixed, one of them is always dominant.

However, there are at least three respects in which these treatments of rhetoric seem to me to raise serious difficulties: their approach to description; the basis upon which they determine the rubrics applicable to their selected texts; and the fact, obvious from the headings in tables of contents (and sometimes explicitly stated) that they do not all agree that the four modes are exhaustive.

Let us begin with the first point. The authors I have quoted, and most others who write and edit this kind of text, contend that description is a subordinate mode; that is, it is never the dominant mode of any piece of writing but, rather, supportive of one of the other three. The most interesting formulation of this position occurs in Daniel:

> The peculiar status of description stems from the contradictory nature of the human mind: while it is impossible to know anything without to some extent abstracting from reality, most people's minds are uncomfortable with abstractions and long to return to the concrete. (Confronted with a puzzling explanation, we say automatically, "Can't you give an example?") Pictures and popularity go together; the most widely sold books are comic books, and the most popular literary forms are novels and biographies, which are mainly occupied with picturing action. But as anything entirely concrete would be without significance, a piece of pure description would have only limited interest. (p. 175)

One wonders whether Daniel would consider a painting, surely "a piece of pure description," to be insignificant. Daniel differs from the others, however, only in being more explicit. They all agree that description alone does not communicate meaningfully. Much more important, of course, is what his formulation reveals about the prevailing conception of the four modes of rhetoric as a whole.

The second difficulty, at first glance unrelated to the question of description, has to do with criteria for determining what is the dominant mode of discourse in a given case. Archer and Schwartz pose questions that determine the author's intention:

Did he wish to give information, clarify meaning, or explain an idea? Did he wish to influence the reader to accept a certain point of view or a particular attitude, or to assent to one possibility among many? Did he wish to give the reader a word picture, a verbal representation, to capture direct experience through sense impressions? Did he wish to tell what happened as a result of a sequence of events? As we answer each of these questions affirmatively, we discover a different primary intention. Each intention corresponds with one of the traditional forms of discourse—exposition, argument, description, and narration. . . .

In most writing, intentions are mixed; seldom do we find a pure form. But in any mixture brewed by a responsible writer, the reader can discover a primary intention or purpose. Each fulfills for the writer some fundamental need in his desire to communicate. Also, although a mixture of forms ordinarily is found in any piece of writing, each form is best studied in isolation. (p. 39)

Daniel doesn't stress intention but says, rather, that a work contains "writing" of one sort for the most part (p. 166), while Brooks and Warren do emphasize intention (pp. 38–39). However, it is difficult to grasp a clear notion from any one of the three books cited, a way of deciding how to classify a single work except by perceiving that there seems to be a lot more explanation than there is story-telling in it, and so on.

An examination of the readings listed under the four rubrics is only a little more enlightening. Brooks and Warren, at the end of their own explanatory sections, refer the student to selected readings in the anthology section. Interestingly enough, the references are consistently directed to *parts* of any essay, to a given paragraph, or to devices, rather than to the reading as a whole (e.g. pp. 120, 191, 225, 266).

Daniel's book is almost entirely explanatory; he quotes selected passages throughout for illustrative purposes. Archer and Schwartz, whose book is wholly an anthology accompanied by brief introductory essays for each section, list expository essays under the traditional rubrics of cause and effect, comparison and contrast, classification and division, etc. It is not always easy to determine, however, why a given essay appears under exposition and not under argument, and of course the reverse. For example, "The Story of Service," by Jessica Mitford, is listed under exposition, process analysis. It is taken from *The American Way of Death*.[4] Since the selections under argument seem to be chosen because their subject matters are, or once were, controversial ("A Modest Proposal" is also there; also pairs of essays, each of which reflects a point of view apparently opposed to the other, although their authors may well have written them simply for explanatory purposes), it is hard to see Miss Mitford's discussion of undertakers' services as intended

(Archer's and Schwartz's criterion) to be an analysis of a process.

Their selections under description are consistent with the belief that it is a subordinate mode; they are taken for the most part from longer works of fiction. Archer and Schwartz, moreover, find it necessary to add categories of classification. They have a section on personal narrative (which apparently does not seem to them to belong under narrative "proper") that is divided into factual and fictional; and they have a section on familiar essays and reviews ("Some Additional Patterns: Special Types") that presumably do not simply explain, argue, narrate, or describe.

Finally, a most interesting anthology in terms of its principles of classification is called *Rendezvous: A Prose Reader,* by John J. McShea and Joseph W. Ratigan.[5] McShea and Ratigan wish to use only selections pertinent to literary studies. Their arrangement is in strict accord with the four modes of discourse; they have four sections, each preceded by a discussion of the mode to be illustrated in the following selections. What is unusual is the way the exposition section is set up and what it contains. Not technique but content seems to determine the subsections under exposition. Comparison-contrast, cause-effect— these are gone, and in their place are essays under art ("Art Criticism"), literary criticism, drama, reviews, diversions (these are humorous essays), personal essays, and a long opening section entitled "Biography and Autobiography" (which includes Theophrastus). Why have biography and autobiography, usually classified under narration, become expository? McShea and Ratigan have perfectly good reasons: "Exposition is that type of writing which explains or clarifies whatever it is considering. . . . In the most explicit sense of the term the biographer *explains* best when he selects the most enlightening events and evaluates them intelligently." (p. 1)

I have tried to explore in some detail these few examples of current treatments of the four modes of rhetoric because they illustrate a problem analogous to the one I discussed earlier with respect to modes of literary criticism. The need of Archer and Schwartz to include additional patterns, of Daniel to add a fifth mode, the dramatic, of all of these authors (McShea and Ratigan concur, p. 221) to insist that description is intrinsically a subordinate mode—these are symptomatic, it seems to me, of a tendency to treat a process as if it were an entity. (McShea and Ratigan are simply idiosyncratic in their treatment of biography, and do not seem to recognize what their arrangement implies.) All these writers see the modes of discourse as somehow substantive. Thus, they can speak of "mixed modes" which are literally contained in varying quantities in a literary text. The predominant mode seems to be the mode that is present in greatest quantity. A well-organized work has the subordinate mode gracefully distributed in the interstices of the dominant. To put it another way, if there is more explanation in an essay than there is "telling what happened" or "arguing" that A is better or truer than B, then the "telling what happened" part and the "arguing" part are interpreted as functioning in support of exposition which is seen as the organizing mode. Yet, aside from its quantitative superiority, it is hard to see in these treatments of rhetoric how the so-called dominant mode does in fact characterize a given text.

It is important to keep in mind that rhetoric is not a system of categories for the classification of substances. It does not have to do with things and their fixed properties; nor does it deal with fixed intentions imbedded in entities called literary texts. I suggested earlier that since narration in poetic is a part of the art object, the "telling" in novels or epics, etc., that corresponds to spectacle or direct presentation in plays, it is not the same as the ethical proof in rhetoric, the author as invented in the text and functioning as part of the argument. Even this formulation is inaccurate; from the perspective of audience there is no fixed text until we construe an argument and thereby make a text. From the perspective of audience, we are examining an ongoing activity in which perceivers make particulars and render them consequential by means of their structured interrelationship. Particulars are simply variables that can be interpreted only by virtue of relations to one another in some mode of connection. Therefore, the four modes of rhetoric are not categories of existent things. It is treating them as such that leads to the recurrent need for new and different categories and to the confusion attendant upon the obviously common experience that no literary text ever seems to belong unequivocally to a single category.

What is being experienced as "mixed modes," it seems to me, is not what the phrase implies. A discursive whole, as artificial or expressive object, may be seen to have a single structure to be discovered by those who examine it. They will disagree about these structures precisely when they are convinced that only one formulation can be correct—an object is what it is; an author expressed in his work what he intended to express or what he himself was. But what is communicated varies with circumstances. When the writers on rhetoric experience mixed modes, they are responding intuitively to the fact that a variety of arguments might interpret the text as communicative object, while formulating that response in terms of a nonrhetorical perspective which reduces the many arguments roughly perceived as possible to quantitative parts of a stable, fixed entity.

Both the "mixed modes" and the multiplication of categories, on the other hand, are an astonishing echo of the theory and practice of literary criticism translated into a pedagogy—albeit a pedagogy which radically reduces the conceptual richness of literary criticism. For it is the case that the methods, mixed and unmixed, used often brilliantly and productively by literary critics in order to do justice to both form and content in literature and to the unique internalities of works and their persistently engaging referential aspects, are the same critical methods transformed, flattened and petrified into exposition, description, narration and argument to fit a pedagogy that had completely desiccated the art of rhetoric and made it synonymous with language or discourse alone until the second half of the twentieth century.

This curious sort of identity can be clearly seen if we consider the arts or methods of criticism side by side with modes of discourse. A dialectical criticism explains how any manifestation of discourse must be assimilated to a mythic or value structure embodied in it. That is the way in which dialectical criticisms interpret literary works (or, rather, "literature"). Exposition assimilates cause and effect, classification, definition, and so on to itself. It is the "explaining in terms of something else" method which bears the analogical stamp of its dialectical origin. The art or method of grammar interprets literary works by accumulating the stuff of the nature of things as does the mode of description. The agents who act and do what they do to change what was into what will be in resolving their complications in poetic arts or methods of interpretation reappear in the mode of narration. Only the art of rhetoric, curiously enough, is not echoed in the translation to argument, since the reduction of its scope to the study of tropes has characterized the rhetoric of literary critics (Booth is a notable exception). As the mode of argument, rhetoric is once again the primary mode of reasoned discourse.

It is because rhetoric as mode of argument restores to the art of rhetoric its full methodological resources that we can reexamine and revise our estimate of the modes of exposition, description, and narration and recognize that although they are identical with the arts of dialectic, grammar, and poetic, they are also quite different. As modes of discourse, as *rhetorical* methods, they are the various arguments, giving the thought of the whole, which function as parts to be unified in any interpretation of a discursive whole. To put it another way, a whole is dialectically unified through parts which are complete instances of the whole which is itself, in turn, an instance of the macrocosm. A grammatically unified whole has been constructed of parts which are indivisible elements. Poetic unifies parts which are themselves structures different from one another. Rhetoric unifies parts which are dialectical, grammatical, poetic, and rhetorical arguments.

In order to discriminate those three rhetorical arguments from the three modes of criticism they resemble, we will treat them rhetorically as exposition, description, and narration and the rhetorical argument as, of course, argument. We must begin by examining the modes of discourse as modes of organization, recognizing that exposition, description, narration, and argument are not things with properties, to be discovered in other things called texts; rather they are modes of connection, ways of relating variables so that the latter may take on particularity and consequence by virtue of their structural interrelations. Instead of discovering the nature of kinds of things, we will invent arguments, keeping in mind that any discursive whole can be read and interpreted expositorily, descriptively, narratively, and argumentatively; and finally keeping in mind as well that until we have invented an argument or reading, from the perspective of communication there is, in fact, no intelligible discursive whole at all.

Let me begin by formulating an argument according to a *causal* model in order to focus attention on a sequence as consequential: *As* the course of war depends in part on natural causes and on the ambitions and hopes of states and individuals, *so* when the ambitions of men lead to the neglect of basic realities, disaster results. Before commenting on this argument, let me offer another: *As* the way of life of a strong, intelligent man depends in part on natural causes and on his own ambitions and hopes and those of other persons, *so* when ambitions lead to the neglect of basic realities, disaster results.

First of all, these two arguments are clearly variations on a theme; but the theme cannot be specified since to attempt to do so is to produce still another variation. However, it can be seen that I have, in each case, composed elements into a structure that is not viable because it violates reality, i.e., the very nature of things. I might read these by moving another way, that is, by building a viable structure instead. Let me illustrate by constructing such a variation of the first argument: *As* the ambitions of men often lead to neglect of basic realities, *so* the defeat of those ambitions in war is an apparent disaster but a real victory. The second argument can also be varied in the same way: *As* ambition leads a man to betray natural needs by denying them, *so* the frustration and relinquishing of ambition are an apparent disaster but a real triumph.

In the case of both arguments, I have begun with elements and constructed a whole. The mode of discourse by means of which one does this is the mode of description. Elements are connected in sequence to produce "pictures." The first argument in each pair I will identify as variant arguments for reading Thucydides' *Peloponnesian War,* the second for Shakespeare's *Antony and Cleopatra.* To begin with, it is important to keep in mind that either text can be read by means of the other three modes, but with that qualification in mind, let me try to elaborate these arguments somewhat in order to show that the structures have been justifiably articulated. In *The Peloponnesian War,* Thucydides gives an account of the war that eventually destroyed the civilization that produced some of the greatest intellectual, political, and cultural achievements of mankind. After briefly recounting the early history of the Greeks, Thucydides distinguishes between the grounds of complaint and points of difference which were the immediate cause of the war and what he takes to be the real cause, "the one which was formally most kept out of sight. The growth of the power of Athens, and the alarm which this inspired in Lacedaemon, made war inevitable. Still it is well to give the grounds alleged by either side, which led to the dissolution of the treaty and the breaking out of the war."[6] The power of Athens was the result of the strength of character of the Athenians, adumbrated in the funeral oration of Pericles, combined with their fortunate material circumstances, a result of their position as a maritime people. This strength didn't save them from military disaster; Thucydides tells us why when he discusses the plague at Athens and Pericles' virtues as a leader. In brief, the Athenians, contrary to the advice of Pericles, embarked on projects that could be advantageous only to private interests and ambitions at the expense of Athens as a whole and her allies (pp. 109–21).

Obviously, from this perspective, I have read Thucydides as building a picture of Athens, the Athenians and their circumstances, and showing how the opposition of Sparta and its allies provoked responses from Athens which in turn led to its defeat. The picture is one of a people who, given what they are shown to be, react consistently with what they are and thereby defeat themselves. By the time it is obvious that they have done the wrong things, it is too late. Let me be even more specific. I am arguing that the Athenians became a great and powerful people precisely because of the aggressiveness of individual persons in pursuit of personal wealth. It must have seemed compelling, in the face of opposition and adversity, to keep doing, even more intensively, the kinds of things that had worked so successfully for them in defeating the Persians and increasing the power and wealth of Athens and its citizens. But the great society, once achieved, couldn't be maintained by the same means which were appropriate for the building, i.e., individuals in an unrestrained pursuit of private wealth. In other words, the public protections for private wealth were destroyed, and with them the private wealth. This account is a detailed picture of a process of defective, unnatural growth, swollen by ambition and distorted by the neglect of realities not fully apparent. Athens refused to see that her wealth and power were exploitative and menacing in the eyes of others. Nor would the Athenians see what reality required of them to maintain their status despite opposition: the temporary sacrifice of personal gain for the sake of the polity.

The theme of *Antony and Cleopatra*, as I have constructed it, is the same. A picture is constructed of both a man and a woman who have great natural gifts and develop them successfully to achieve political and personal power. They use sexual power as well in the service of political gain. When they do in fact fall in love with each other, and want to express that love in a natural way by living together, it is too late. For Antony to leave Octavia, whom he married (a sexual action) for political reasons, in order to remain with Cleopatra (a political figure as well as a sexual partner) is seen as political unreliability, and they are destroyed by his political rivals. In this sequence, I have built a whole (the man, the woman, the relationship) which is damaged irreversibly by its unnatural growth.

These descriptive arguments are clearly variants, as I have elaborated them, on a tragic theme. However, as I tried to show in the brief formulations, they can be read descriptively as arguments that are not tragic. I am simply suggesting that the political defeat of Athenian civilization is tragic only if one makes the account such that the sequence ends with the clearly apparent defeat in the war as consequent. If we place elements such that the whole is built as it was in the second descriptive reading, it is perfectly clear that the inevitable defeat in war corrected the unnatural growth caused by unbridled ambition, and permitted a return to natural development that resulted in a cultural Athens that has never been destroyed. In other words, I have read Thucydides' work as a description of the vulnerable elements of a civilization and how they are destroyed with the result that the permanent, indestructible elements are reconstituted into a civilization that endures.[7]

To read Shakespeare's play that way may seem perverse, and it is certainly an uncommon reading. However, I believe we can argue that the fifth act provides sufficient warrant for insisting that it can be legitimately read as an account of the triumph of love over politics. I am suggesting here only that a sequence can be termed tragic in the mode of description if it ends in destruction. Since, from the rhetorical perspective, I am constructing the sequences, I would point out again that any experience, including discourse, can be interpreted in a great many ways. We can read any text "tragically" in any mode of discourse; but, rhetorically, we cannot say that something *is* or *is not* a tragedy. I shall have something more to say about description, but let us turn now to another mode of discourse, exposition.

In the holistic mode of exposition, variables are arranged hierarchically, leading through varying conflicts and assimilations toward knowledge of the truth. Consider the following: *Because* scientists, conducting their research according to a given theoretical framework, eventually achieve results anomalous with respect to that framework, *therefore* they develop another theory to account for these anomalies, discard the former theory, and assimilate the anomalies to the new theory, which leads to new knowledge. Compare this expository reading of Thomas S. Kuhn's *The Structure of Scientific Revolutions*[8] with the following reading of Karl Menninger's *Love Against Hate*.[9] *Because* men and women interacting in terms of received norms of interpersonal behavior are unhappy and in conflict, *therefore* they inquire into and learn to understand aggression and sexuality, reject their old ways of living, assimilating aggression and sexuality into new modes of activity in terms of a new understanding of love.

The structural similarities of these sequences are apparent: conflict is not resolved by accumulating increments of knowledge; rather, it is dissolved in the light of a truth to which oppositions are assimilated, thereby transforming them. We can support this reading of Menninger by pointing out, for example, that love, the life instinct, serves to sublimate aggression and extend the power of sexuality, thus transforming both (p. 263). We can point similarly to Kuhn's insistence that a new "paradigm" is a transformation of a scientist's world, so that even aspects that seem to remain untouched are in fact altered in being assimilated to the new paradigm.[10]

There is a sense in which the mode of exposition, too, admits of two contrary stresses. The assimilation to a more inclusive formulation as consequent is a sanguine mode of expository reading when the elimination of conflict (as in our reading of Menninger), or the abolition of anomaly (as in our reading of Kuhn), is stressed. However, every assimilation, in transforming circumstance, opens up the possibility of new areas of conflict; if we read with this stress, the mode is what we might call "tragic." Let me explain that in terms of the characteristic structure of an expository sequence. Since conflicting positions *and* assimilations characterize discourse in the expository mode, assimilation implies simultaneously both dissolution of conflict and generation of conflict, insofar as to assimilate is not simply to fuse but to transform conflicting positions such that they become, in effect, a new position, which may then be countered by still another position, which emerges only in the light of the transformation. Such a reading of Kuhn offers a concrete example. "Normal" science, in our interpretation or expository reading, depends on paradigms, conceptual boxes into which a scientist attempts to force nature; these attempts are what is meant by research. Paradigms are theoretical positions to which all previous knowledge in a field has been assimilated, a body or set of received beliefs which determine research problems, methods, and the range of acceptable solutions:

> Nevertheless . . . the very nature of normal research ensures that novelty shall not be suppressed for very long. Sometimes a normal problem, one that ought to be solvable by known rules and procedures, resists the reiterated onslaught of the ablest members of the group within whose competence it falls. On other occasions a piece of equipment de-

signed and constructed for the purpose of normal research fails to perform in the anticipated manner, revealing an anomaly that cannot, despite repeated effort, be aligned with professional expectation. In these and other ways besides, normal science repeatedly goes astray. And when it does—when, that is, the profession can no longer evade anomalies that subvert the existing tradition of scientific practice—then begin the extraordinary investigations that lead the profession at last to a new set of commitments, a new basis for the practice of science. (pp. 5–6)

The new set of commitments, generating new activities and new puzzles, will inevitably generate new anomalies as well in a continuing dynamic process. Increasing knowledge is assured, but no final achievement of truth. If we stress the continuing generation of new ignorance, consequent upon new knowledge, we are reading from a tragic perspective.

Let us turn now to the third or sequential mode of discourse, narration, by considering the following: *Before* an aggregate of individuals can satisfy their needs, they must set out to investigate the remote consequences of their various actions; *after* learning in the process that what they have been doing is in fact self-defeating in terms of the impact of this new self-knowledge, they can act differently in new circumstances to invent instruments and activities to achieve satisfaction. This is a narrative reading of John Dewey's *The Public and Its Problems*. [11]

Here is another formulation in the mode of narration: *Before* a woman can find appropriate husbands for herself and her sisters, she must set out to inquire into and understand the behavior of the young men she is considering; *after* gaining in the process new insights into herself as well, in terms of the impact of this self-knowledge, her subsequent actions in new circumstances will be radically altered. This is a narrative reading of Jane Austen's *Pride and Prejudice*.

The texts for which I have ordered these narrative readings may be experienced as quite remote from one another. However, if we arrange variables narratively, relative to complication or problem and resolution, the structural similarity of all such arrangements becomes striking. For example, resolution involves some kind of discovery and reversal, or else nothing is resolved. When we order both the philosophical treatise and the novel in this mode, we are interpreting them in the mode of narration. We say the group must discover the remote, not immediately evident, consequences of actions undertaken, in order to act effectively; the discovery involves new awareness of wants because it involves a recognition of the errors made as errors of understanding and action. This conscious awareness of what they want as a group and not just as individuals distinguishes a genuine community or public from an aggregate and makes for an ability to act in a totally new way. In other words, communal awareness involves reversal. Obviously, had there been no error to begin with, nothing (if human error is not applicable) to disturb the even tenor of events, there would be no complication, no problem. A new complication now emerges: how to invent new ways of getting what the community now knows it wants. The reversal is action to resolve new complication. What I am stressing here is simply that discovery in a narrative sequence involves a reversal in modes of activity consequent upon the discovery of hitherto unknown facts and leads to new action in an ongoing process.

Elizabeth Bennet may be said to encounter difficulties as part of the larger problem of how to get a husband, in this reading a very serious problem in the circumstances of that novel. Her discovery that Darcy is not a scoundrel is then read as a discovery of hitherto unknown information, but it is also a discovery about herself, an understanding of her past behavior and attitudes, i.e., her prejudice, which alters her action with respect to him so that she is moved to visit Pemberley. Her later discovery that he has furnished the money to rescue Lydia from disgrace again affords insight into her previous error in assuming the Lydia-Wickham episode must harden him against her, and reverses her action so that she refuses to assure Lady Catherine that she will never marry Darcy. In terms of Darcy as well, the narrative sequence may be read to present a series of discoveries of information which are simultaneously insights into his own character and pride and reversals of his mode of action.

In both of these arguments in the mode of narration, ongoing action is stressed. For example, we would say that as circumstances alter, the public will have to be found, again and again, because new complications will arise to require a new community and new awareness of wants relative to the new circumstances. Elizabeth will go on coping with her family in new circumstances. The discovery of information brings insights into past error that cannot be wiped out, although the complications that led to these insights may be resolved. In the concrete, the public's awareness may lead to revolutionary change, not without some pain or loss. Elizabeth marries Darcy, but the deficiencies of her parents and sisters cannot be wiped out; they leave a permanent scar once she has been forced to face them for what they are. In this sense there is something like a theme of tragedy that runs through narrative structures. There is no problem unless something has gone awry, and if the resolution involves new knowledge of self and a new way of acting, there would seem to be always some kind of concomitant distress. Nevertheless, a variant reading in this mode is equally feasible and corresponds, in a sense, to the descriptive sequence, which moves toward a naturally strong, viable whole, the defects of which have been successfully cured. If we stress the reversal as opening up new possibility of further complication, and focus on discovery as involving insight that will render the effort to analyze and resolve new complications more effective, we shift the perspective from the tragic in a narrative reading. Complication becomes a consequent without which there is no ongoing dynamic process; that is, complication is seen as "good."

Let us now turn to the fourth mode of discourse, the hypothetical mode of argument, and begin by noting what it does not do. Variables are not connected in the mode of argument by building elements into a picture that accounts for the nature of things; agents do not encounter complications which must be resolved, nor do they deal with conflicts, or the exemplifications of oppositions which must be dissolved by assimilation to truer or more inclusive positions. Variables are treated in the mode of argument as perspectives discriminated in terms of an agent or agents by whom they are made or encountered and dealt with through speech and action. We should expect this to be the case because the mode of argument *is* the art of rhetoric, an art of persuasion which depends on an agent to *invent* appropriate arguments for his purposes, with respect to matters that seem to allow for alternative conclusions.[12]

Let me illustrate first with an argument constructed for Richard Hofstadter's *Anti-intellectualism in American Life*.[13] *If* Americans believe that all men are equal, yet the intellectual excellence of some men, seeming an implicit contradiction of that belief, often leads Americans to deny intellectuals the opportunity for political leadership, *then* intellectuals must keep trying to find some way to implement their ideas in effective action by continuing to express them verbally.

This is a formulation of an argumentative, rhetorical structure by means of which I have "made" that text. Here is another argument: *If* the rich of a country grow richer at the expense of the poor, who increase in number, creating two nations, rich and poor, in bitter conflict, and the political system makes it impossible for government to act to effect the welfare of the nation as a whole, *then* those who realize the danger in the situation must act to restructure the political party system and debate all the issues openly. This reading of Michael Harrington's *The Other America*[14] discloses a similar structure. Agents act in terms of their own perspectives, which are, in turn, encountered as contingencies to be dealt with by agents otherwise oriented. Some agents acquire wealth; this makes others poor. The poor do what they can, but their poverty deprives them of the knowledge and power to act effectively. The orientation of the rich, in turn, is to stay rich and get richer. Those who are oriented such that they are aware of the situation and deplore it must speak and act to make government help the poor instead of helping the rich.

In both readings variables are interrelated in ways that make perspectives clash, and these clashes are dealt with sometimes action-ally, sometimes verbally. In the mode of argument, too, we can recognize contrary stresses; for example, if we stress, in a reading of Hofstadter in the mode of argument, that the continuing effort to express ideas and make them understood will eventually make opportunities for intellectuals to implement ideas in action, we are offering a sanguine, "happy ending" reading. If we stress the ongoing process, one in which saying and doing may be brought together for a while but surely come apart again as new contingencies arise, the stress is tragic. We can formulate this for Harrington as well. There is a way in which agents can deal with the conflict between rich and poor; they can bring saying and doing together by altering party structure so that debate on issues is possible, thereby making improvement possible. But here, too, contingencies arise in the form of the opposing orientation—let us say, of congressmen who will not permit structural changes that would diminish their power to keep government on the side of the rich. Thus agents desiring change must speak out and contrive to call attention to the situation in, among other ways, books like *The Other America.* To stress the possibility of dealing with the situation, to stress the "answer," is a sanguine reading. To stress the continuing conflict is to read tragically. Finally, we must keep in mind that these variants are not a function of the text I have used in illustration. They are produced by interrelating any variables according to the mode of argument.

Any one of the eight texts I have used to illustrate the four modes of discourse may be read in all four modes, as may any discursive whole. This seems to account, as I suggested earlier, for the emphasis on mixed modes in the rhetoric texts, and for the inconsistencies among anthologies in the matter of the rubrics under which given selections ought to be considered. I will return to the matter of variant readings later, but it would be useful now to try, in a more general way, to characterize the four modes of discourse, and see whether there are not still other aspects of fictive argument that remain to be uncovered in light of the discussion thus far.

THREE

MAKING FICTIVE ARGUMENTS

This, then, is how the four modes of discourse work: we construct an argument in the mode of description by building constituent elements into the argument of a communicative whole, which is what it is by virtue of being composed of those elements as it is composed; the construction may avoid unnatural or contingent constituents and cure consequent distortions of the whole and its activities. Why is it necessary to speak of "cure" or "avoidance"? Why not say simply that we can build a whole which is natural, healthy, and requires no cure? Again it is important to go back to our origins in the art of rhetoric. The mode of description is a mode of argument, a process rooted in the assumption that alternative conclusions are possible, and such an assumption, in turn, implies choosing, consciously or not. To go "the natural way" *is to avoid* the unnatural for which a cure is required as soon as its very possibility has tainted the natural by being entertained. To put it another way, "natural" and "unnatural" are empty variables, rhetorical commonplaces which cannot take on meaning except in terms of one another. Thus, given the minimal duality of stress we have seen to be characteristic of any rhetorical mode, given the contrarieties of empty rhetorical commonplaces, every argument suggests its alternative; and therefore we may also construct an unnatural whole which we show to be beyond the help of therapy. In this way we construct what I called earlier a tragic reading in the descriptive mode.

The other three modes of argument also suggest alternative versions. We generate an argument in the mode of exposition by assimilating conflicting positions of partial truth or opinion to greater, more inclusive truths, which transform them from adversary opposition to coherence. On the other hand, we can vary this "affirmative" reading by noting that to the new, coherent position a new opposition may well arise since the new, more inclusive truth, in being new, has generated more inclusive truths. In the mode of narration we derive thought and action from characters and predicaments of which agents are not fully aware, but which they come to recognize as problematic situations to be resolved. However, since the discoveries which resolve problematic situations are also insights into themselves achieved by agents, resolution of a problematic situation leads to new predicaments and new complications. Consequently, an affirmative reading implies the legitimacy of a "tragic" reading as well. Finally, we invent an argument in the mode of argument by discriminating positions held and relating them in feelings and actions which lead to new insights and perceptions and the discovery of new facts. But the dualism characteristic of all modes of rhetoric suggests that the new facts discovered by any agent may be challenged by another, and in the ensuing debate agents must again discriminate positions and so on. In this way we stress the "tragedy" of ceaseless struggle rather than the equally legitimate satisfaction of positive achievement.

I have given this summary in language that may seem unduly awkward in order to point out as clearly as I can that we are dealing with modes of discourse as modes of distinguishing and relating, *and not* as structures of particulars related. That is, the "agents" who encounter other perspectives or resolve complications, the oppositions assimilated, the elements or pictures composed—these may be discourse about persons or peoples, men or animals, molecules or ideas, events or unicorns. We are concerned with modes of discourse as they operate; since we do not encounter modes of discourse or arguments experientially except as we use them to inform the matter of discourse, we must examine them functionally. In other words, if we want to appreciate the formal workings of modes of discriminating and relating, we must apply them. The use of the modes of discourse is simultaneously the making of particulars which cannot be experienced independently of a process of "informing." Consequently, *there are no particulars in any communicative sense; they must be made.* We will look more closely at the implications of this presently. What should be clearer at this point is the sense in which all arguments, because they *make* particulars, are fictive arguments, and fictive arguments cut across generic distinctions. Both *Pride and Prejudice* and *The Structure of Scientific Revolutions* are made communicative because we interpret them by means of fictive arguments regardless of whether one is called a novel and the other is not. Both are equally "fictional."

We must also bear this in mind: that discourse about anything is always both formal and material, and that means that arguments may be characterized by *what* they talk about as well as by *how* they talk about it. At the beginning of the last chapter we examined the question of *what novels are* according to literary critics; the kinds of answers we identified are not relevant to literary criticism alone, but imply broader conceptual contexts in which we could locate, among other possibilities, what it is that arguments talk about. However, we have seen that analyses that begin with a commitment to defining an object lead to fixed interpretations—*the* pattern, *the* plot, *the* archetypal or mythic structure, even *the* argument; for we can conceive of an object as communicative and then proceed to a grammatical analysis that will correct faulty perception and show what the object really does communicate when its audience perceives naturally and correctly. We needn't try to imagine how that would work; we need only recall I. A. Richards's *Practical Criticism*, [1] an extraordinarily fine example of grammatical corrective therapy applied to achieve rhetorical purposes.

It is the case, then, that we characterize the modes of discourse by *how* rather than *what* in order to be able to develop critical resources that will enable us, in turn, to treat discursive wholes as dynamic rather than fixed communicative structures. We choose the modes of discourse proper to rhetoric because, as we noted earlier, argument unifies parts which are themselves, formally, rhetorical modes of grammatical, poetic, dialectical, and rhetorical criticism. This means we have a method permitting us to do coherent interpretations that will integrate a plurality of arguments in a unified whole. To say this, however, is to anticipate a step in our inquiry, and we will have to return to it later; for thus far we have not yet examined the problem of how to make whole discursive objects but have confined our discussion to making arguments, which are not objects but modes of activity or processes.

I should like to stress at this point that rejecting particulars as a way of characterizing arguments (rejecting what the arguments "are about") is by no means a denial of the critical truism about the inseparability of form and content. Because they are inseparable in our experience we can characterize arguments in terms of content or form, and because they are inseparable we *must* separate them for purposes of analysis in order precisely to understand what it means to say that they are inseparable. We see then that a stance from the perspective of content points to fixities (not to speak of classifications and reclassifications ad infinitum); discursive form is dynamic. The *what* tells us "it" is *this;* the *how* tells us "it" is as many things as we can discern by moving across it in a variety of ways.

As the next step in this inquiry it is important to clarify any remaining ambiguity as to the choice of the art of rhetoric and its four modes of discourse as critical method. Can we achieve rhetorical purposes with other methods? If rhetoric can incorporate the functions of other methods, can one "do" rhetoric using one of the others? In fact we have seen that grammar can be used for rhetorical purposes, as I. A. Richards does, and what is true of grammar must be true of poetic and dialectic which are also dynamic discursive forms. If we turn for corroboration to the practice of literary critics, we see that Northrop Frye uses dialectic for rhetorical purposes in the section on "theory of genres," in *Anatomy of Criticism* (pp. 243–337),[2] as Wayne Booth uses poetic for rhetorical purposes in *The Rhetoric of Fiction* (see chapter 1 above). Having rejected content in favor of form, why do we choose as our "form" rhetorical modes of discourse rather then grammatical, poetic, or dialectical modes? Certainly not because they cannot be adapted such that they, too, can internalize author and audience (as rhetoric does primarily, without adaptation)—Richards internalizes audience, Booth author, as we have seen.

I have shown how rhetoric permits us to disclose many structures in a single work (not simply the three represented by author–work–audience); cannot the other methods do this? Obviously they can; but we must examine closely the ways in which they can perform this function. Let me again use examples to explain the special ways in which grammatical, poetic, and dialectical modes of criticism can be used to discover multiple communicative structures. With respect to grammar, the example of Richards points to a single interpretation for any communicative object; on the other hand, David Lodge recognizes the possibility of variant readings for a single text, using his approach, which I characterized earlier as grammatical. However, the variant readings are the result of the use of a grammatical method by different critics. Of course the mention of more than one critic brings in the rhetorical—audience, or the text as commmunicative object. But although Lodge doesn't reject the idea of potential multiple readings as Richards seems to, the readings are nonetheless separate and to some extent conceived as mutually exclusive.[3]

R. S. Crane used a poetic method to treat communicative objects, although he called the latter didactic and didn't consider "mimetic" wholes qua communicative. Nevertheless, as I pointed out at length in chapter 1, he treats *Tom Jones* as a whole made of effect-producing parts. Although I believe that Crane's work and Booth's are examples of poetic methods used to achieve rhetorical purposes, they cannot be said to meet our requirement with respect to multiple structures since the criterion of the "neo-Aristotelian" poetic critics for a valid reading is "the author's intention";[4] this is by no means to be construed as in any way simplistic, and no one acquainted with the argument of Crane's essay on Gulliver's Houyhnhnms could do so. My point here, however, is simply that such a criterion again points to a commitment to one correct reading even in the case of supposedly "rhetorical" works, those classified as didactic. Indeed, Booth's concept of the implied author, aside from being a translation of the ethical proof in rhetoric, is also an internalizing in the work of the criterion of intentionality, and consequently also points to at least a "preferred" reading for any text.

As for dialectic, Northrop Frye admits rhetoric, as is clear from the fourth essay, "Rhetorical Criticism: Theory of Genres," but he also affirms a kind of critical pluralism by setting up a system of multiple critical approaches in the *Anatomy of Criticism* (pp. ix–x).[5] Yet for all that, archetypal criticism is explicitly preferred. In all three examples, in fact, separate readings result from the use of the method by separate users, different critic-audiences using substantially the same method separately to achieve different results. These are indubitably examples of grammar, poetic, and dialectic "doing" rhetoric—Richards for therapy, Crane to analyze "didactic" poems, Frye to do genre criticism and assimilate it to the hierarchy crowned by archetypal criticism. But none of these critics recognizes the full validity of multiple readings of a single text—Richards not at all, Crane insisting that the method based on the *Poetics* is ultimately superior,[6] Frye similarly, insisting that "archetypal criticism has a central role."[7] What neither the critics nor these modes of criticism can do is recognize and deal with plurality of response to literary works not as aberration or the imperfection to be expected in any human enterprise but as the richly complex internality of a text itself.

We choose the rhetorical modes of discourse, then, and characterize them formally, in order to accomplish the particular task we have set ourselves, a task rhetorical criticism, rooted in a long tradition of theory of argument, is peculiarly fitted to accomplish: that is, examination of the dynamic structure of discursive wholes qua communicative objects, a task for which we require a critical apparatus that will discover the *thought of the whole* in all its complexity.

As we turn our attention again to our review of the modes of discourse, an interesting question arises which seems to me to deserve careful consideration. In terms of the formal structure of fictive arguments as consequential, we have identified four basic modes of discourse, or four kinds of argument. But an argument is not a thing; it is rather an activity or process, and that suggests the question: Does the argument really end formally? In other words, what does consequence really imply? The descriptive argument may seem to end most conclusively; a natural whole of some sort is built, unnatural, contingent constituents avoided and distortions cured. Yet, formally, if "contingencies to be avoided" is part of a dynamic process, there is the implication that contingencies will continue to arise in an ongoing process perceived in this mode. It is important to bear in mind that the mode of description qua process, qua "how," is purely formal. If we were characterizing description in terms of content, we might argue that death, in ending Antony and ending Cleopatra, ends our descriptive reading. An argument is not a person or a thing, however, and formally its ending is always somehow arbitrary, although we can "stop" comfortably whenever we are aware of having achieved signification or meaning, a point marked out for us by consequence.

An interpretation in the mode of narration ends with the resolution of a problem or complication and the change in direction consequent upon it. But that change in direction itself is an indication that when a problem is solved the resolution in turn alters the situation such that new problems arise. The reading in the mode of exposition involves assimilations to closer approximations of truth or "knowledge," but, as we have seen, new truth generates new occasions for assimilations to even closer approximations, and absolute truth is never finally achieved. Scientists, having transcended earlier conflicts, in this kind of reading must go on to further conflict. In the mode of argument conflicting orientations are not assimilated but discriminated in terms of the feelings and actions of agents, and agents, if not an individual agent, persist. The argument in the mode of argument ends as arbitrarily as it begins with the removal of the agent to a new situation—for example, the intellectuals encountering renewed hostility in the course of time—or it may end when action or doing is completely blocked by the conflicting orientations of other agents, and the protagonists must continue to reiterate their warnings, as they must in this reading of *The Other America*.

Some literary critics have noted this sense of open-endedness, particularly in connection with the twentieth-century novel. Alan Friedman,[8] for example, has contended that it marks a structural change from that of earlier fiction and attempts to account for it in terms of broad cultural changes that mark the twentieth century. Without addressing myself to his very interesting discussion, I would simply point out that the rhetorical modes of discourse are formal and universally modes of argument. I would suggest that, in fact, the sense of open-endedness is a function of the dynamic nature of argument as an ongoing process of changing variables into particulars in consequential structures in all four modes. Thus open-endedness is as true of the arguments of eighteenth- and nineteenth-century novels as it is of the arguments of twentieth-century novels. That we feel the great novels of the remoter past, as well as those more recent, as somehow suggesting more than they seem to contain, seems to me to be a truism the source of which is at least in some part the dynamic nature of fictive argument. To move for a moment to the perspective of the author who furnishes us with the matter of discourse that we actively organize according to the modes of discourse, the difference between contemporary novels and those of past centuries is not a difference in structure, but a difference in the convention used to deal with open-endedness. Twentieth-century novels have seemed to us to stop when the consequence of a sequence is reached; as if one were to say, "Very well, I've shown how this sort of thing goes and that is all I contracted to do." In fact, they do not always stop altogether. Joyce wrote *Ulysses* after *Portrait of the Artist as a Young Man*. Sartre wrote a trilogy, each book of which is susceptible of reading as a single work. We can point to Joyce Cary, Anthony Powell, and many others. Nonetheless, many contemporary novelists do simply stop, and even the trilogies and the tetralogies eventually stop appearing. On the other hand, we might also recall that Greek tragedy was much given to trilogy, even if no critic, regardless of his critical method, has argued that *Oedipus the King*, alone, lacks coherence and unity.

Novelists before the twentieth century had another way of dealing with the sense of open-endedness, a device recognized by critics as a convention, but more often deplored than understood, it seems to me, for what it is. I am referring to the summarizing paragraphs or chapters in which we are told what happened to the principals after the point at which any argument or reading of the novel comes to an end. A list of novels in which we could find this device would be very long indeed. Let me mention only *Pride and Prejudice* since I have touched on it earlier. I read the novel in the mode of narration; clearly, when Elizabeth and Darcy are engaged to be married and Jane and Bingley are united, their misunderstandings cleared up, the argument in this mode has ended with its consequent, and Elizabeth has come to know herself and that she should marry Darcy after all. In that reading the following matter is, in fact, not "informed," but disappears in the formulation of the novel's argument as experienced. Chapters 18 and 19, in which we learn of Elizabeth's relations with Georgiana, and that Kitty lived thereafter with Jane and Elizabeth, are really unnecessary. Yet they are a response to a felt need that can never really be satisfactorily met.

Rhetoric is the art of paradox. From the rhetorician for whom, with pairs of contraries and contradictories, Aristotle furnished the means for arguing either side of a question, to the critic who tries to see that there are many ways to interpret the fictive arguments made by novelists, rhetoric permits us to explore the ambiguous realm of experience. The paradox we have uncovered here cannot be resolved. With respect to their structures of argument, novels stop; they cannot really end. Earlier novelists concede this openly; by tying loose ends in a last chapter, they admit that there *are* loose ends—that arguments are, in a sense, open-ended. Twentieth-century novelists make the same confession by stopping abruptly and leaving the loose ends in the lap of the reader. These are differences of convention, not of structure.

We can discern the open-endedness of fictive arguments very clearly in those discursive structures we call history. Historians know that sharply demarcated time periods are artificial in one way, thematic organizations in another, and so on. Yet they are constrained to make historical arguments in terms that lead to consequents with which they can end a given work.[9] The modes of argument we have examined are also histories, and as such they also differ from one another.

The history we read descriptively is causal history. A whole is constructed of its constituent elements, and once it is thoroughly described, we know what causes it to be what it is. Thus, we read Thucydides as describing all the elements that make up the Peloponnesian War, and we know what caused it. Narrative history would include only the particulars relative to resolving a complication or a problematic situation. If we read *Pride and Prejudice* in that mode, we will say that the history of past events is the information that will make it possible to resolve the complication and furnish the protagonist concomitantly with insight into herself: did something happen to make Darcy refuse Wickham the living at Darcy's disposal? Did Bingley know Jane was in London? The events, we point out, are recounted only when necessary. The history of the Bennet's marriage we will not encounter until late in the novel, when Mr. Bennet's shortcomings must be understood so that the complication will now be fully understood: not just getting husbands, but getting suitable husbands—in other words, making good marriages. The novel itself, we point out, as a history of that problem, its related problems and their various resolutions, does not dwell on events not directly relevant. Why Mr. Bennet's land was entailed need not be explained, only the fact that it is entailed is germane. The account of Mrs. Bennet's relations and their sources of income will be given because the social circumstances they reveal are germane to the complication. (If we read it in the descriptive mode, we will construe the placement of particulars in terms of the building up of Elizabeth's nature and the character of the entire world that makes her and Darcy what they are. As a result, the particulars will in fact become quite different particulars.) We will read Dewey as giving us a history of ideas about the relation of the individual to society and the state in order to show why these ideas are inadequate for formulating the problem of the public, and we will construct this in the early part of the argument. Subsequently, the history of past events and how they have been interpreted will be recurrently brought in whenever this information contributes to an understanding of the complication in the account.

History, in the mode of exposition, is epochal in some sense. When we read him in this mode, we see Kuhn running through the history of science in terms of epochs characterized by a major paradigm which gives the epoch or period its developmental focus and its world view. Pre-paradigmatic science is, in fact, not developmental at all, while the end of an epoch is marked by a crisis of theoretical conflict similar to the pre-paradigm state of the science. The crisis is ended in the dissolving of conflict by assimilating anomalies to a new paradigm, and development can resume. Menninger, in this mode, tells a history of aggression and sexuality in terms of epochs of individual development, beginning with infancy and childhood.

In the mode of argument perspectives are made and feelings related to actions experienced by agents, and argumentative history explains what agents have said and done. It is not told in terms of the necessary elements that make things what they are, or in terms of complications and their resolution, or in terms of movements toward greater knowledge and inclusiveness. Hofstadter was read in this mode as dealing with individual men and groups, all of whom exemplify typical orientations to the "intellectual" with respect to learning, religion, business, and politics.

The temporality of discourse determines that all the modes of discourse must involve historicity—that, in effect, to make particulars by connecting variables in a consequential sequence is (in some sense) to do history. It is this same temporality, it seems to me, that lies at the root of a universality we sense in a discursive sequence in any mode, regardless of the particulars made. When we have successfully made a communicative structure, the response might be formulated as "this is the way things are," rather than, "this is the way *this* thing is." Perhaps this universality is a result first of the open-endedness of a discursive sequence, of the fact that we may stop connecting variables but that connecting is a process and, like time, it never really ends. *Thus, the paradox: we make an argument, and because it is consequential, it is marked as discrete, but because it is sequential, it is adumbrated beyond consequence and never really ends.* Therefore, the communicative structure from the perspective of audience is not the same kind of structure we recognize as a poetic structure. Therefore, the modes of discourse are themes, endlessly varied throughout the universe of discourse, intensifying our sense of their universality; and when we construct *The Peloponnesian War* in the mode of description, it is a variation on the theme of *Antony and Cleopatra* so constructed, as *Pride and Prejudice* is a variation on the theme of *The Public and Its Problems* when we form them both in the mode of narration.

However, it is also the case that, rhetorically, any instance of discourse can be interpreted in a great many ways, any one of which will yield a new constellation of particulars. In other words, variables may be related in any one of the four modes of discourse thus giving rise to four different kinds of particulars. I should like to illustrate this briefly by offering alternative arguments for some of the exemplary texts I dealt with earlier, beginning with a narrative reading of *The Structure of Scientific Revolutions*, which I read initially in the mode of exposition.

Before scientists can solve unusual problems in the course of their research, they must examine their instruments, procedures, and assumptions; *after* discovering during this process new information that casts doubt on the adequacy of their theoretical assumptions, they must alter those assumptions to resolve their problems, thereby altering radically their subsequent research in new circumstances. The history of this account will be quite different from the history appropriate to the expository account. The history of any given science becomes an account of successive attempts to resolve problems by determining the data relevant to their resolution, resolving them, and going on to new problems which emerge in the light of what is now known that was heretofore unknown. At any given time different sciences are at different stages of development, and it is also true that what occurs in one science may be totally irrelevant to the problems of another.[10] This reading of *The Structure of Scientific Revolutions* is a variation on the theme of *Pride and Prejudice* as I read it initially.

Suppose we were to interpret *Pride and Prejudice* in the descriptive mode? *As* young women have grown up in a society in which marriage offers the only viable future for them, and they encounter contingencies in the form of men who are not what they seem, *so* those who have developed their natural intelligence and corrected unhealthy faults will choose and be chosen by the better-natured men, and those who have become foolish and frivolous will not marry well. It is not difficult to support this reading of *Pride and Prejudice*, and in doing so we will make particulars quite different from those structured in the mode of narration. Consider the history this account determines. Elizabeth and Jane are shown to be naturally good, beautiful, and intelligent. Although Jane is less intelligent than Elizabeth, it is an excess of kindness and charity that makes her so. The two sisters are naturally endowed, since clearly parental guidance can be seen to be entirely inadequate to account for their virtues. They are described, their social circumstances are described. Lydia stands in contrast to them. When contingencies are introduced in the persons of Darcy, Bingley, and Wickham, each girl acts according to her nature as it has developed, corrects its faults if she can and given that nature and the nature of the world in which they live, each inevitably finds her proper mate.

The success of the Athenian cause, in the descriptive reading, depends on the nature of things and the behavior of men; when Athenians ignore the realities to pursue the goods of ambition, the very nature of Athens has been betrayed. The Bennet sisters are what they are because of nature and the twin circumstances of a world that has determined what they must aspire to and parents who, despite their faults, cannot prevent two sisters from cultivating natural gifts of concern and discernment to make up for parental shortcomings and who lead an unendowed daughter to a deterioration of her already meager capacities. Elizabeth and Jane do not betray themselves, and they thus overcome the obstacles created by misunderstanding and lack of virtue on the part of others. Structurally, the two accounts as descriptive arguments are variations on a theme.

The Peloponnesian War may be read in the mode of argument; in such a reading the underlying natural causes become a meaningless notion. The Athenians ran up against the Spartan orientation and interests and those of their own allies and Sparta's while pursuing policies that made sense from their own perspective. As such, *The Peloponnesian War* is a variation on the theme of *Anti-intellectualism in American Life*.

Variables may be interrelated in any one of the four modes of discourse, and the mode determines what kind of particular will emerge. Formally, then, we can construe any text in four different ways. But the four ways of connecting four kinds of particular in a consequential structure do not by any means exhaust the variety of interpretations possible for a given instance of discourse.

When we examine the relation between a mode of discourse and the particular made in the statement of the sequence, we are apt to think of it as an analysis of the way in which the sequence would be seen in particular instances. But this is quite misleading. Certainly a descriptive argument (one of the four modes of *how*) will always be about (the *what*) the natural and unnatural, the characteristic kind of particular that description conjures up on its therapeutic way; and a narrative argument will form problematic situations, an expository argument generate truths or knowledge, an argumentative argument invent positions in conflict. But an analysis of a given instance of discourse in terms of one of the four modes will not simply turn up a given version of nature, problematic situations, truths, or a debate.

Agents engaged in debate (in the widest sense of that term), coping with problematic situations, holding fast to truths, living in circumstances that reflect the nature of things—these are the materials of argument in all four modes of discourse. A narrative account makes particulars as problematic situations, but it can be formed alternatively with respect to agents in conflict, ideas, or circumstantial reality. A descriptive account making particulars as the nature of things or circumstance can be constructed alternatively with respect to ideas, agents in conflict, or problems to be resolved. To put it another way, the four modes of discourse we have been discussing are reflected in *materials* which embody arguments. In order to make as clear as possible the structural similarities between accounts given in each of the four modes as well as the formal distinctions that separate the modes, I have focused on agents in all the accounts given. Different accounts can be offered for all eight texts I have used, in all four modes, by focusing on problems to be resolved, circumstantial reality, or ideas. For example, a circumstantial interpretation of Thucydides might focus on a constellation of economic circumstances or, alternatively, political or social circumstances, and so on. We can then make four variations—in the four modes of argument—on an economic, a political, or a social theme.

Similarly, a social, political or economic reading of *Antony and*

Cleopatra, Pride and Prejudice, Love Against Hate, or, indeed, any text, is possible. Moreover, the reading that focuses on circumstance will invoke particulars that do not emerge in other readings. For example, I offered expository and narrative accounts for *The Structure of Scientific Revolutions;* in both cases I considered scientists as agents engaging in activities. Were I to focus on the circumstantiality of sciences in formation, the lines of argument in both modes would be quite different. A shift to social circumstance would lead to totally different interpretations of *Love Against Hate,* in which, for example, the apparently arbitrary social dominance of men over women could organize the accounts in four formal variations. A competitive economic system would give still another theme that could be varied through the four modes of argument.

How we make particulars to render texts communicative is a rhetorical question, and its answer depends on the perceiver, both materially and formally. The perceiver, if he would justify his argument, must support it by persuading other perceivers that it is indeed valid. If they, in turn, make particulars such that his argument coincides with theirs, there is in fact "communication" in an ongoing process. Of course it is important to bear in mind that "critics" (perceivers *particularized* by being interpreted in terms of an activity, a characteristic and directed way of moving) do not systematically compare their made particulars. They interpret fictive argument X by means of their own fictive arguments. In effect, a particular established systematically in one reading can often be seen to make sense—perhaps for totally different reasons—in another context. The critic or reader will then presumably integrate such a particular into his own reading, furnishing a radically different "why" if called upon to explain.

However, some arguments cannot be justified or validated in this way, and some interpretations (some "novels," some "philosophies," some "scientific theories") disappear forever, while others may re-emerge when changes in circumstance have somehow lent them new cogency.

That this is, in fact, the critical interpretive process is evident from the variety of ways in which given discursive sequences have been interpreted. Jane Austen's novels have been read as romantic narratives, as descriptive of a social world (the "novel of manners"), as expository essays on moral values, as arguments setting forth conflict among agents. In each of these modes in turn the perspective has varied from agents, their language and action, to problematic events such as courtships, marriages, family histories, the pursuit of money, to circumstance—early nineteenth-century rural England, middle-class society, economics—to ideas—freedom, love, responsibility, etc.[11] Thomas Kuhn's book provoked considerable negative response; yet each critic had "read" a different argument. Kuhn was attacked with respect to agents: he didn't understand what the scientist does; with respect to problematic situations: how scientific theories develop, what happens in "normal science," how "paradigms" work—he had got them all wrong; with respect to circumstance: he was wrong about the nature of the universe, about scientific communities, and about what does in fact lead to scientific revolutions; and, of course, he had failed to understand the objective reality of truth.[12]

In both these cases, apparently so far removed from one another, the process of integrating discourse by means of formally distinct modes of connection and material loci of organization is the same. Let us take these as exemplary of the process and see what emerges. We have already noted that any text can be read in all four or any one of the modes of discourse, and that readings are further varied with respect to a focus on agents, problems, circumstances, and ideas. However, it is clear that a choice of agents—Antony, Cleopatra, or both; three Bennet sisters, two, or Elizabeth; Athenians, Spartans, or both, etc.—does not eliminate problematic situations, circumstances, or ideas. Rather, the three are brought into an account relative to agents and what they are shown to be, or agents and the complications or problems that they must resolve, or agents and the accepted positions and feelings from which they speak and act. Similarly, focus on problematic events brings agents, their speech and action, their ideas and circumstances into the account relative to those events, while the focus on circumstance places agents in them acting with respect to problems and in terms of their ideas, all of these seen relative to the circumstances they serve to illuminate. Agents do not love and hate in a vacuum; circumstance is meaningless unless it is the circumstance of someone and something; ideas are of something and held by someone; nature enters into scientific discourse only when it is *said* to be what it is, and agents say what it is, in the course of resolving problems under given circumstances and on the basis of their ideas.

Moreover, the four material aspects of argument merge into one another in a multiplicity of ways. Agents may be construed as part of the circumstance that conditions the development of love in Menninger, that produces conflict in Hofstadter, that keeps the poor in their poverty in Harrington, that produces the problem of the public in Dewey, that complicates the relations of Elizabeth and Darcy in Austen. Nature may be construed as providing the *problematic situation* of science, but it is also the *circumstance* that conditions investigation and the *agent* of physical change and the *idea* that explains it. Agents and their speech and action can be construed as constituting the problems of Dewey, Harrington, Menninger, Kuhn, and the other authors I have discussed. Indeed, we can construct an argument in any mode formally, in terms of agent, problem, circumstance or idea. But just as an argument is not a fixed entity, neither is an agent, a problem, a circumstance, or an idea. They are, rather, perspectives from which we invent the universe of discourse to render it communicative, just as the universe of discourse is a perspective from which we create the universe itself to render it communicative in endless variety.

If it is the case, as I have contended, that the matters of fictive argument can be both discriminated from one another and merged, this suggests a question concerning a fictive argument as formal mode of discourse: is it correct to say, as has been said here, that argument in the mode of description builds a "picture," constructs from elements an account of a natural whole cured of its unnatural distortions? That in the mode of narration problematic situations are resolved? That in the mode of exposition conflicting opinions are assimilated to positions conceived as closer approximations to truth? That in the mode of argument opposing and conflicting orientations are discriminated, related to one another, and dealt with by means of action and speech? Is it correct, after all, to say that these are four distinct modes of making and relating particulars in consequential discursive structures? I think it is quite correct to say that these are four separate and distinct modes of connection. But if we mean that they are distinct in the sense that in the narrative mode, for example, we cannot describe or argue or explain; that each of the modes necessarily excludes the *functions* of the others, then the distinction we have insisted upon would be false.

However, I have not come by a devious way to affirm the traditional notion of mixed modes. To do so would be to conceive of the modes of discourse as fixed entities which supplement one another in varying combinations of bits and pieces. The modes of discourse are ways of connecting, of arranging in structures, ways of doing and not things. But a way of doing something is functional, and each mode of discourse, distinct from the way of others, nonetheless performs the same functions. Let me try to explain why this is so.

First we must see clearly what is going on when we invent an argument, and it is useful to begin with what we are not doing. The practice of literary criticism will furnish a good example. We know that in formal, poetic analysis a literary work is taken to be an artifact distinguished from other artifacts on the basis of its material, language. It is carefully examined to determine the kind of whole it is, since it is recognized as a distinct whole because it has a beginning, a middle, and an end. What ensues is a part-whole analysis to determine finally whether it is excellent in terms of criteria appropriate to the kind of whole it is. However difficult it may be to eliminate the inevitable bias of the critic and his private responses, to do so is nevertheless the aim, the same aim, we might remember, as that of the scientist who interprets nature. Grammatical critics contend that the literary object is a natural or linguistic artifact such that language is its form rather than its material, while some critics—let us call them dialectical—see the literary object as the embodiment of a preexistent form or model or myth. What they all have in common is the attempt to determine what the literary object truly or really or essentially is regardless of how it may be variously experienced. Therefore, although they are all faced with the obvious difficulty of dealing with an object that cannot be encompassed immediately in its wholeness, and that cannot be *retained* wholly, they can engage in the laborious task (it goes without saying that it is a richly rewarding task) of reading and rereading, of treating as a whole what can never be experienced in its wholeness. Critics do this job in a great many ways, but the goal they hold in common: to analyze the work such that the resulting interpretation is commensurate with what the work is in itself.

It is only in terms of the treatment of literary works *as if* they could be encompassed in their wholeness that the notion of spatial form in the novel could make any sense.[13] In discourse as it is experienced, spatial form is impossible. Temporality governs the experience of discourse; and in rhetorical analysis, in contrast to the other critical approaches, it is especially important to bear this in mind, for an argument is a structure of interrelations in which particulars are arranged in terms of consequence. When we are in the process of experiencing any instance of discourse we are simply experiencing. When we state the argument we are arranging particulars in a structure that is consequential and therefore communicative. But to state an argument is not to reproduce a whole in itself, an artificial object, but to produce an argument, an experienced whole, which is quite different. This is why discursive wholes from the rhetorical perspective have many arguments or structures rather than the one assumed by the poetic, grammatical and dialectical critics. It is, of course, the fact that discourse must be interpreted and is never univocal in meaning that gives rise to disputes in other modes of criticism as to what the structure of the work really is and how it should be interpreted.

For when the critic interprets a novel or any natural or artifical object, he too is engaging in fictive argument. Like all others who construct fictive arguments, he has his goal in a series of univocal statements about an identified entity. Other critics engaged in like enterprises will disagree with him both in their univocal statements and the identified objects presented in those statements. And when critics disagree, they undertake to reveal the errors of statements and identifications different from their own. This is the first step of adversary rhetorical dispute, and on this relativistic level one finds aphorisms such as "there's no disputing taste," or "to each his own taste," as the only alternatives to rejecting errors of poor taste.[14]

But in rhetorical criticism the approach is deliberative rather than adversary, and the alternatives are made to suggest neglected aspects of the artificial object which are observed and taken into account as a consequence of the fictive argument presented. It is not a question in rhetorical criticism of attributing a plurality of structures presented in a plurality of interpretations to a single object with a single structure, but rather an exploratory discovery of levels of interrelated structures, aspects, and values. From a nonadversarial rhetorical perspective, then, alternative interpretations are not conceived as a problem.

The statement of the argument, then, is analogous to the statement of the formal principle or plot in poetic criticism or the statement of the pattern in grammatical criticism or of the "myth," for example, in some modes of dialectical criticism. The argument formally stated is a statement about the communicative structure. It tells how an instance of discourse has been experienced as communicative. It says, "This is how I put it together to make it mean something." It is, in and by itself, a formulation, in a sense, of what is retained in the mind of the perceiver that will permit him to point to a book and affirm that he has read it and knows what it's about. Only the structured is perceived and retained as meaningful or communicative. To validate the argument as stated requires a thorough analysis, which means a more exhaustive interpretation in terms of arguments linked in a mode of discourse. When this is done in a rhetorical analysis, the particulars are, in effect, being made.

When we engage in this critical task, then, what do we discover about the way in which the modes of discourse function? A concrete example should make this clear. I stated the argument of Menninger's *Love Against Hate* in the expository mode, and it will serve to make the point, but first let us consider the mode of exposition. In it, conflicts are assimilated to a truth that transforms them. Exposition is the mode of explanation, the mode that seeks to "expose" the way things truly are. The rhetoric texts seem to indicate the movement toward increasing comprehensiveness characteristic of this mode: "The exposition or explanation of a subject can be developed in many ways, probably in as many ways as there are expository essays. Some of the ways of developing a subject in an expository manner are so common, however, that they can be isolated and studied separately. These are: definition, example, comparison and contrast, process analysis, classification and division, cause and effect."[15]

If we turn now to our expository reading of Menninger, we can indeed see that all the modes mentioned are functioning. Sexuality and aggression are *comparable* insofar as both are primary instincts the gratification of which is frustrated by society. But aggression, in *contrast* to sexuality, may be destructive. *Because* sexual drives have been distorted by severe repression, men are personally unhappy; *because* aggressive drives have been similarly distorted, men are in conflict with one another in society. As we fill out this reading, we find the psychological developmental *processes* explained, hate and love *defined*, modes of sublimation *classified*, and case histories cited which *exemplify* the struggle of love against hate.

I want to make it clear here that I am not suggesting that exposition is a mixed mode, that these are techniques used supportively of each other in succession. I am saying that the definitions of love and hate can be shown to be inextricable from the analysis of the process of psychological development, which is, in turn, the substance of the classification and exemplification; and the comparison and contrast are part of the definition. In other words, at the risk of laboring this point, to define *is* to classify, to specify the cause of the effect, to furnish terms of comparison, to exemplify, and to explicate a process. Each performs the functions of all the others.

But it is also the case that this expository development, leading to greater insights into the truth and to achievements of value through sublimation, is nonetheless, at the same time, a description of the human psyche and human society, an argument setting forth the conflicts and difficulties encountered by agents in growing up—in effect, a biography of humankind—and a narrative account of problems encountered by men in society, of the ways in which these have been solved, and of the problems that emerge in the wake of earlier resolutions.

The account I have constructed is distinctly an expository account; it is structured in the mode of exposition. But functionally, in terms of the expository mode of connection, the account does accomplish what the other modes accomplish by relating particulars in a different way. To describe fully is to explain, to narrate, to argue. Explaining is a mode of arguing, describing, and narrating. To tell what occurred is to describe what occurred and explain what occurred and resolve problems in the light of insight achieved. The four modes of discourse, then, are formally distinct, but functionally identical.

I have tried in this inquiry to show that, rhetorically, the universe of discourse is a universe of themes and variations in which a novel can be treated as a treatise and a treatise as a novel because both are interpreted by means of fictive arguments, as all communicative structures must be, including the universe itself. Yet if we choose to take a stance from the perspective of experience, we are bound to acknowledge that experientially, for the most part, we do distinguish a "novel" from a treatise; we experience them as somehow different. If they cannot be distinguished by means of the structures of argument we use to make them intelligible to us, we must inquire further to try to discover what it is that does distinguish novels from other discursive structures.

F O U R

MAKING DISCURSIVE WHOLES

All arguments are fictive arguments because they are *made* structures of meaning; and just as arguments in all four modes—description, exposition, narration, and argument—can be discriminated one from the other formally (and/or materially), so do they merge with one another functionally. Similarly, since the formal activity of making does not depend upon whether or not a maker is called author or reader, speaker, or audience, in order to inquire into "making," we can merge author and reader without prejudice. To avoid ambiguity, let me stress the word *formal*. As long as we consider the process, author and reader do the same thing: they relate variables in a structure that is meaningful because it is in some way consequential (the way, as we have seen, depends on the mode of argument). Presumably, author and reader can be distinguished insofar as an author makes his experience communicative by making written arguments and discursive wholes, which are then part of the experience that the reader, in his turn, renders communicative to himself by means of fictive argument. In other words, an author's particulars become variables for me to cope with, variables that I did not have to deal with before he dealt with *his* experience through written discourse. However, this distinction does not alter at all the way in which arguments are made formally.

But we do more than this when we read. Not only do we arrange particulars in a consequential structure according to one of the modes of discourse, such that the particulars take on meaning—indeed, such that particulars are in fact made by virtue of the arrangement; we usually also constitute a self-contained whole separate from other self-contained wholes in the sense that we can point to it and identify it by its title. Thus, for example, while I made descriptive arguments which read *Antony and Cleopatra* as a variation on the theme of *The Peloponnesian War*, I may also constitute organized wholes identifiable as *Antony and Cleopatra* or *The Peloponnesian War*, each uniquely itself. This must be done in order to fully interpret any single literary work, a point we will consider in detail later.

That criticism and interpretation do involve such organization is self-evident, we identify books as separate from other books. But we also confirm and validate this activity negatively when we sometimes write interpretive essays with titles like "The World of William Faulkner" or "The Poetic Vision of So-and-So." Implicit in these titles, in the "world" and the "vision," there are probably separate works that have been constituted, whose singularity we are for the moment ignoring. The implication of this common and often fruitful enterprise is most important. It indicates, it seems to me, that just as we make fictive arguments, we make linguistic wholes. Books are not to be taken as ineluctably "given." The experiencer participates in the making of his experience; he makes the arguments that render experience communicative, and he makes communicative objects that constitute that experience.

We must ask now how we make wholes, since, from the rhetorical perspective, they are not in fact given to us, and we might just as well experience "worlds" or "visions" or nothing at all organized such that we could specify this as a novel called *Emma*, that as a different novel called *Mansfield Park*. Before we can explore this question, however, we must consider whether or not it will be possible to make a whole not only as itself, a singular whole of discourse named in its singularity—we know we can do that because we do it all the time; but can we make such a whole and specify it also as a whole of a particular kind, that is, a "novel"?

Thus far in the argument of this essay I have tried to show that rhetorically we cannot distinguish the "novel" from other instances of discourse in terms of a dichotomy between "fact" and "fiction." Materially, in terms of content, the distinction is patently untenable. That novels have been interpreted as treating of any and all subject matter is evident in the proliferation of subcategories variously attributed to prose fiction; we have had political and psychological novels, picaresque and historical, romantic and realistic novels, the bildungsroman and the naturalistic novel, and many more including innumerable combinations of those I have mentioned. Moreover, any single novel may be and probably has been read as belonging to more than one category.

Formally, the dichotomy is equally untenable. The modes of discourse which render experience meaningful as structures of fictive argument are formally the universal modes of discourse. Consequently, all argument is a "making," all argument is fictive. In other words, a treatise is as "fictional" as a novel, a novel as "factual" as a treatise.

We often resort to the accidental criterion of intention, a criterion accidental precisely because, as we have seen in examining the modes of discourse, it cannot be embodied formally. Thus Frank Kermode, to cite only one example, affirms the fictiveness of discourse but distinguishes "conscious" from "unconscious" fictions, the former comprising imaginative literature.[1] But unless we know, from some source outside of the work itself, what that intention was, we cannot ever infer *with certainty* the "fictional" status of a work from the work itself.

It would be well to elaborate somewhat on this matter. To distinguish novels and short stories as fiction and not fact, and to do so in terms of the author's intention, is to say that the author "consciously" invented people and events, that he meant to write an imaginary story rather than a story about "real" people and events that "really" happened. It is not my purpose to deny that such intentions are possible, even probable. Nor would I object to calling the products of such intentions fictional. But the evidence of, for example, more than one biography of a single person indicates, it seems to me, the converse: that the supposedly nonfictional genre of biography is also fictional. Is the subject of one biographer's interpretation more "real" than the often very different subject of the second biographer? What shall we say about the fictional status of characters in a work identified (again, the criterion is clearly extrinsic) as a roman à clef?

What is most important is that from either extreme of the dichotomy it is impossible to make a *formal* distinction between fiction and nonfiction, qua structures of communication, on the basis of the author's intention. It is easy to document this impossibility with examples of novels that seem to be barely veiled autobiographies, and may or may not be, according to the "invented people and events" criterion, if only we knew—but we do not. Let me cite two interesting and very different examples, and then I will stop laboring the point. Jorge Luis Borges wrote what seems to be a highly tendentious critical essay on one Pierre Menard, "author of *Don Quixote*."[2] It looks like what we conventionally call an essay, complete with scholarly apparatus. We will probably decide that Menard and his strange project never existed, but only because the editor of the collection in which it appears lists the title under "fictions" rather than under essays. In any case, the designation is based on a criterion external to the work.

The second example poses another kind of problem altogether. William Carlos Williams wrote a beautiful little story called "The Use of Force." It is, in its extreme brevity and evocative intensity, almost like a lyric poem. The nameless first-person narrator is a doctor who visits a young school child in a rural district during a diphtheria epidemic and subsequently describes his feelings on being compelled to use force in order to examine her throat, which does in fact disclose the disease. The artistry of the account is unmistakable, and the story appears in anthologies of fiction.[3] However, it suggests a very complex ambiguity with respect to "intention," the fact-fiction dichotomy, and the range of response it evokes. To begin with the latter, the sheer beauty of its language and the economy within which so much rich suggestiveness is achieved is very impressive. On the other hand, it is impressive, too, in terms of the psychological and moral insight the beautiful language conveys. It can be read as a personal essay, albeit unusual among personal essays in its intensity, because of the first-person narration. It can be read as a short story, for aside from the gifted use of language and the style, any account of what happened can be said to be a "story." Did Williams "intend" to give the "facts," to tell what really happened to him once? Maybe he intended to write a story, but "used facts." How can we know, and in a sense, if the story was based on a particular experience he had had, how could he know? Because *we* have a piece of external information, that William Carlos Williams was a country doctor, his first-person narrative of a physician's encounter may be thought to be autobiographical. Similarly, if a first-person narrator is a woman, and the author is known to be a man, we feel sure that the story is "fictional" and meant to be. The truth is that, internally, neither "fact" nor "fiction" can be formally discerned, and neither can intention.

However, supposing we agree to discard both the author's intention and the terms fiction and nonfiction as means by which we can isolate novels for critical consideration. Let us agree that all arguments—rhetorical structures—are fictive arguments and, as consequential, meaningful structures, are formally distinguishable only in terms of the four universal modes of discourse. We have already seen that any one instance of discourse, for example any book, can be interpreted in a great many ways in all four modes. Consequently, it is also clear that "fictive argument" and "novel" are by no means synonymous terms. Let us then consider how we *can* examine novels without resorting to a dichotomy that will not serve. To begin with, a novel, amenable to interpretation in terms of all four modes of discourse, is not in itself a single argument by means of which particulars are arranged. Since most novels which have been interpreted at all have been interpreted in a variety of ways, usually seen as mutually exclusive or contradictory, we can say, at the very least, that a novel is a gathering of fictive arguments related by (if by nothing else) their identification under the rubric of a single title. It is also the case that any such group of arguments is expressive, communicative discourse. When such discourse has sufficient magnitude to be complete and unified in significance, to borrow from Aristotle (perhaps we might suggest that the magnitude is achieved when the discourse accommodates a variety of arguments together with the complexity that results from the functional merging of each and all), we have a written text that can be read as a separate whole, a novel. However, the novel we have identified thus far is not the novel as literary critics see it but only a kind of separate text, a discursive whole as opposed to an argument. For we have distinguished fictive arguments of all kinds from those expressed in books, and to the extent that we may be said to "have" the novel, it is still only a gathering of arguments expressed in a book. We must find a way to discriminate among discursive wholes *kinds* of texts among which will be novels as the term is commonly understood.

Having found neither formal nor material criteria adequate to the purpose, and having found intention fruitless as well, we might do well to turn our attention to the art of rhetoric which governs this enterprise. Form and matter with respect to the "speech" will not do, nor will the "speaker," as we have seen; what remains is audience, the perspective from which we have already derived multiple structures for any single text. Furthermore it seems clear that what we have been doing all along is merging audience and speaker in the sense that we have been treating the reader as engaged in the creative activity of making arguments, an unexceptionable activity engaged in by all literary critics as they interpret texts and an activity dignified for some time now much further afield than literary criticism alone, under the aegis of "the science of hermeneutics." Finally, since for rhetoric it is legitimate "in principle" to presume more than one way of arguing on any issue, there is a sense in which the discriminating of kinds of texts is arbitrary, i.e., depends on the intention of the agent who discriminates. But this sense of intention is not quite the same as that of the term we just rejected.

In effect, intention will not distinguish between "fact" and "fiction" with respect to the alleged nature of any single, signifiable discursive whole, or text, as produced by the intention of any single, signifiable maker of that text (if the text is said to have two or more makers, the point is the same). A maker's or an author's mind and desire do not concern us—they may be a poetic or a grammatical or a dialectical concern or they may not be, but they are most certainly not a rhetorical concern; multiple structure has its critical genesis in the perspective of audience. In any case, the minds and desires of authors are highly problematic. The difficulty can be overcome, however, if we avail ourselves of the full resources of traditional rhetoric, and these are both rich and illuminating.

Let us recall, first of all, that there are two sides—pro and con—in any debate, whether in the legislature or the courtroom, and there is a presumptive opposition even to the position taken in any ceremonial speech of praise or blame. But the two sides of an argument, pro and con, do not limit debate to two possible lines of argument; on the contrary, there is an indefinite number of possible lines of argument, depending on the ingenuity of the speakers in choosing commonplaces with which to invent their arguments. In fact, to put all our cards on the table, in the discussion of fictive argument and the ways in which all four modes of discourse can be varied with respect to agents, problematic situations, circumstances, and ideas, we were relying on single-term commonplaces—agent, idea, etc.—to generate a matrix of argument together with the four modes of discourse, because the "material" terms as well as the "formal" terms—description, narration, exposition, and argument—are all empty "places" until we act in using them, just as the activity relates variables, and only *in the process of the connecting* do they become particulars. If the formal modes of discourse and the four *kinds* of particulars they make were not empty commonplaces, they could not merge functionally as they do. Moreover, within the matrix of argument, indefinitely many variations can occur through the use of different two-term commonplaces used as contraries or contradictories, because, for example, arguments formed in the mode of narration with respect to ideas may be invented in terms of freedom and necessity, or nature and art, or objectivity and subjectivity, and so on.

Commonplaces, then, have been our chief critical resource from the outset. In order to distinguish the sense of intention that can lead us in turn to discriminating *kinds* of texts, among which we will find novels, let us make explicit a commonplace already implicit in the argument of this essay; for all along we have been using the notion of the *one* and the *many*, which discriminated rhetoric and its many structures for a named text from other critical methods and their one, and which now reminds us that a speaker or author is one, but the audience is many. Furthermore, we can ask about the "intention" of audiences, but not with respect to one, single, signifiable text (we can't exhaust the possibilities for a single text because, among other things, audience alters with time); in any case, our problem is not a single text, but an ongoing process of making discursive wholes designated as specific *kinds*. Thus, just as we could say that formally there are four modes of making meaningful discourse, so can we talk about how wholes can be designated as kinds. For in talking about fictive argument and the modes of discourse at length, we did in fact merge audience and author or, treat audience, the many, as maker, a one, without any commitment about any singular maker and his intention. In this sense of intention, the term is essential to our enterprise because in rhetoric, since either side of a controversy is in principle equally defensible, initial choices are arbitrary, a result of the intention of the chooser. We need only bear in mind that we are not concerned with an exclusive, singular intention but with a kind of range of discursive intentionality with respect to the designation of discursive wholes.

The notion of a "range of intentionality," a parameter within which lie possible designations for discursive wholes, is a device for bringing within the compass of inquiry what might seem to be beyond it, the arbitrary intentions of agents. This operation is somewhat analogous to that of discovering the four modes of discourse as an empty, formal matrix of communication. However, it is only analogous; there is a curious and troublesome difference between the two. Until fictive arguments are made in modes of discourse there is no communication at all; therefore the making of argument in written discourse and/or with respect to written discourse brings nominal texts into being (a named text is not the same as a real, or interpreted, constituted text—a distinction that will be clarified presently). But the designating of a text as a novel or a treatise, and so on, is independent of fictive arguments—modes of discourse cut across discriminations of kind—which *make meaning;* thus it is, in a sense, prior to experience because there is nothing about a written text, a bundle of fictive arguments and possible fictive arguments, that can determine its designation. It would seem, then, that the "range of intentionality" must be a nonsensical notion, and the designating of texts completely spontaneous and arbitrary, or at least mysterious, unavailable for rational scrutiny; or else, we must gather it a posteriori, without formal rigor, by listing categories used in libraries, for example—a very unsatisfactory expedient leading to endlessly confusing mixed categories much like the "mixed modes" of the modern rhetoric and composition anthologies.[4]

However, although it may seem impossible to solve, let us state the problem briefly. We must find a way of generating a formal matrix exhaustive of the range of intentionality with respect to designating texts as kinds, such that any discursive whole or bundle of arguments may be designated in as many ways as the matrix permits, just as we discovered that any instance of discourse may be made communicative by rendering it consequential in any one or all four modes of discourse. Only such a matrix affords the flexibility required for interpretation in a context of increasing cultural complexity.

Resolving the difficulty requires a careful reexamination of some aspects of traditional rhetoric, and it is best to begin with Aristotle who provides at the outset the basic terms of an exhaustive matrix. There are three *kinds* of rhetoric: forensic, dealing with actions done in the *past;* political, dealing with action to be taken in the *future;* and epideictic, dealing with the *present.*[5] I have omitted the ends of each, giving only the names and times in order to emphasize the "times" because, since we experience discourse temporally, a temporally rooted matrix seems especially felicitous; however, more important is the fact that it is obviously exhaustive. Nonetheless, before we decide that there is no need to search further, we ought to review the basic features of rhetorical theory to be certain we haven't neglected any relevant aspect of it. As we know, rhetoric as "theory of argument" rests on the assumption that any position may be affirmed or denied legitimately, without prejudice. In consequence, lines of argument are structured by means of commonplaces, pairs of variables used as contraries or contradictories, and any argument of necessity implies its contrary or contradictory, supplementary or independent. Therefore our matrix, which seems to fall outside of this fundamental rhetorical duality, ought to give us pause. We might reason as follows: we have an exhaustive matrix with respect to time—three kinds of rhetoric oriented to past, present, and future, which means three kinds of speech and thus means that we can propose three ways of designating a named text as a "kind" of discursive whole. But isn't *time* itself part of a commonplace? In fact it is part of more than one commonplace; if we look for its contrary we are apt to suggest *space*, and together they have been used to structure discussion of both art and science. If we look for its contradictory, we will find *eternity*, the timeless; finally, if we look for its supplementary, we will find *duration*, for its independent, *the instant*. The arguments which convey meaning are structured by commonplaces, empty terms (they take on meaning only in concrete application) which make no sense at all except in pairs (what does eternity mean if there is no such notion as time?). Therefore, a temporally exhaustive matrix of intentionality is not truly exhaustive unless it is completed by a term which will encompass the atemporal. Again Aristotle provides the missing dimension in the term *dialectic*, of which rhetoric with its three temporally exhaustive kinds is said to be the counterpart in the first sentence of his *Rhetoric*.

Furthermore, what rhetoric and dialectic are said to have in common guarantees the congruity of the latter with the other three terms, whereas the respects in which they differ indicate that dialectic is the appropriate term to complete the matrix. It is important that the necessity of that fourth term be absolutely clear before we return to Aristotle to examine the evidence for the choice of dialectic because, on the face of it, as I said earlier, the three modes of time which govern forensic, political, and epideictic rhetoric are exhaustive in themselves. The crux of the argument is really quite simple, but I will risk repeating it once more in a slightly different way. That is, the fundamental operational tool of a rhetorical method, however it may be and must be elaborated as the activity goes on, is the empty topic or commonplace which consists of a pair of variables. Aristotle tells us that the rhetorician ought to have a lot of them at his command so that he can choose the best ones for his purpose as the need may arise;[6] indeed, the first two books of the treatise are devoted on the whole to lines of argument and the commonplaces which produce them. If that is so, it is clear that we cannot treat time as substantive in some sense in the context of a rhetorical enterprise. Varieties of *times* give us a very good "place" as part of the commonplace time-space taken as contraries; but if that is the case, we cannot ignore the same commonplaces taken as contradictories. It is interesting to note that we haven't really ignored its contrary either! We "judged" (a rhetorical function) *space* irrelevant when we limited our discussion to discourse, which, whether spoken or written, cannot be made communicative by the use of extensional criteria. Nor is it frivolous or arbitrary to say that we must, once we make an initial choice of *time*, take into account its contradictory, *eternity* or *timelessness*. We are now engaged in a method of debate, and, having chosen the method, we have set into motion an activity that will inevitably generate opponents—*since it is legitimate to argue on either side of a question.* To remain for the present within the conceptual context of Aristotelian rhetoric, as long as we are concerned with contingencies—what isn't necessarily thus and no other—we can engage in debate.[7] If I say, then, for example, "Great works of literature in time are forgotten," someone may and probably will reply, "Nonsense. Great works of literature are eternal, as meaningful to one generation as to another." However, in constructing a matrix of intentionality, I want to avoid controversy. I don't want to set up a system in terms of which I shall have to say that one of these two positions is wrong. I don't want to win a debate; therefore, I must avoid debate altogether because what I do want is to find a method of literary analysis that will permit a pluralism of interpretations in some kind of harmonious interplay. Therefore I must deal with the contradictory of time (wherein past, present, and future are exhaustive) by incorporating it as part of the matrix, a perfectly satisfactory solution from every point of view.[8] I have a pluralistic instrument because it is inclusive of all possibilities with respect to time and timelessness, and I have a formal matrix, empty and exhaustive, with which to inquire into the range of intentionality for designating named, written texts.

It remains to see whether dialectic will meet the requirement. As I noted before, for Aristotle rhetoric is a counterpart of dialectic. The crucial similarities of the two are these: "No other of the arts draws opposite conclusions: dialectic and rhetoric alone do this" (*Rhetoric* 1.1.1355a35). "Neither rhetoric nor dialectic is the scientific study of any one separate subject: both are faculties for providing arguments" (1.2.1356a34–35). As long as dialectic is a way of making arguments and draws opposite conclusions (ergo, proceeds by means of commonplaces), it is a congruent part of the matrix. On the other hand, dialectic differs from rhetoric insofar as "the consideration of syllogisms of all kinds, without distinction, is the business of dialectic" (1.1.1355a9), whereas the enthymeme only, a sort of syllogism, is proper to rhetoric. "The function of [rhetoric is] to discern the real and the apparent means of persuasion, just as it is the function of dialectic to discern the real and the apparent syllogism" (1.1.1355b15–16). This means that whereas rhetoric is concerned with what communicates best (Aristotle, incidentally, believes that what is true naturally tends to persuade best (1.1.1355a21), but the end of rhetoric is persuasion, not truth), dialectic is concerned with valid argument regardless of its persuasiveness in a particular instance. Dialectic, thus, tests premises and determines whether arguments are or are not specious, even though it is a universal art and not a method for discovering truth in a science.[9] Obviously, then, since what is *persuasive* at any given time is contingent upon many circumstances, rhetoric may be said to be timebound, whereas dialectic, concerned with valid argument—a formal question—is not time-bound. Consequently, dialectic will indeed meet our requirements for completing the matrix of intentionality.

From Aristotle's *Rhetoric*, then, we have devised a means of determining the range of choices available to audiences or readers or critics for designating named texts, or named bundles of fictive arguments or possible fictive arguments, as kinds, and, in consequence of which designation is made, finding in them or attributing to them certain kinds of properties. We are saying, then, that we can treat a named text dialectically, forensically, deliberatively,[10] or epideictically. We are especially indebted to Aristotle, as well, because of his distinction, which we noted in chapter 1, with respect to epideictic: that the audience does not judge what the ceremonial speech of praise and blame is *about,* does not judge the content of the speech, but rather observes the speech itself for itself. In other words, we do not say, yes, what is being praised is a value and praiseworthy, or no, it is not; we say, rather, whether the speech itself is a good speech. The distinction is important because forensic and deliberative speeches lead to a judgment about their content, one which can at most only imply the excellence of the speech qua speech if it was successful in persuading to action; yet its success or failure might have been attributable at least in part to something beyond the speaker's control. On the other hand, the epideictic speech is judged only qua speech. It is, so to speak, the rhetorical kind of rhetoric, the rhetorician's rhetoric, and when we treat a named text epideictically, we are calling it a novel in the strict sense of the word.

Before we can develop the four kinds and show more concretely how the matrix works, however, we must consider whether or not the four possibilities in any way guarantee the critic or reader or audience freedom to choose among them. Of course, they do not, and unless we can ground the chooser's freedom in a rhetorical system consistent with the matrix of intentionality which we have so painstakingly grounded in Aristotle's *Rhetoric,* we have not accomplished what we undertook to do in this part of our inquiry: that is, to show that a full use of traditional rhetoric, of "argument" as well as "tropes," will enable us to distinguish novels from other kinds of texts despite the fact that all meaningful discourse must be fictive argument. Our difficulty here is that Aristotelian rhetoric really will not allow for that freedom.

In order to examine the sense in which it will not and the reasons, I should have to discuss Aristotle's philosophy to an extent far beyond what is germane to this inquiry. It should suffice to point out that nowhere in the *Rhetoric* is there any device for making a choice or any discussion of the possibility of doing so. The rhetorician is free to exercise his powers of invention to the fullest—but he is not free to choose the context in which he will exercise them. That context is determined by complex of institutional, societal realities. Nevertheless, the Aristotelian concepts of the three kinds of rhetoric and dialectic are flexible enough so that the *Rhetoric* affords material relevant to deliberating, judging, displaying, and discerning logical connections in much wider senses than those explicitly touched on in the text itself. This flexibility will permit us to use the matrix of intentionality for our own purposes. But in order to ground the freedom to choose in the rhetorical tradition we must turn to another rhetorician, who extends the range of rhetoric and furnishes a device which implies that freedom we are seeking.

In the *De Inventione* (1.6.8), Cicero repeated the three kinds of rhetoric he had from Aristotle, but the resemblance ends there. For Cicero, rhetoric was part of political science, a science which had need of eloquence (1.5.6); indeed, the first four chapters of the first book concern the very origin of human civility, an origin attributed to a wise man's *spontaneous* awareness that men needn't be savage and to his combining his wisdom with eloquence to persuade them to engage in civilizing pursuits; and the chapters conclude with an account of the separation of wisdom and eloquence or philosophy and rhetoric, and the need to reunite them. For Cicero, then, rhetoric and dialectic are not universal arts with no special subject matter but universal arts applicable to all subject matters. Rhetoric is the art of invention, and dialectic the art of judgment of the validity of arguments invented.[11] The change from Aristotle to Cicero is profound. Aristotle says of dialectic and rhetoric that they deal "simply with words and forms of reasoning," unlike "sciences dealing with definite subjects."[12] For Cicero, rhetoric is the method of the practical sciences, philosophy the method of theoretic sciences; for, as he tells us, general questions not involving individual persons and actions are reserved to philosophy.[13] However, we discover that the instrument of inquiry remains the commonplace or topic which always involves two opposing positions.[14] Consequently, it is in Cicero that we find full support for our contention that we make sense of the chaos of experience by inventing fictive arguments linked in modes of discourse which, in effect, invent the world for us, at least the world as significantly communicated. In Cicero, Aristotle's arts of words have become the methods by which all substantive knowledge is acquired.

But Cicero does something else for us as well. In the seventh chapter of the first book of *De Inventione*, after listing the divisions of rhetoric or its parts as Invention, Arrangement, Expression, Memory, and Delivery, he decides to treat invention first which is "the most important of all the divisions, and above all is used in every kind of pleading" (1.7.9). What is important for us here is Cicero's blurring of the very careful distinctions Aristotle made among deliberative, judicial, and demonstrative rhetoric (judicial and demonstrative correspond to Aristotle's forensic and epideictic), a blurring that results from his emphasis throughout on the aspects of rhetoric as he sees it that are equally applicable to all three kinds. The measure of the radical conceptual change can be taken in these alterations of terms, although they are made with the casualness of a simple translation from one language to another. Epideictic means display in Greek, as opposed to apodictic, which refers to scientific demonstration of the true nature of things. When the arts of words *are* arts of things, when we get to things only through the words about them, demonstrative rhetoric is not at all misleading and a distinction would be meaningless. Since the three kinds of rhetoric have lost their complicated distinguishing marks set against methodological similarities that we find in Aristotle (in fact Cicero devotes only sections 155–77 of the second book to political and epideictic speeches, running to something under twelve pages; section 178 concludes the treatise), we would expect other kinds of discriminations to organize the work, and we find the schematism we are looking for in the chapter following the divisions of the art of rhetoric.

Cicero begins *De Inventione* by saying that "every subject which contains in itself a controversy to be resolved by speech and debate involves a question about a fact...a definition...the nature of an act...or about legal processes" (1.8.10). These are the four "issues" which form the basis of dispute: briefly, the *conjectural*—what is the fact; the *definitive*—how to describe or characterize the fact; the *qualitative*—what special circumstances must be taken into account; the *translative*—what is the proper procedure, or under what jurisdiction ought the issue to be debated and resolved. We can explain these best in terms of an example from judicial rhetoric: the conjectural issue would ask, Did A kill B? The definitive asks, Was it murder, or manslaughter, or justifiable homicide, etc.? The qualitative might ask, Granting that A did it and that it was murder, was he driven to it by B's persecution of him? If it was murder, did A do it for money, or was it a mercy killing? The translative asks whether a change of venue would be more apt to guarantee a fair trial, or whether the case ought to be tried under federal or state law, or as murder or violation of civil rights, etc. We need add only two additional citations from Cicero. At the end of the passage in which he first introduces the issues, Cicero says that, with respect to the issues, "where none applies, there can be no controversy"

(1.8.10). The second occurs immediately following, at the beginning of the next section: "As to the dispute about a fact, this can be assigned to any time. For the question can be 'What has been done?' ... and 'What is being done?' ... and what is going to occur..." (1.8.11).

The passages I have cited make clear the real significance for this inquiry of the kind of expansion of the art of rhetoric that Cicero effected. If all controversy is governed by the same four issues, either one or more for any given dispute, then dialectic and the three kinds of rhetoric are indeed, in terms of Ciceronian rhetoric, a matrix of intentionality because any one of the issues can be debated dialectically, judicially, deliberatively, or demonstratively, depending on the rhetorician's choice. Cicero's remark about the issue of fact and its applicability to any "time" is quite conclusive. Moreover, that the rhetorician must consider his objectives and determine the appropriate arena for his debate is confirmed by and embedded in the system itself with the translative issue, the device which focuses attention on the problem of choice that concerns us.

It would be disingenuous to suggest that Cicero conceived of the translative issue precisely as I have treated it here, or that he meant to say that any *one particular* issue of fact necessarily could be treated with respect to the past, present, or future indifferently. It is also the case that at any given time a rhetorician's choices may be limited by the prior choice of his opponents. A lawyer must defend his client in court if the client has been charged with a crime even if he would prefer to have the law changed under which his client was arrested. But in general rather than in particular the range of possible choice remains, and the innovations of Cicero, if they were perhaps opaque in an age of oratory, have long since been realized in the concrete.

In our time laws have been changed, not through the *deliberative* process of the assembly only, but through breaking the law or filing suit in the courts in order to make it possible to have a law declared unconstitutional when there is little hope that a legislature will repeal it. On the other hand, in the United States, criminal activities that cannot be prosecuted in the courts for lack of appropriate evidence are often exposed, and, in a sense the criminals are "persecuted" in Congress, in quasi-*judicial* hearings held in the name of legislation. *Demonstrations* of the present consequences of past injustice are held in lieu of criminal proceedings that cannot be held for a variety of reasons. The *dialectical* exchanges of philosophers to determine values in ongoing discussions give way to deliberations on values in international bodies. If these are not examples of the *translative* issue as it is dealt with in the concrete in the twentieth century, they are examples of something close enough to it to be indistinguishable from it. And it is precisely because we can often choose to deal with our world in action in any one of the four ways, regardless of what is at issue, that we can choose to designate written named texts in any one of the four ways that constitute and exhaust the range of intentionality. Thus, a named text can be read dialectically as philosophy about ideas; it can be read judicially as science about things; it can be read deliberatively as history about occurrences; or it can be read demonstratively as a novel, embodying styles and manners.

A text read *dialectically* is read in terms of ideas. For Aristotle it is the function of dialectic to examine reasonings, syllogisms, to discern the real and the apparent;[15] for Cicero, general questions are the pursuit of philosophy, dialectic the means of judging the validity of inventions, the only mode of reasoning his philosophy accommodates.[16] It is dialectic that rises above the particularities of audience to be "used in formulation of problems for inquiry and in disputation between positions asserted and questioned . . . ," and "to secure agreement with, or refutation of, common . . . or expert opinions."[17]

A text read *judicially* is read as science about things. The scientist questions nature rather than merely observing; and a question posed is a crucial experiment and must be answered one way or the other. The scientist judges then whether things were and are necessarily thus or so. The necessity attaching to what is conceived as scientific truth or fact is achieved in discourse in the rhetorical mode concerned with the past, the one mode in which, in a contingent world, necessity obtains, since what was must necessarily be what it was beyond possibility of alteration.

A text read *deliberatively* is read as a history of occurrences; it is read in terms of sequences which extend beyond the work to sequences conditioning it as well as giving it subject matter. If it seems paradoxical that deliberation, oriented to the future, should be the rhetoric of history, it is only apparently so. Deliberation is a way of dealing with the past and present to project to the future. Aristotle tells us that it is useful for the political speaker to know the history of his country (*Rhetoric* 1.4.1360a30); when he comes to discuss argument common to all kinds of oratory, the two main classifications are example, which is like induction, and enthymeme, which is like syllogism. The chapter on example is concerned almost entirely with political oratory (2.20.1393a31–1394a20), and he says toward the end that rather than inventing examples (like fables) it is better for the political speaker to quote "what has actually happened, since in most respects the future will be like what the past has been" (2.20.1394a6–9). From our point of view we need bear in mind simply that the "content" of deliberation is always, inevitably, an account or accounts of past occurrences, since the future is unknown except by extrapolation from the past.

Finally, when we read a text *demonstratively*, we read it as a novel, we designate it as a discursive whole and attribute characteristics to it not with respect to what it says about the nature of things, or in terms of the sequence of occurrences dealt with, or in terms of a world of ideas of which it is an instance; rather we attribute to it characteristics of discourse itself: style, arrangement, manners of speech and what they imply, linguistic devices or tropes, and so on.

Let me try to illustrate this formulation with some brief examples. If we designate *The Brothers Karamazov* as a novel by reading it demonstratively, there are various questions we might ask respecting the chapter in it devoted to Ivan's poem of the Grand Inquisitor. We might ask, for example, about its relation to what precedes it, and its relation to the text as a whole. We might inquire into the chapter's function with respect to the integration of all parts we have discerned, or we might look at its language, tracing patterns of imagery and their relation to other patterns of imagery we think we have discerned throughout the book.

If we ask, however, about the doctrine it seems to express, the theological and philosophical view it advances, and then discuss the implications of that view, as we have construed it, I take it we are not treating the work as a novel. We would be reading it dialectically as philosophy about ideas, and that chapter as part of a philosophic work is radically different functionally, and therefore virtually, from what it is as part of a novel. Again our analysis and judgment of the final sections of *War and Peace* will vary depending upon whether we read that named text demonstratively as a novel, deliberatively as a history of the Napoleonic invasion of Russia, judicially as a sociological study of early nineteenth-century Russia, or dialectically as philosophy of history.

A named text may be designated, obviously, in a variety of ways such that it may "belong" now to this "kind," now to that. Benjamin Disraeli's *Sybil* may be read demonstratively as a novel. We happen to know in this case that the author's intention was somewhat ambiguous. He meant to write a novel and called it that, but meant it also to express his political views, so that it might be said to embody[18] intentions both deliberative and judicial as well as demonstrative, since it was to show what is the nature of things with respect to the structure of society and to counsel those who could effect change in the future by an analysis of occurrences in the past.[19] Although *Sybil* has not enjoyed the acclaim of literary critics, it has been treated as a novel. However, it has also been treated as if it were a work in political science and as an accurate history and explanation of the events that led to the Chartist movement.[20]

This is not to say, and the point needs to be stressed, that to treat a work as a novel precludes history, the discussion of ideas, or a vision of social reality and the nature of things. It is to say that of a text we call a novel we ask primarily about itself qua text, qua discursive whole. The way in which the dialectical, deliberative, and judicial are clothed in a novel, we shall see presently. What seems to me indisputable is that only in virtue of a favorable judgment with respect to the disposition of its parts, its style, and its language are we even likely to say a novel has engendered a true vision of social reality and of the nature of things and human nature, of accurate history, and of good philosophy.

We designate novels, then, by reading texts demonstratively, that is, focusing on the discourse itself, on disposition, on manners of speech depicted, and on the qualities of language and style. Before we go on, however, it will be useful to recall what was mentioned earlier; that we do in fact often talk about the work of an author we read as novelist *as if* it consisted in a rich variety of themes quite independent of any systematic, self-contained, separate wholes or named texts. As I have said before, a whole, a single novel, is by no means necessarily a *given;* we must intend to make it and must do so. We can talk about events that occur and people who live in Yoknapatawpha county; to point to and talk about named texts such as *Absalom, Absalom* or *The Hamlet* is to do quite another thing. That other thing is precisely the making of boundaries which will permit us to separate discourse into novels distinct from one another. To be sure, unless we do this, we may have, in effect, designated a single named novel called "Yoknapatawpha County," or "The World of William Faulkner," or something of the sort.

Having separated novels from other kinds of discursive wholes or named texts, we must go on to indicate the ways in which we organize the wholes we call novels—in effect, make bundles of fictive arguments of indefinite number into separate wholes. Since wholes can be organized in more than one way, we shall find that the novels we make can also be differentiated by their formal mode of organization into genres—philosophical novels of ideas and opinions, narrative novels of action, sequential novels of natural events and human nature, and demonstrative novels of style and invention, characters and manners. How we organize and generically designate novelistic wholes, which we will subsequently interpret by means of connected fictive arguments in four modes of discourse, is the next step in our inquiry.

FIVE

MAKING NOVELS

Any novel can be made in any one of the four modes of organization, just as it can be read in any mode of discourse; and in any *given* organization a named text designated demonstratively must be organized in only one of the four modes, as we shall see presently. However, it is usually organized in the same way by most critics who discuss it, whatever their other differences may be; that is, most named texts said to be novels are usually read by readers and critics at a given time either as philosophical or as sequential novels, for example—the psychological or sociological novels characteristic of some kinds of criticism—as the result of cultural influences which may condition all modes of criticism at that time.

In any case, granting that cultural contingencies limit what critics *do,* we must continue to explore what can be done, and there are two problems to address at this stage of our inquiry: that of how to organize discourse to make separate discursive wholes, and how to differentiate kinds of novels. Before we begin it is important to emphasize that dialectic and the three kinds of rhetoric provided an exhaustive *formal* matrix for differentiating the novel from all other kinds of discursive wholes that might be chosen as designations for any named texts. However, the problem of making perceptibly separate discursive wholes is a purely formal one, having *nothing* to do with the way in which an instance of discourse is designated and *everything* to do with the temporality of all discourse. Consequently, the formal process of making discursive wholes would be equally applicable to the three possible kinds of texts—dialectical, deliberative, and judicial—we are not now concerned with organizing, and we can confine our illustrations of the process to making novels. We should expect, too, that if there is more than one way of organizing a discursive whole, each way of doing so will make a different kind of novel, as, no doubt, it would make a different kind of history, if we were reading deliberatively, a different kind of science if we read judicially, and a different kind of philosophy dialectically. Finally, we would also expect that the genres of the novel, as was suggested at the end of the last chapter, will resemble in some way forms of dialectic and of each of the three kinds of rhetoric, since those exhaust the possible kinds of discursive wholes from the perspective of discourse qua communication, which is obviously the perspective of any rhetorical enterprise including one concerned with literary criticism.

First of all, then, we must find a way of making separate, identifiable wholes, and since discourse is a temporal medium, the boundaries available to us are *beginning, end,* and *middle,* the area which intervenes between beginning and end. These will provide us with principles by means of which we can make separate, identifiable novels and discriminate kinds of novels as well; and since the novel once made is self-evidently an instance of itself, the principle that organizes it clearly gives it the unity of a separate whole and provides the coherence that makes sense of the relations among variables which give us the particulars of any fictive arguments according to which the novel may be interpreted.

We can organize a novel in terms of *beginning,* and when we do this, "beginning" infuses the novel, functioning throughout to give it unity and coherence. We say that the beginning of anything is unconditioned, that is, is discourse before which there is nothing. Consequently, the beginning is spontaneous, arbitrary. If we organize in terms of end, we may indeed argue that the beginning is not arbitrary at all, as we shall see. But beginning, qua beginning, and thus characterized as unconditioned by anything preceding it, is contextually free. Why is "something" begun? Because an agent desires, is emotionally moved to say, to do, to think, to make, and so on. When we organize a novel *in terms of* beginning, therefore, we are organizing it in terms of what agents do, and feel, and say, seen as spontaneous and arbitrary; these provide the rationale for the connections among particulars in any mode of discourse, any fictive argument we use to structure the novel. We show that what agents do, feel, and say determines what the world really is and what is desirable. Middle is not functional in this mode of organization; it is as if the whole in its entirety is a congeries of beginnings, of what is said, done, and felt. The end is simply the end of those feelings determined and set into motion by the initial desire of the agent. To organize in terms of *beginning* is to organize a discursive whole which presents doing, speech, and feeling limited only by the initial discriminations of the agent's unconditioned beginning; and the novel organized in terms of beginning is clearly the demonstrative novel of style and invention, of characters and manners. Why? Because the novel of "beginning," of the unconditioned, exists by virtue of an agent's invention. Like an epideictic speech in Aristotle, it communicates itself as object to be appreciated; like a demonstrative speech in Cicero, it displays the values for which it argues. But its values are the values of discourse qua discourse (as the values of a philosophical novel, as we shall see, will be the values of discourse qua ideas expressed); thus they are style, manners of speech, and the characters of worlds and of what agents do and feel as these are invented by language, what they say.

The novel that takes its beginning from an unconditioned agent I shall call, borrowing Cicero's term, a *conjectural* novel, because the conjectural issue which asks whether someone did or does or will do something is the issue that initiates controversy insofar as there is nothing to communicate until agents act, or speak, or contemplate acting. And I mean controversy in its broadest sense, variety of opinion on any issue, because in the absence of divergent opinion human beings would not need to communicate with one another at all. Finally, the conjectural novel is, above all, the "novelist's novel," just as epideictic is the rhetorician's rhetoric.

Any novel may be organized as a conjectural novel of style and manners. Let me offer two illustrations of such an organization, beginning, however, with an admonition: what I say about these two novels as systematic wholes ordered by doing and feeling and speaking—the principle of beginning—is determined by my decision to organize them this way. Until they are organized, there are no two novels. But that they are to be organized in terms of beginning is my choice, and that choice determines what I will select and order to illustrate the principle of organization and support my argument that it "makes sense" to organize them this way.

It is essential to emphasize this because the reader of this discussion will inevitably identify the conjectural novel with what he sees as a major trend in twentieth-century fiction, and I shall compound the error by using two twentieth-century novels as examples of how one organizes a novel in terms of beginning. Indeed, there is a sense in which he will be quite right to do so. As I noted at the beginning of this chapter, in a given culture, texts are designated and organized in one way for the most part; and the complex interrelations among novelists and readers, authors and critics, tend to foster cultural homogeneity. Novelists are also readers, and critics make fictive arguments in written discourse just as novelists do. Nevertheless, the overall difference we may perceive between twentieth-century novels and those written in the eighteenth or nineteenth centuries is not really as radical as it sometimes seems. Let me offer some random observations that seem to me to bear out my contention.

First of all, cultural homogeneity is always more evident at a distance; close up it is often full of holes. Fictive argument in modes of discourse and the making of discursive texts are always an inventive business. It is the case that novels like Beckett's *Molloy* or *Malone Dies* are apt to "feel" very twentieth-century. Yet Forster's *A Passage to India* and Lawrence's *Sons and Lovers* or any Hemingway can be said to be equally twentieth-century, and they "feel" radically unlike Beckett or Joyce or Woolf or Faulkner. Then, consider Sterne's *Tristram Shandy* and its near-forgotten close relations: how did they get written in the eighteenth century? On the other hand, consider the plight of the nineteenth-century novelist who lacked twentieth-century linguistic preoccupations and twentieth-century linguistic criticism as part of his cultural milieu. Did his achievement suffer? Apparently not. I would simply call the reader's attention to Charles Dickens and an essay by Dorothy Van Ghent on *Great Expectations*, which she analyzes as a world and the agents in it created entirely by its language.[1] In all seriousness, I find it one of the most illuminating essays on Dickens that I know of, and it offers a highly laudatory interpretation of consequences of Dickens's style, technique, and language, which have more frequently been deplored as failure to rise above caricature. I hope Dickens would have found the essay illuminating; but I imagine he might have found it strange.

In short, the conjectural novel of style and manners is any novel organized in terms of beginning whether by a novelist, a critic, or any other reader; and since audience will organize and thereby make novels more frequently for all named texts than authors will, we shall bear in mind that any text can be organized in any one of the four modes of organization we shall be examining, and that just as no text bears the mark of its author's intention, no text bears an indisputable mark of its author's world when we examine it as a communicative structure. Indeed, there are no novels until we make them. Let us begin by making *The Tin Drum*.

We can organize *The Tin Drum*, by Günter Grass, as a conjectural novel by pointing out that the narrator, Oskar Matzerath, begins to tell the story of his life from his bed in a mental hospital, establishing almost simultaneously that he is free to begin where he chooses, that he is writing the story of his life, that he is writing a novel. There is no relation implied between the freedom to begin anywhere and novels and autobiographies; nor is there any distinction made between a novel and the story of one's life. Neither are they said to be identical. Oskar simply says what he says:

> How shall I begin?
> You can begin a story in the middle and create confusion by striking out boldly, backward and forward. You can be modern, put aside all mention of time and distance and, when the whole thing is done, proclaim, or let someone else proclaim, that you have finally, at the last moment, solved the space-time problem. Or you can declare at the very start

that it's impossible to write a novel nowadays, but then, behind your own back so to speak, give birth to a whopper, a novel to end all novels. . . .

I shall begin far away from me; for no one ought to tell the story of his life who hasn't the patience to say a word or two about at least half of his grandparents before plunging into his own existence.[2]

There is no limitation on what the world of the novel may be beyond the inventive gift of its maker, and no relation between particulars beyond his making them. "I tell him incidents from my life, so he can get to know me. . . . He seems to treasure my stories, because every time I tell him some fairy tale, he shows his gratitude by bringing out his latest knot construction" (p. 15). Reality and fairy tale are indistinguishable because they are used interchangeably and *not* distinguished by the agent who uses them. They are connected because he desires that they should be.

In the beginning there is an agent starting to tell his life story. He is clearly making it in the telling when we organize the novel in terms of beginning. The agent does what he does by means of three instruments, which enable him to make things happen: his drum, his vocal power to shatter glass, and his self-made identity as an emotionally, intellectually mature three-year-old. The end of *The Tin Drum* is the end of the agent's statement of what happened to him and what he did:

What more shall I say: born under light bulbs deliberately stopped growing at age of three, given drum, sang glass to pieces, smelled vanilla, coughed in churches, observed ants, decided to grow, buried drum, emigrated to the West, lost the East . . . celebrating this day my thirtieth birthday and still afraid of the Black Witch. . . . I am running out of words, and still I cannot help wondering what Oskar is going to do after his inevitable discharge from the mental hospital. (p. 587)

The principle of the unconditioned beginning makes sense of this because it is a principle of creativity validated by the creation of the novel itself.

Since I have begun with the example of *The Tin Drum,* in which I have treated what is done and felt and said in terms of a single agent, let me point out that this "kind" of novel is not meant to be identified as what is sometimes called picaresque. It is not simply that picaresque usually denotes a fixed category whereas I have contended that any novel may be variously organized; it is also that I have organized the whole out of a series of feelings, assertions, and actions operating as principles, and not in terms of an agent with a fixed identity who *encounters* a series of events not otherwise connected than by his participation in them. In what I am calling the conjectural novel, the feeling and desire are central; indeed, the "agent" may be conceived as multiple agents as well as a single agent.

Jean-Paul Sartre's *The Reprieve*[3] can serve as an illustration. We would select things done, words spoken, and emotions felt that connect persons and events occurring in widely separated locales and may be conceived in this mode of organization as arbitrary with respect to those persons and events. We would point to chapter headings, which are dated beginning with Friday, September 23, and ending with Friday, September 30. But it is not the chronological notation that connects people and events, but rather the deeds, pronouncements, and passions of those agents suggested by the dates and referred to briefly throughout—Hitler, Daladier, Chamberlain, Masarik.

If we organize in terms of beginning, we see that here, to the persons of the novel, anything can happen, and nothing suggests what must occur, or what persons or kinds of locale must be or will be introduced, or how what occurs must be accounted for beyond feelings or desires which move men to act in some way or other. We know only that what connects them, whoever or whatever they may be, are what those agents feel and do who initiate the novel, make it a novel, and then the disparate responses, the feelings, of other agents whose behavior is, in turn, not *in principle* predictable. What we have then, if we organize *The Reprieve* as a conjectural novel, is a plurality of actional principles which arouse emotions. These emotions or passions fit together by arousing a series of actions in turn.

The end of the novel can be seen as juxtaposing many simples related through the emotions:

> Let them sheathe their swords if they so pleased, let them have their war, or not, I don't care; I am not duped. The accordian was mute. Mathieu resumed his walk round the yard. "I'm free, and shall remain so," he thought....
> Daladier took a look; it was the first time he had spoken since their departure from Munich:
> "They are going to mob me, I suppose."
> Leger did not protest....
> He came into the room with the newspapers; Ivich was sitting on the bed.
> "It's all right, they signed last night."
> She raised her eyes, he looked pleased, but said no more, daunted by the expression in her eyes.
> "Do you mean there won't be a war?" she asked.
> "Yes."
> No war; no planes over Paris; no bomb-shattered ceilings; life must now be lived....

The plane had grounded. Daladier climbed heavily out of the cabin and set his foot on the ladder; he was pale. A vast clamor greeted him, the crowd surged through the cordon of police and swept the barriers away; Milan drank and said with a laugh: "To France! To England! To our glorious allies!" Then he flung the glass against the wall; they shouted: "Hurrah for France! Hurrah for England! Hurrah for peace!" They were carrying flags and flowers. Daladier stood on the top step and looked at them dumbfounded. Then he turned to Leger and said between his teeth: "The God-damned fools!" (pp. 344–45)

The novel organized in terms of *end* is, first of all, a whole which is logically prior to parts, its ordering different from that of the conjectural novel; for we do not use beginning, an agent or agents who spontaneously do, feel, and speak, to organize the whole. Rather, the novel organized in terms of *end* is organized by a principle which affords insight into prior complications which is a simultaneous insight into the resolution, and integrates complication and resolution into a unified whole. Thus, to organize in terms of *end* is to organize a *qualitative* novel of action, for the ordering is of parts as "actions-leading-up-to" discoveries each of which makes sense of what precedes it—the beginnings—and "actions-moving-out-from," reversals making probable the end, which may then be seen as necessary. *End* is the exhaustion of the possibilities generated by the beginning; but these are not cumulations of continuously generated feelings. Rather, the discoveries and reversals organize the whole such that the necessary end is related to the beginning, almost in the mode of syllogistic argument, through the middle. The qualitative novel doesn't begin at the end in temporal terms; but its nontemporal beginning really is the end because *end qualifies* everything that precedes, and determines the real significance of action that might otherwise suggest only a definitional meaning (a meaning we will explore in detail presently). The most obvious example is a qualitative ordering of *Oedipus the King,* in which, to take only one point, the quick temper of Oedipus and his failure to really pay attention to what Tiresias is saying might be the sort of natural arrogance and impatience that lend him verisimilitude as a proud monarch. The resonance these characteristics of behavior take on later is a function of end; indeed, Oedipus doesn't himself know the meaning of his actions until the end. The qualitative mode of organization lends itself very well to tragic irony because it stresses action that is meaningful not simply in itself but in the light of an end yet unknown by the agents when the action occurs. (There are many ways to organize *Oedipus,* but I would guess that Sophocles did it in terms of end because that way the use of a widely known story would work to enhance effect rather than diminish it; novelty would be no advantage.)

Let me turn now to a second and different sort of example and treat it in some detail. I would begin to organize James Joyce's *Portrait of the Artist as a Young Man* as a qualitative novel of action by considering the implication of the title. Since "young man" and "artist" are not synonymous (not all young men are or will be artists), how can or how does it happen that the young man will become an artist? In the first part of the novel, Stephen Dedalus struggles with hypotheses about the universe, about God: "What was after the universe? Nothing." "God's real name was God."[4] Most of all, he wonders about language: "Words which he did not understand he said over and over to himself till he had learned them by heart: and through them he had glimpses of the real world about him" (p. 62).

Sex and religion involve a struggle for him because both are profoundly seductive, the former with all the power of nature, the latter with another kind of power: "He listened in reverent silence now to the priest's appeal and through the words he heard even more distinctly a voice bidding him approach, offering him secret knowledge and secret power. . . . He would know obscure things, hidden from others, from those who were conceived and born children of wrath." (p. 159). Discarding both, he turns to learning, preparing to enter the university: "The end he had been born to serve yet did not see had led him to escape by an unseen path: and now it beckoned to him once more and a new adventure was about to be opened to him" (p. 165).

The significance of these various struggles and discoveries, however, is opaque in this reading until we grasp the qualifying principle in terms of which they cohere. The last passage cited is important in this light. Stephen has struggled with hypothesis after hypothesis as to the "end he had been born to serve." They have not satisfied him. Then he does recognize that end: "Yes! Yes! Yes! He would create proudly out of the freedom and power of his soul, as the great artificer whose name he bore, a living thing, new and soaring and beautiful, impalpable, imperishable" (p. 170).

Now he begins to understand what he has become, and what remains for him to discover: How can he become an artist? Final recognition and the reversal in action which it engenders do not emerge, however, until the long conversation with Lynch on aesthetics in which Stephen achieves the insight which organizes the novel (given this way of organizing it), unifies it and tells us why, in effect, these parts belong together. He recognizes that there are things which must be perceived:

> When you have apprehended that basket as one thing and have then analyzed it according to its form and apprehended it as a thing you make the only synthesis which is logically and esthetically permissible. You see that it is that thing which it is and no other thing. The radiance of which he

speaks is the scholastic *quidditas,* the *whatness* of a thing. This supreme quality is felt by the artist when the esthetic image is first conceived in his imagination. . . . The instant wherein that supreme quality of beauty, the clear radiance of the esthetic image, is apprehended luminously by the mind which has been arrested by its wholeness and fascinated by its harmony is the luminous silent stasis of esthetic pleasure. (p. 213)

To be an artist one must be in a position to perceive the beautiful. Thus, this insight or discovery leads to the reversal which is the necessary departure from Ireland. This nexus of discovery and reversal is the principle of wholeness in a qualitative novel of action, and by determining and validating the necessity of the end provides the reference and meaning for the parts in their interrelations. The way in which *end* performs the qualifying function is worth looking at closely. The "parts" unified are "quantitative" parts in two senses, the first of which is simply the temporal sense of beginning, middle, and end which are unified in some way or other to produce any discursive whole. In the second sense, there are five parts: three parts of the novel devoted, roughly, to language, sex, and religion, followed by a fourth part, in which the discovery of his true vocation follows a reversal of behavior with respect to sex: he "falls" after a phase of pious chastity—and religion; he rejects the priesthood and knows he will, in fact, reject religion as well. In part five, a quarrel over religion at home (reported to Lynch) and with Lynch, and the aesthetics discussion with Lynch, underline the artistic vocation and lead to the discovery and simultaneous reversal, i.e., the need to leave Ireland, and finally to the *end,* which validates the insight and the reversal's "turn" by the *action* of departure.

I want to stress all this because, as we have seen throughout this inquiry, the unique feature of rhetorical criticism is its incorporation within a rigorous theoretical structure of a systematic critical pluralism: the reader will recall from chapter 2 that "rhetoric unifies parts which are dialectical, grammatical, poetic, and rhetorical arguments." This should remind us that the kinds of wholes we organize are *like,* but not exactly the same as the kinds of texts we designate, just as the modes of discourse are only *like* modes of literary criticism.

The wholes we organize are like dialectical, demonstrative, deliberative, and judicial wholes because the four issues apply to all speeches, all communicative discourse. To say it formally, all discursive wholes, whether dialectical, demonstrative, deliberative, or judicial must be organized by means of beginning, middle, and end. Consequently, for example, conjectural novels will resemble conjectural philosophy, conjectural science, conjectural history, and so on; and as a final example, just as the conjectural organization in terms of beginning is quintessentially demonstrative, so is the qualitative organization in terms of end quintessentially deliberative, and the qualitative novel will most resemble both qualitative history and deliberative rhetoric, those extraordinary, paradoxical rhetorical modes in which one must look backward in order to look forward, to explore the past in order to determine the future.

Moreover, the wholes we organize are also *like*, but not the same as the modes of discourse. To take only the qualitative whole we have been discussing, the mode of discourse of narration involves complications and their resolutions through insight, a structure similar to the discoveries and reversals of the qualitative novel. But resolution implies further complication, and "ending" isn't really germane to modes of discourse. In addition, modes of discourse link fictive arguments together to make particulars emerge in consequential interrelation. Modes of organization deal with the disposition of parts in discursive wholes; it is rather like the difference between Aristotle's treatment of argument in books 1 and 2 of the *Rhetoric* and his treatment of the speech in book 3. Yet all three books are about persuasive, communicative structures, or speeches. Finally, as we saw in detail in chapter 2, the modes of discourse are *like* and *unlike* the modes of criticism because they are, in a sense, the modes of criticism transformed into argument in the process of being treated qua communication.

Thus if the qualitative novel seems to echo the mode of discourse of narration, and the rhetoric of deliberation, it will also seem to echo poetic criticism, and that is the point I have been aiming at here. In Aristotle's *Poetics*, however, the most important "parts" are plot, character, thought, diction, melody, and spectacle, not the quantitative parts from the prologue through the exode (12.1452b15). Terms like "insight," "discovery," and "reversal" do echo poetic criticism; but we are close to poetic only insofar as an organization in terms of *end* makes formally necessary a disposition of possibilities at the outset, which must be eliminated because of the determination of the end, which is necessary in principle. However, poetic is concerned with an artificial object, and its principle is plot, the soul of tragedy, a complex of action to which the other parts are subordinate. For us, the end is an arbitrary necessary principle. We can and will organize in terms of all the principles temporality makes available to us. Our teleological principle in this case is part of the pluralism of principles appropriate to the art of rhetoric; Aristotle's teleological principle is substantive and real. Thus, instead of being organized by plot derived from imitating the actions of men to produce an artificial object, the qualitative novel, organized in terms of *end* too, takes agent as prior, character as source of thought, action, feeling, and speech. For the qualitative novel is not an artificial object but a communication, and agents make communications not by imitating but by expressing.

If we return now to the disposition of "parts" in Joyce's novel, and how they are made meaningful in terms of *end*, we can see that in the absence of any principle to govern selectivity (whether an author's in writing or ours in interpreting) we could not attribute significance to them. They may have a loose relevance through a named agent who is seen at various stages of childhood and early youth, but that is not enough to lend them genuine coherence. The principle of *end*, particularized here as the artist's vocation, which demands exile for its fulfillment, unifies these five parts, giving to them attributes of developmental progression, and gives coherence to their juxtaposition and meaning to a selection of detail.

I said that the first three parts might be said to be devoted to language, then sex, then religion. If *end* is the "real" beginning in such an organization, we can see that when a young man who wants to be an artist leaves friends, family, country, to venture out into an unknown, perhaps harsh world, we must immediately ask how it is that the vocation—his expressed reason for leaving Ireland—necessitates exile? In the light of this puzzling necessity we go back to the beginning to *discover* the answer. Now we see that the author-artist begins, without any control at all, by wetting his bed. He is only an agent, empty. He will develop character in part one by expressing himself, defining himself in every way he can; roughly the "language" section. Then he brings himself to further development by coming into relation with other characters, culminating in the quintessentially intimate relation with another, the sexual. In the third part he gives unity to the world in his struggles with and acceptance of religion. In the fourth part he realizes his vocation and must discover how to pursue it in the context of external circumstances. In the fifth part he discovers at home and in conversation with Lynch that circumstances in Ireland will not permit him to be an artist, and at the end he leaves. The discovery of vocation expressed, and *thus made real,* in the conversation with Lynch, is the final discovery and simultaneously the final reversal of the novel. Stephen, in knowing that there are things the beauty of which is a function of their "whatness," also knows himself—what he is and what he must do. Thus the unity of the qualitative novel of action is also the reflexive interrelation of the protagonist and his world. In light of this principle of the whole, the parts are seen as ordered and interrelated, beginning and middle illuminated by the necessity of end.

The qualitative novel is organized in terms of *end* in such a way that there are many discoveries and reversals as well as one discovery and reversal which is culminative, ends the novel and shows where the others have been tending all along. At each stage Stephen Dedalus looks back and discovers what the past meant (as he discovers what Father Dolan really thought when Stephen complained of being unjustly punished), reverses his attitude and direction as a result of discovery, then goes on to new discoveries until the vocation is at last discovered and the last action taken. And, whereas the *conjectural* novel of style and manners, organized in terms of *beginning,* also involves discovery, the discovery is not insight into oneself and one's problems; it is rather discovery of what has never been seen before, creative discovery of a world of possibilities, a world, as we have seen, of endless beginnings. Thus the companion term, reversal, does not figure in the conjectural novel.

Finally, although the parts of a novel organized as a qualitative novel of action are quantitative parts, the sections or chapters of *Portrait...,* corresponding to the quantitative parts enumerated by Aristotle—Prologue, Parode, Episode, and Exode—they are, as we have seen, genuinely structural parts, as they are not for Aristotle, who simply mentions them pointing out that they are not the "formative elements" (*Poetics* 12.1452b15). Quantitative parts, however, *become qualitative parts* in the organization of a qualitative novel in terms of *end,* taking on quality from the wholeness structured by *end.* This difference from poetic, which the qualitative organization resembles, is more than simply a convenient mark of distinction between two modes of organizing temporal wholes in terms of *end.* It sheds light in still another way on the different aims of poetic and rhetorical literary criticism. A poetic organization points to "thought" as just one of the "formative elements" of an artificial object. A qualitative organization points to empty, "meaningless" quantitative parts, which, when qualified by *end,* take on meaning as part of a whole the structure of which *is* thought because it is the structure of a communication.

If we organize a novel in terms of *middle,* we are organizing it such that the principle of its wholeness is perceived in terms of being, of an englobing presentness without beginning or end. All beginning seems spontaneous or arbitrary. The novel organized as a conjectural novel of style and manners is seen as infused throughout with the spontaneity of feeling and expression that generated it in the beginning. When a novel is organized in terms of *middle,* the beginning will be seen as having been only apparently arbitrary, the end as only apparently final. The parts will be transformed by the character of middle so that the novel is unified by an intellectual structure coincident with the being of the universe; then the novel throughout, beginning and end as well as middle, is seen as an exemplary instance of that intelligible being.

Middle, taken as principle, implies an intellectual structure because it presupposes that what—as we have seen with respect to beginning and end as loci of principle—might very well be viewed as still other arbitrary desires (in effect, beginnings) in a series of feelings and expressions, or a link with beginning the final significance of which depends on the necessary end, has rather been seen as furnishing an illumination which transforms the whole. To see it this way is to abstract an idea to serve as the principle of wholeness, and in light of this principle to transform the parts. This transformation is an organization in terms of middle because it is an organization affirming an intellectual structure coincident with the intelligible structure of the universe, a structure without discernible, finite beginning or end. A novel so organized may be called a *translative* novel of ideas, because the translative issue concerns the jurisdiction under which a controversy ought to be resolved. Its appropriateness as a term for the "philosophical" novel is best explored in the light of *beginning* and *end*, and the kinds of novels they make, for the implications of *middle* as organizing principle are very different from those of *beginning* and *end*.

The conjectural issue is concerned only with whether or not a deed was done by an agent, disregarding any characterizing of the deed or any rationale for the doing of it: this unconditioned issue suggests a novel wholly creative in a beginning self-conditioned. The result, as we have seen, is the conjectural novel, the inventive expression of an agent, *the inventive qua inventive*. In a sense, this novel I called earlier the "novelist's novel" is not really a text because its terminal boundary is fortuitous; the discussions of *The Tin Drum* and *The Reprieve* as conjectural novels make that clear. Since beginning is unconditioned, wherever the novel *does* begin, it *must* have begun; but its end must simply coincide with the beginning which provides the only really fixed boundary. Similarly, as I noted earlier, the qualitative novel begins properly at the *end*, which qualifies *beginning* and *middle*; however, the similarity ends there. When we organize a novel as qualitative, we are organizing a whole prior to its parts—obviously, since the whole must be fully made before the parts can be interpreted, in contrast to the conjectural novel, the "parts" of which, the continuously generated "beginnings," determine what the made whole will be said to be. Thus with *end* as principle of wholeness, the whole of the qualitative novel is finite. That is, we can and do go back to discover what led up to *end*; but when we have fully accounted for it, we've reached a fully qualified, significant beginning. The novel's organizing principle has lent its authority, so to speak, to the second terminus, in this case beginning, and the novel is fully bounded. To do this, to see a "novel" this way, is to focus on a *text qua whole text*, something analogous to the art object of poetic. When we look at a named text as a conjectural novel, we see a whole, but a whole organized by beginning and implying the possibility of an indefinite extension of inventive expression.

The *translative* novel of ideas and feelings, like the conjectural novel of style and manners, points beyond itself because its organizing principle, *middle*, like *beginning* in its particular way, *does not* accommodate the finite. However, unlike beginning, *middle* doubly excludes the finite by excluding both *beginning* and *end*. This double exclusion results in a peculiar paradox in that the principle of a translative novel both gives to it and locates unity and coherence not in the novel itself as organized by *middle*, but outside the novel in the intelligible structure of the universe the novel is said to exemplify. Thus the novel of ideas is a translative novel because its principle of organization translates the text from the universe of expressive discourse to the context of the universe itself in order to give it unity and coherence; and, when we see a discursive whole as a translative novel, we are not looking at a text but at an instance of intelligibility.

Thomas Mann has dealt with this mode of organization in his remarks on *The Magic Mountain*, in which he uses the term *leitmotiv* rather than intellectual structure: "The leitmotiv is the technique employed to preserve the inward unity and abiding presentness of the whole at each moment... and thus seeks to abrogate time itself by means of the technical device that attempts to give complete presentness at any given moment to the entire world of ideas that it comprises.... its aim is always and consistently to *be* that of which it speaks."[5] He suggests, in fact, that the novel should be read twice: "That is why I make my presumptuous plea to my readers to read the book twice. Only so can one really penetrate and enjoy its musical association of ideas. The first time, the reader learns the thematic material; he is then in a position to read the symbolic and allusive formulas both forwards and backwards" (p. 725). In terms of a second reading, then, always a more critical reading in some sense, one would see the idea of the whole as of course present throughout.

Let us consider as an example of this mode of organization Mann's *Death in Venice*. If I were to organize it as a conjectural novel of style and manners, in terms of beginning, I might say that we begin with a man going out for a walk and being seized with sudden, spontaneous desire: "True, what he felt was no more than a longing to travel; yet coming upon him with such suddenness and passion as to resemble a seizure, almost a hallucination."[6] I should then show that this beginning, initiating a sequence of acts, speeches, and emotions, infuses the story throughout, giving it unity and coherence. If I organize it in terms of middle, however, as a translative novel of ideas and feelings, a very different whole is made. First of all, can we discern concretely the "abiding presentness of the whole" if we organize *Death in Venice* this way? The choice of the translative mode of organization points out to us the painted old man seen on the ship which takes Aschenbach to Venice, a mirror image of the painted Aschenbach of the end, eager to reach out for the young Tadzio just as the old man gravitates to the young men on the ship (p. 349); then the gondola Aschenbach enters, "black as nothing else on earth except a coffin," calling up "visions of death itself" (p. 352).

Death in fact pervades the story in this view; it beckons throughout. The end does not "follow" from the middle:

> It seemed to him the pale and lovely Summoner [Tadzio] out there smiled at him and beckoned; as though, with the hand he lifted from his hip, he pointed outward as he hovered on before into an immensity of richest expectation. . . . Some minutes passed before anyone hastened to the aid of the elderly man sitting there collapsed in his chair. They bore him to his room. And before nightfall a shocked and respectful world received the news of his decease. (p. 397)

The end is simply still another embodiment of the whole. Of this translative whole we do not say that Aschenbach remains in a plague-infested city simply because he desires passionately to do so. We see now that spontaneous desire is not, after all, the point. The passages quoted tell us, by virtue of our decision to organize in terms of middle, that the beckoning of the boy is a beckoning of death; that throughout, the cohesive force of the story derives from the compelling attraction of death. The beginning, then, must be reevaluated in this light. The description of the man Aschenbach sees during his walk at the outset takes on sinister overtones. After a life devoted to order and discipline, Aschenbach succumbs finally to disorder and thus to death, and his succumbing is "present" throughout.

In terms of middle, then, the wholeness of this story becomes, in principle, an intellectual structure having to do with a conflict between life and death. As it happens, Mann, in the role of critic, read it this way: "[it] portrays the fascination of the death idea, the triumph of drunken disorder over the forces of a life consecrated to rule and discipline."[7]

If the "idea" of the translative novel must be somehow coincident with the intelligible structure of the universe, perhaps we can generalize this principle by asserting as the principle of all existence a constant tension and conflict between death or dissolution and life or order. Such a principle could be seen as organizing any discursive whole, not to speak of the universe itself. Let us try to organize another novel this way.

Nikos Kazantzakis' *The Greek Passion*[8] can be organized in terms of middle to illustrate an apparent difficulty. Let us point out, first, that the novel concerns the village's acting out of the events of Holy Week at the end of which Manolios, the appointed Christ, is to act out the

Crucifixion. Manolios's role, then, once assumed in the course of the novel, transforms or "translates" the events of the novel, long before Holy Week, into exemplary instances of the events in the passion and death of Jesus Christ. An eternally present enactment, implicit in the very structure of the universe, according to Christian doctrine, determines the wholeness and therefore the interrelation of parts.

But in this case we would have a "story" (what is sometimes called a myth) serving as paradigm for a novel. In what way can we see the paradigmatic story—the passion and death of Christ—as an intellectual structure? As we know from Plato, the intellectual structure as englobing principle, the "idea," is often expounded by means of a "story." Consequently, we will transform the "story" in order to discover a way of using it as intellectual structure to organize the novel. Richard Mc-Keon has discussed this distinction in another context:

> It is a mistake to suppose that we encounter individual things as given elements in immediate experience. . . . It is a mistake to suppose that "myths" or the accounts of happenings deal with particulars in a peculiar sense distinct from the generality of "arguments," that is, of discursive inferences from premises. Rather, the two employ different means of achieving particularity by means of different modes of generality. The construction of an argument concerning particulars depends on the establishment of premises from causally related particular instances; the construction of a likely story depends on the use and suggestion of causes to relate the incidents or the parts of the narrative plausibly. . . . For although argument is . . . not a story, the plot or the "myth" of a tragedy is its "argument."[9]

What, then, does the story of the life and death of Jesus Christ convey, and how can it be shown to be, or used as, an all-encompassing principle rooted in the structure of the universe? Let me formulate the thesis this way: the universal principle of man's existence consists in a constant conflict between good and evil, innocence and guilt, and men are redeemed from guilt only through engaging in conflict with evil, a conflict characterized by suffering modeled upon that of Jesus Christ, the very principle of goodness. *The Greek Passion,* in this light, embodies this principle throughout the whole. The principle, Christ as englobing middle, makes the whole and the interrelation among all the parts. Good and evil, the innocent and the guilty, in this light will all be seen to be present when the eternal events are set in motion:

> Christ is risen, but He is still crucified in our flesh. Let us see to it that He rise in us also. . . . So listen: it is an old custom . . . in our village, to name, every seven years, five or six of our fellow citizens to revive in their persons, when Holy

Week comes around, the Passion of Christ.... We must today—we, the heads of the village—choose those who are worthiest to incarnate the three great apostles, Peter, James, John and Judas Iscariot and Mary Magdalen, the prostitute. And above all, Lord forgive me, the man who, by keeping his heart pure throughout the year, may represent Christ Crucified.[10]

The persons chosen immediately become the persons of the eternal conflict and live out the lives of Christ and the Apostles. The middle, the acting out, implies the beginning and the end—it is a recurrent action embedded in the life of the novel and life as the novel exemplifies it. The beginning can now be seen to imply the end, the end to imply the beginning, as both are contained in and given signification by the middle, the eternal life of Christ; for in the conflict of good and evil Christ is inevitably crucified because redemption from guilt *is* the suffering of innocence.

What seems to characterize middle as principle of organization, and the intellectual structure it imposes, is a polarity of terms that comprehend the universe in a complex reflexivity that admits of all possibility, is at one and the same time the ground of movement and conflict and yet unchanging; thus, in their omnipresence and eternity these terms serve as the abiding principle in the light of which movement and conflict are intelligible. In addition, it is not difficult to distinguish the translative organization from its expository counterpart since the latter is characterized by an assimilative movement, the former by a recurrence of event which is, in effect, a denial of movement. It is much more difficult to distinguish the translative organization from dialectical criticism, which it also resembles. That is, dialectic is always characterized by opposing terms, whether the commonplaces of its rhetorical manifestations or the theses and antitheses of, for example, Hegelian and Marxian dialectics. Thus a clearcut distinction like the one between a poetic organization, which does not involve commonplaces, and a qualitative organization, which does, is not possible, and it is quite easy to confuse the dialectical and the translative.

Nevertheless, there is a difference. A dialectical organization of a novel would suggest the embodiment of an unambiguous truth or value, and *The Greek Passion*, for example, might be said to reflect the redemptive passion of Christ, or rather the redemptive power of goodness as made manifest in Manolios, who is good throughout. The conflict between good and evil is also unambiguous in this view, the characters representing good in lesser degrees being clearly distinguishable from those who represent evil. We can make out a very good case for this interpretation, pointing out, too, that even for those who deliberately assume the roles of Jesus and his disciples, the mysterious power of God is terrible, overwhelming, and unexpected—especially mysterious. Events perfectly realistic for the world of turn of the twentieth-century Greece, under Turkish domination, are suddenly invested with the aura of the model—ancient Israel, under Roman domination, with a corrupt church hierarchy; for priest Grigoris is a pharisee, priest Fotis a kind of John the Baptist. And both the Greek pharisees and the conquerors misinterpret the defenders of the poor as politically motivated, as pharisees and Romans misinterpreted Jesus. Furthermore, as the model takes over "real" life, we see that to "assume" the life of Christ is dangerous and terrible.[11]

The rhetorical translative organization shares with the dialectical the formal characteristic of the englobing middle as principle, as I have already indicated; therefore, the infinite, timeless, two-termed nature of the principle is the same. However, the terms of a dialectical dichotomy are perceived as substantive; the terms of a translative dichotomy are a rhetorical commonplace. Therefore they are empty until used to organize a novel, and above all they are interchangeable. I mean by this that when a commonplace is used, let us take good and evil, one may argue without prejudice that A is good or that A is evil. This means that although we may organize *The Greek Passion* as a translative novel of ideas, the statement that "men are redeemed from guilt only through engaging in conflict with evil" is ambiguous, and we cannot be sure who is guilty or what is evil all of the time. For example, Michelis, the young archon, is moved to follow Manolios, desert his betrothed, Mariori, the "bad" priest's (Grigoris's) daughter, and to give his property to the homeless wanderers from Sarakina, banished from their village by the Turks. Now Mariori is in a hospital, dying, and writes to her father: "It's because of you I grieve, and also because of the man to whom I was betrothed. Perhaps he doesn't grieve at seeing me go, but I can't stop weeping when I think of him. Why? Why? What have I done? I only wanted a house and a child... and now..." (p. 337). Michelis hates priest Grigoris, but when he sees the letter he hates God too. And of course Grigoris hates Michelis and Manolios and the thin, ascetic, ragged priest Fotis, who leads the starving outcasts, makes Grigoris seem worldly in his prosperity, and seems responsible for destroying his daughter's life. Priest Fotis speaks to Manolios as they contemplate fighting for the land given by Michelis which Grigoris and the townspeople will not permit Sarakina to take:

> It is worth while, it is worth while, Manolios!... There was a time when I, too, used to say: "Why struggle for this life here below? what does this world matter to me?"... But later I understood. No one can go to heaven unless he has first been victorious upon earth, and no one can be victorious upon earth if he does not struggle against it with fire, with pa-

tience, without resting.... All the priest Grigorises, the Ladases, the Aghas, the big proprietors, are the forces of evil which it has been allotted us to combat. (p. 347)

As soon as we think in terms of the principle of conflict as ambiguous, this passage speaks for itself. Manolios does die at the hands of the "pharisee," and his enraged followers with the approval of the Agha, the Pilate figure. But we must point out that he dies on Christmas Eve, the eve of the *birth* of Christ. Why? Because Christ's death and birth are inextricably one? Or is it because Jesus must be born before he can die his redemptive death, and Manolios, dying before the birth instead of at Easter, is a false Messiah, a follower of a false prophet, Fotis, who preached the kingdom of this world? Perhaps Fotis's words reflect the Christ who said he came to bring a sword, not peace. They do not in any case reflect the Christ whose kingdom was not of this world. We cannot be sure about Fotis and Manolios, just as we are left with a puzzle with respect to *Death in Venice*, since the disordered depths, the yielding to which kills Aschenbach, are the same depths without access to which no artist can realize his art. Dialectical organizations take into account ambiguity and tension and conflict, but the statement of principle which organizes the whole is a statement about the *truth* structure of the universe in which ambiguity, tension, and conflict are made intelligible. Ambiguity, tension, and conflict are in themselves the translative version of the intelligible structure of the universe.

How, finally, do we order a novel in terms of all three, *beginning, middle,* and *end?* We know that a discursive, a temporal *whole,* cannot be brought into existence at all without a beginning, a middle, and an end. All novels "have" these, and they are the loci of principles of the wholeness of discursive wholes. We have seen that when novels are organized in terms of *beginning,* the character of *beginning* as unconditioned necessarily provides the cohesive force which binds up the novel and marks it off as itself. Thus the middle is undifferentiated; the emotions generated by desiring, saying, and doing in the beginning are present throughout, and the end is the end of a series of passions. The conjectural novel of style and manners is, so to speak, "empassioned." When *end* is seen as the organizing principle, *beginning* is stripped of arbitrariness and infused potentially with the character of *end. Middle* then is seen as reflexively embodying the wholeness determined by *end.* The end provides the actualization of the necessary through which the whole is unified and cohesive. The qualitative novel of action, then, may be said to be "integrated." Finally, we can see that when novels are organized in terms of *middle,* neither the beginning nor the end can have any separate status; they are assimilated to the intellectual structure reflected by such an organization. The translative novel, thus "ideated," mirrors the universe and cannot be said, functionally, to begin or end.

The novel we organize in terms of *beginning, middle,* and *end* is quite different from the translative novel of ideas; like the conjectural novel of style, it is a whole the character of which is determined by its parts. The parts are not emotions generated by doing and saying, however; they are, rather, simple elements related to one another to form a composite that may be read on one level as the constructed self of a protagonist, on another as the construction of the entire underlying nature of which he is a part. Since the composite of related simples gives us the nature of the world as it is said to be, it is replete with beginnings, middles, and ends. It can be conceived of as expanded to the ultimate inclusiveness or reduced to the compass of *this* novel. As *this* novel, ordered in terms of *beginning, middle,* and *end,* the novel defines nature and human nature seen in a sequence of natural events. In the *definitive* novel of sequence, the beginning is arbitrary not in the sense of spontaneous or unconditioned but only in the sense that the composition could have been expanded to begin further back, and extended to end later.

Simple elements functioning as inventive principles can be used to order Virginia Woolf's *Mrs. Dalloway,*[12] and when we order it that way we constitute a composite which is not only Clarissa Dalloway and her nature but the totality of natural events and circumstances of which she is a part. We begin by noting that Mrs. Dalloway goes out to buy flowers for a party. A man notices her and thinks her charming (p. 8). She hears Big Ben strike and thinks: "For Heaven only knows why one loves it so, how one sees it so, making it up, building it round one, tumbling it, creating it every moment afresh . . . in the bellow and the uproar; the carriages, motor cars, omnibuses, vans, sandwich men shuffling and swinging; brass bands; barrel organs; in the triumph and the jingle and the strange high singing of some aeroplane overhead was what she loved; life; London; this moment of June" (p. 9).

Simultaneously, a woman and a world create one another. Gradually, her human milieu emerges—her intimates, touched on in thought during her excursion and throughout, and the various inhabitants of the city included during the excursion, whether she notices them or not. They appear, too, when she does not; as Peter Walsh dozes in the park, for example (pp. 85 ff). Is there a significant sequence in the building of this world? Certainly; but what it is said to be depends on the mode of discourse we use to arrange the particulars. We are not concerned with that. Whatever the arrangement, we are concerned with the connections that validate it in any mode. The composition of elements which provide connections and are rooted in the character of beginning, middle, and end as composed in sequence are present throughout, giving the novel its special kind of wholeness.

Clarissa Dalloway may be said to be constructed through the interplay of opposed forces, action and reaction, emerging as fully herself, affirming life—rejected by Septimus Warren Smith—and the value of her parties, which bring people together and give them pleasure. Although Peter says that her parties are trivial and Richard that they are too demanding of her, she accepts herself and her way of life as valuable because they are a source of pleasure, which is a natural good. None of the elements in the passage cited, for example, has any privileged status, so to speak, in virtue of a whole of which they are parts, a whole that determines function and priority. Rather, the whole is a composition of the simple elements themselves in their interplay of forces, of action and reaction. The whole, then, is Mrs. Dalloway's world and Mrs. Dalloway. At the end:

> "I will come," said Peter, but he sat on for a moment. What is
> this terror? what is this ecstasy? he thought to himself. What
> is it that fills me with extraordinary excitement?
> It is Clarissa, he said.
> For there she was. (p. 293)

There she is, at the "end" as she was there in the passage cited from the beginning, as she is there in the middle, and just as the world she is a part of is there at the beginning, in the middle and at the end; she is "there" because the *definitive* novel of sequence has been organized as a composite which, *functionally*, just *is*.

The definitive mode of organization resembles the descriptive mode of discourse in that both compose elements into "wholes"; but the two are in fact quite different. The descriptive mode of discourse is a process in which, beginning with commonplaces, fictive arguments are made, and these in turn are connected in an additive sequence such that concrete particulars emerge as the elements which compose an ongoing description that is, in effect, endless. The definitive novel is a whole that is composed; and, although it has no real beginning, middle, and end as in any way distinct one from the other, a particular composed definitive novel—as contracted to constitute *this* novel—is bounded, all its parts simultaneously present and not in process of being built out of or into anything.

The definitive mode of organizing a novel is also different from the grammatical criticism it resembles. Although the formal structure in terms of *beginning, middle,* and *end* is of necessity the same (whether or not these are part of the grammatical critic's vocabulary), the elements of a novel organized grammatically are radically different because they are conceived of as real entities. A grammatical organization begins with the assumption that there are realities, a nature of things and of persons to be discerned in a novel; the interpretation will be the recovery of these elements which "cause" the thoughts, words, and feelings that are one's first experience of a novel's surface. One recovers the reality beneath the surface, and then the real whole can be composed as the surface is interpreted in terms of the reality it reflects through a glass darkly. The novel, finally, is constructed through the interplay of forces, and thus we find *who and what Clarissa Dalloway really is* by comparing her thoughts with what others think of her.

A definitive organization also composes simple elements serving as principles. But the universe is not composed of existent things the consequences of which are thoughts, words, and feelings; rather it is a universe of "things" said, thought, and felt in which the things or elements are inventive. Now, we have seen that the principle of the translative novel, good versus evil in one of our examples, was inventive—the evil priest Grigoris invented the good Manolios as Jesus Christ. The good Manolios invented the evil of Mariori's decline and death, and so on. The principle of the qualitative novel, in its end, was the principle of invention whereby an empty agent, Stephen Dedalus, invented himself. In the conjectural novel the desires of agents invent agents and their world.

The elements of Mrs. Dalloway are the empty, single topics—things, thoughts, words, and actions. At the beginning we encounter a curious confusion about things and words for things as different persons use them. Through thoughts attributed to an agent, Clarissa, we learn that Peter Walsh, another agent, spoke about vegetables or didn't, exactly: "'Musing among the vegetables?'—was that it?—'I prefer men to cauliflowers'—was that it?" The passage continues identifying Peter Walsh and his whereabouts, observing that "it was his sayings one remembered," and ending finally with: "—how strange it was!—a few sayings like this about cabbages" (p. 8). We encounter actions through thoughts attributed to agents. Let us consider Clarissa as an element inventing herself and others. She meets Hugh Whitbread and feels "oddly conscious at the same time of her hat. Not the right hat for the early morning, was that it?" Hugh made her feel "skimpy" (p. 11). Recollections of Peter Walsh follow: "The perfect hostess he called her (she had cried over it in her bedroom), she had the makings of the perfect hostess, he said. . . . She would not say of any one . . . that they were this or were that. She felt very young; at the same time unspeakably aged" (pp. 13–15). When she returns home she discovers that Lady Bruton has asked Richard to lunch, but not her. She feels alone and that her body is shriveled and aged and failed "since Lady Bruton . . . had not asked her" (p. 48). Later, when Sir William and Lady Bradshaw speak of the suicide of Septimus Warren Smith, she thinks, "What business had the Bradshaws to talk of death at her party?" (p. 277). But she doesn't pity him. "She felt glad that he had done it;

thrown it away while they went on living" (p. 280).

These are selected, almost random examples, and so many more are available, which show Clarissa Dalloway being invented by an extended—occasionally interrupted—interior monologue, by thoughts identified as "Clarissa." If we look at it this way, what suddenly emerges is an insight that tends to be suppressed when the elements are all simply parts of a composition, without any active function, the latter being attributed to a "narrator," or "narration." For it is the case that Clarissa Dalloway *defines* herself entirely in terms of her invention of how others perceive her. That is perhaps clearest in connection with Hugh Whitbread and Lady Bruton. They make her by responding to her as they do, but she has herself invented them by inventing their attitudes. Other passages indicate that they do not judge her as she imagines they do. Peter Walsh's judgments of her and her parties are more admiring than she guesses, and so on. Yet her responses to Peter on the basis of how she has invented him, invent herself and evoke responses in him that will in turn reinforce her self-created self insofar as her behavior toward him makes him what she thinks he is. In this sense the novel is composed through what I earlier called "an interplay of opposed forces, action and reaction."

We get the world, and what are purported to be the natural events and circumstances reflected in this novel because the simple principles of the definitive novel are all inventions inventing to compose a world. It is the lack of agreement between these opposing forces that composes a world in motion, created by all the perspectives taken together. There is no "real" Clarissa at the beginning, middle, or end; we are not looking for such a person. She is what she feels at any moment and what others feel her to be. The definitive whole is never reductive; rather the perspectives are indefinitely expandable, and as part of *this* novel, Clarissa is what she is said to be at the beginning, the middle, and the end.

It is worth calling attention here to a similarity between the translative novel and the definitive novel. Both seem to imply a breadth and depth, a multiplicity of levels absent in novels ordered as conjectural or qualitative novels. The special power of the latter stems from the generating force of *beginning* as principle in the one and the force of necessity that characterizes *end* in the other. The limitation of particularity that arises from the sharp clarity of beginning and end as boundaries is at the same time a source of concentrated power.

On the other hand, the sequential composite of the definitive novel includes by implication the universe, natural, social, and so on, with its multiplicity of beginnings, middles, and ends. Its power lies in an expansiveness and breadth we have only touched on in our brief discussion of Clarissa Dalloway and her world. Finally, the translative novel of ideas, organized by *middle*, also obliterates the sharp focus of beginnings and ends to achieve, in their place, a breadth coincident with the universe. It does so not by implying an expansion to inclusiveness, but rather by postulating a single, englobing concept that is the structure of the universe and of which this novel is but one concrete instance, as each part of the novel itself is still another concrete instance of that self-same whole.

As it is the case, then, that any discursive whole may be read in any of the four modes of discourse, it is also the case, as I have tried to emphasize, that any novel may be organized as a conjectural, qualitative, translative, or definitive novel. I treated *The Tin Drum* as a conjectural novel of style and manners; it can be organized as a translative novel of ideas in terms, for example, of a parodied version of the "Divine Child" myth, an interpretation offered in a very interesting essay by E. H. Friedrichsmeyer. He argues that Oskar, who remains a child, has an unusual birth—he believes Matzerath is not his father—and possesses a drum, counterpart to the lyre of Hermes, conforms to the divine child myth; Oskar is victimized by other children, but has the ability to shatter glass with his voice and thus possesses a powerful device for self-protection. Further, Oskar identifies himself with the child Jesus.[13] However, he points out, citing Jung:

> The divine child archetype is "...ein die Gegensätze vereinigendes Symbol, ein Mediator, ein Heilbringer, d.h. Ganzmacher." Oskar, the shatterer of glass, the thief and murderer cannot but be a symbol of the precise opposite. If we further take into account that the divine child is viewed as a "Kulturbringer" in Jung's and Kerenyi's treatise and if we remind ourselves of the era in which Oskar lived, we may readily see perspectives of interpretation of *Die Blechtrommel* in terms of "zeitkritik."[14]

The intellectual structure in this interpretation is strikingly like Mann's formulation of his own for *Death in Venice*. The steps in making it might go something like this: we can equate eternal childhood with a refusal to act in terms of the order of the adult ego, instead acting out of the destructive disorder of the id—witness Oskar's behavior throughout. Attributes of the divine child characterize Oskar, but his behavior parodies the redemptive function of the divine child in the myth. We have thus an intellectual structure—particularized in the myth—which can be formulated as a thesis concerning the eternal conflict between order (life, good) and disorder (death, evil) in which disorder is constantly triumphant.

As one more brief example, we can organize *A Portrait of the Artist as a Young Man* as a definitive novel of sequence by showing that the whole is a composite constructed by elements in action and reaction to constitute not only the human nature of Stephen Dedalus, but the natural events of the world of which he is a part. Religious dogma, national loyalties, filial piety clash with sexual need, artistic sensibility, intellectual insight, and so on—these are forces in opposition and from their encounters are composed a man and a world.

To summarize then, the possible boundaries of a temporal whole are the loci of principles in terms of which that whole may be ordered and its parts interrelated. To make a qualitative novel of action we organize in terms of *end*, achieving unity by means of the way in which a "necessary" end is accounted for and related to beginning through middle. If *beginning* is the organizing principle, the connecting links of the conjectural novel partake of the unconditioned character of beginning, and middle and end disappear functionally. When *middle* organizes the translative novel, its character as englobing principle, without beginning or end, constitutes a whole that is present *in its wholeness* in all parts. When *beginning, middle,* and *end* organize the definitive novel, we have an expandable or contractable composition implicitly embodying and thus defining the underlying nature of the universe.

Although middle clearly implies an intellectual structure coincident with the intelligible being of the universe, it is the case that the other three also involve theses relevant beyond any particular whole each may be used to order. For if *a* whole may be ordered in terms of (1) the desires and expressions that characterize the beginning, (2) the composite of simple elements that characterizes the beginning, the middle, and the end, and (3) the actions, discoveries, and reversals that characterize the end, any whole may be so ordered, including the universe itself. And that these principles do indeed organize identifiable wholes is demonstrated by the identifiable wholes we organize with them.

The four kinds of discursive whole these principles give rise to are, then, in themselves "eternal" because the parts of a novel in their modes of disposition are simultaneously present. This ordering and the principles that determine it are independent of fictive arguments and modes of discourse, and any novel once constituted may be read by means of any mode of discourse. Principle provides a systematic framework, a "real world" that verifies consequence by "showing" *why* particulars are interrelated. It does not tell *how* particulars are arranged such that they *are* consequentially related. To put it another way, principle doesn't tell us how anything moves; it does tell us that no matter how an argument is said to move, it makes sense that variables should be linked together in that movement to make particulars and to make meaning because the discourse is consequential.

The ordering of novels is, let me reiterate, independent of the making of fictive argument in modes of discourse. On the other hand, each mode of organizing a novel resembles one of the modes of discourse and, in turn, a kind of literary criticism. I discussed the latter resemblance in some detail in connection with the qualitative novel of action, and will let that discussion serve as illustrative. That there should be these resemblances is simply a result of the nature of this inquiry. All literary criticism is concerned with named texts and with discourse, and the formal imperatives of discourse impose themselves upon all critics alike. Discourse can be treated *poetically* as one sort of material for making art objects, *grammatically* as one sort of form for making art objects, and *dialectically* as a realm of values transcending the particular discourse of particular texts which only reflect it. Since we are treating discourse *rhetorically*, we are examining its communicative structure, i.e., treating discourse as vehicle of meaning. This task imposes the special imperative upon us of always considering our critical terms as topics, and always taking into account both terms of a two-term topic or commonplace. Thus we have been constrained by the temporality of discourse to take into account atemporality as well; but because such commonplaces are always reciprocally *and not otherwise* meaningful, arranging discourse "in motion" is not the same as, but like, ordering discourse "at rest."

The four modes of discourse showed us how discourse is rendered meaningful by means of fictive argument, but we could make fictive arguments without texts, and we could make fictive arguments that might be said to interpret two or three named texts taken together. In other words, fictive argument could not account for another aspect of our experience of discourse, separate named texts. We needed a way to make texts, and for this we turned to that aspect of rhetorical theory which treats kinds of whole speeches. From Aristotle we took a way to make philosophical, historical, scientific, and what we think of as literary texts, the novels we wish to interpret rhetorically. Turning to Cicero, we found that the epideictic or demonstrative speech which communicates itself qua speech, and is what we mean rhetorically when we talk about "novel," has in common with all other kinds of communications the fact that it must be based on at least one of four issues, for in the absence of these there is no divergence of opinion and no communication.[15] It is very important to clarify what that means before we go any further, and why we must do so is quite simple. Cicero's four issues have provided us with an extraordinarily flexible and versatile critical instrument. They showed us that *any* text could be treated dialectically, judicially, deliberatively, or demonstratively by showing that the four issues applied to all texts. They provided a theoretically grounded justification for freedom of choice in designating named texts as kinds through the translative issue which implies an argument for a particular choice of jurisdiction. Finally, they provided a theoretically grounded system for characterizing more thoroughly and thus naming appropriately the kinds of novels we might make by organizing texts in terms of the temporal boundaries available to discourse.

Since Cicero's four issues are heavily implicated in this enterprise, the question that arises at this stage of the inquiry is very important: if a "case" depends, as Cicero says it does, on at least one or at most all four issues, would we be constrained to say that a novel might be organized in four ways simultaneously? Do the four issues, like the four modes of discourse, merge functionally or in some other way? In fact they do not. Cicero makes it clear in the *De Inventione* that the issues *do not merge*, that although we might find ourselves having to argue all four, the case would only turn on one, the last one on which we find ourselves opposed, and the previous issues would be treated seriatim, never simultaneously. With respect to the question of merging he says:

> Furthermore a conjectural argument cannot at one and the same time and from the same point of view and under the same system of classification be both conjectural and definitive, nor can a definitive argument be at one and the same time and from the same point of view and under the same system of classification both definitive and translative. And, to put it generally, no issue . . . can have its own scope and also include the scope of another issue, because each one is studied directly by itself and in its own nature, and if another is added, the number of issues is doubled, but the scope of any one issue is not increased. (1.10.14)

Cicero elaborates on the issues themselves seriatim, always stating that an issue arises when there is no dispute about the previous ones. The conjectural issue is a dispute about a fact, whether an act has been done, is being done, or will be done. "The controversy about a definition arises when there is agreement as to the fact" (1.8.11). "There is a controversy about the nature or character of an act when there is both agreement as to what has been done and certainty as to how the act should be defined" (1.9.12). It is important to note that the later issues arise only when the preceding questions have been agreed upon. In other words, there *is* a sense in which all four issues are pertinent to all speeches. Unless something was done by someone, or is being contemplated, there is literally nothing to argue about. The conjectural issue may not be the crux of a case, but only because there is agreement on the action; yet the action itself with respect to which there could have been disagreement is necessary. Similarly, the definitive issue may not figure if both sides agree that the act was such and such; but there must be a defined act as part of any case. If the qualitative issue is in dispute, the side which loses the case may then raise the translative issue and try to avoid the consequence of losing by shifting ground.

What I hope is clear here is that all four issues cannot simultaneously organize a speech. A case may remain in dispute until a number of speeches have been made; but each one will be made in terms of a single issue.

There is a difference, then, between the modes of discourse which merge functionally, and many of which may serve to interpret a named text, and the modes of organizing discursive wholes, modes which do not merge functionally in the context of a coherent, theoretical system and serve only seriatim to organize and thereby make a novel. Indeed, since separate wholes cannot be made without boundaries, the result of our inquiry into Cicero is not surprising. If the boundaries which are our concrete agency of the organizing issues were to merge, they wouldn't be boundaries, and we would be unable to resolve a very important critical problem: although the kinds of rhetoric—judicial, deliberative, and demonstrative—and dialectic serve to discriminate kinds of texts and furnish the criteria according to which we can designate any named text read demonstratively, as a novel, the designation is only what that term signifies; it is a pointing to and a classificatory naming. But a named text called a novel is not the same as an *interpreted* text, and we require distinct boundaries in order to *make* the interpreted text. Reading demonstratively from the point of view of discourse qua discourse, whole qua "wholeness," we must organize the named text conjecturally, definitively, qualitatively, or translatively to make of a named text a novel of a particular kind. And, of course, any named text demonstratively perceived can be organized four ways so that it is potentially four distinct texts, each one of the four genres of the novel.

At the end of chapter 3 we concluded that "the universe of discourse is a universe of themes and variations in which a novel can be treated as a treatise and a treatise as a novel because both are interpreted by means of fictive argument." We have succeeded now in entering that universe of discourse, of themes and variations which we have constructed, generated, formed, and invented, and we have made novels too, novels in four genres. We are now ready to formulate the relationship between those two activities—making fictive arguments and making novels.

To begin with, a theme or mode of discourse is not a novel, not one of the genres of the novel, although genre may be said to be a kind of stable variation on the temporality of theme, theme a moving variation on the timelessness of genre. Why do we need them both to interpret a literary work? That question can be answered in a variety of ways. I might point out that the fictive arguments which guarantee consequence, i.e., meaning, in discourse, are constructed of two-term commonplaces (as modes of discourse are varied by single-term commonplaces) such as motion and rest, permanence and change, time and eternity—all pairs of terms each of which is meaningless except in light of the other. Since the four modes of discourse are in fact connected, ordered fictive arguments, an exhaustive inquiry into the way we *read* or *interpret* (terms denoting motion, temporality) *novels* (a term denoting a kind of object rather than an activity) must encompass both terms of the time-timelessness commonplace which has played so important a part in the organization of this inquiry.

On the other hand, I might suggest that psychologically we not only need to make our experience by means of argument linked in the several modes of discourse to convey meaning, we also need separate wholes we can distinguish from other wholes. Modes of discourse, themes and their variations, convey meaning, but they are processes and get away from us. Ordered wholes seem clear, can be contemplated, but do not afford any way of dealing adequately with their internal complexities (deeper than disposition and style) or with the complex relations among themselves. Since "issues" and "boundaries" do not merge, they have a stability that makes discursive wholes possible; but because they neither merge functionally nor operate simultaneously, they accommodate only single, simple interpretations.

In fact we need the four modes of discourse *and* the four modes of organization because communicating meaning is a very complicated activity. I tried to show in chapter 3 that there are ways in which dialectical, grammatical, and poetic literary criticisms can be and are adapted for rhetorical purposes. However, our rhetorical criticism is committed *in principle* to affirming multiple structures of any novel and demonstrating multiple structure—if not all possible structures—not as seriatim (as is the case with other kinds of criticism when they allow for multiple structure at all) but as operating simultaneously in a novel.

We have, in our own way, the classical twofold job to do that faces any rhetorician. We have to invent our arguments and put together a speech. Aristotle dealt with kinds of rhetoric—forensic, deliberative, and epideictic—and with aspects of dialectic, in terms of audiences, and kinds of judgments to be rendered, and times relevant to these, in book 1 of his *Rhetoric;* he treated modes of proof in book 2. But he needed book 3 for the speech, the disposition of its parts, its style and diction, and so on. Our task is not the same; but it is like his because implicit in his inquiry is the sense that an argument is not a speech, although a speech without argument can't communicate, and an argument that isn't part of a "speech" is without context and is lost.

In order to develop a rhetorical criticism as I have conceived it, I have had to invent arguments in the several modes of discourse, explain what I was doing and why; I have had to make novels, distinguish their genres, explain what I was doing and why. Now I must explain how novels and modes of discourse are related, and then show the relationship by bringing them together, making novels and interpreting them by means of modes of discourse. The explanation is implicit in the results of the inquiry thus far. Let me refer to a statement that occurred in chapter 2: "Rhetoric unifies parts which are dialectical, grammatical, poetic and rhetorical arguments." How does rhetoric do this? When we have made a novel of a given kind by organizing discourse in terms of a principle derived from the temporal boundaries of beginning, middle, and end, that principle of organization is the principle which unifies any collection of fictive arguments in modes of discourse by means of which we will interpret the novel as communicative of meaning. The last phrase, however, is redundant. A novel may be said to reflect nature, exemplify the universe, be an art object or express its author. If it communicates, however, it communicates meaning. Finally, the principle that unifies the several arguments and has rendered the disposition of parts coherent also validates the relation among the particulars in any and all fictive arguments advanced to interpret the novel.

In part two, then, I shall offer four brief essays in rhetorical criticism, each a reading of a novel as organized in one of the four genres and interpreted by all four modes of discourse.

THE PRACTICE OF
RHETORICAL CRITICISM

Invention, Discovery, Explication,
Evaluation

FICTIVE ARGUMENT AND NOVELS

The art of discourse, according to Cicero, consists of two parts, the art of invention and the art of judgment, and it is used in the treatment of two kinds of questions—general philosophical questions and particular rhetorical questions. We have thus far been concerned with general questions. We have contended that all arguments are fictive arguments, and we have undertaken to separate the art of rhetorical criticism from other arts of discourse and to distinguish the novel as a discursive whole from discursive wholes in general. We have invented or made fictive arguments and we have judged or differentiated the themes or lines they follow and the genres or kinds of wholes to which they are related. Among verbal wholes we have differentiated novels from scientific, philosophical, and historical works, as four kinds of organization, and we have used the same commonplaces to differentiate four kinds of novels. But these are general questions, the theory that enables us to find our subject matter; the answers determine where to place books in a library or bibliography, for the same collection of books may be classified in many ways. According to the Dewey Decimal or the Library of Congress systems, the book called *Tom Jones* will be found among the novels in English literature, but in other classifications it might be among books treating characteristics of men, times, emotions, neuroses, or secular beliefs and practices. Now that we have invented the novel and used rhetorical criticism to classify kinds of novels, we are ready to turn to the particular questions involved in inventing particular novels and judging their characteristics.

For if we take a book called *Tom Jones* from the library in which it is classified as a novel, we accept it as a novel only in a general sense determined by the art of bibliography or by library science. We must invent it as a novel, and that invention must be justified and explored by judgments formed by the art of rhetorical criticism. Moreover, since it is invented, the novel called *Tom Jones* is not predetermined to be a novel of a particular kind. It may be invented as a novel of any of the genres, and it may be judged by any of the modes of rhetorical criticism. Indeed, to appreciate it as a novel, this pluralism of possibilities ought to be explored.

Before we begin, however, to bring theme and genre together in the particularity of practical criticism, we need to examine briefly the full implications of Cicero's conjectural issue for a fully rhetorical literary criticism. In the last chapter we organized wholes in four different ways, and we were able to see how the demonstrative mode, the inventive for its own sake, is most purely embodied in a conjectural organization so that the crucial aspect of the conjectural—its inventiveness—permeates the other three modes of organization because the others, too, are demonstrative since we have designated and treated them as such. Further, one of our early discoveries (see chapter 3) was that fictive arguments in modes of discourse do not really end and cannot. But if the modes of discourse are themes, and genres are variations on those themes, discursive wholes must be discursive sequences as well even though we are treating them qua simultaneously present parts in a given distribution or relationship. The conjectural issue suggests the serious problem of how discursive sequences *can be stopped* because the conjectural novel is, in principle, beginnings only; and the other three kinds of novels present similar difficulties because they are conjectural insofar as they are inventive, as are all rhetorical structures. We saw that in the last chapter as we distinguished these organizations from the grammatical, dialectical, and poetic modes they resemble. Since a genre is a kind of theme stopped, we must show how a discursive sequence in being ordered in terms of a part-whole organization can be stopped.

We did not examine that problem in the last chapter, focusing instead on the characteristics of beginning, middle, and end as boundaries. But the endings of *The Tin Drum* and *The Reprieve* as we construed them conjecturally seem quite arbitrary, as does that of *A Portrait of the Artist as a Young Man*, organized qualitatively. Why is *Mrs. Dalloway* not otherwise expanded or contracted when read definitively? In principle, the translative novel's structure is always present in any part; but we can organize it that way only through our experience of it which is sequential. Therefore, it, too, poses the same problem. When we organize it as a first step toward transforming a named text into an interpreted novel, how can we get a novel organized from middle to end? Again, let me reiterate: we have now uncovered this problem because we are now able to see that the continuous spontaneity of the conjectural as the "pure" demonstrative mode, its "beginningness," lurks in the other three as well because they, too, are modes of demonstrative rhetoric.

Second, having learned that appreciation of novels depends on discovering what was previously overlooked, we must be able to go on to the *judgment* of values that criticism implies. Finally, we must test our invention of a rhetorical literary criticism. We began with the task of finding a way eventually of making the novel out of fictive argument; we will now try to make fictive arguments about novels. That is, we will interpret them in a plurality of ways as communicative discursive structures. To do that, is to do rhetorical literary criticism. Only rhetorical criticism, moreover, can invent a way to stop the inventiveness of its conjectural manifestation, and only rhetorical criticism can judge values, for values are the thought of the whole qua expression and expression qua the thought of the whole.

It is the case, then, that the unity of a novel, its connecting links, are furnished by the principle with which we organize a discursive work as a novel. Further, this principle organizes a whole within which we may trace an indefinite number of thematic structures, varying materially with respect to agents, problems, ideas, and circumstance, and formally with respect to the mode of discourse in which the sequence moves; that is, we find many particularizations of the universal themes of description, exposition, argument, and narration.

We must organize our discursive experience according to a principle that unifies it in order to have a separate, identifiable object that can be a communicative object—in our case a novel. The four distinct ways of organizing discursive wholes in terms of the boundaries appropriate to a temporal medium are the four genres of the novel, are formally determined, and provide four characteristic modes of validation for interpretive readings of a novel.

Genre, then, provides novels as kinds of objects, provides validation of any arguments which render them meaningful (that is, communicative), and provides the unified wholeness in terms of which the many thematic structures we trace in a novel may be seen as coherently interrelated. Genre functions in the latter sense because the *one* kind of principle according to which we organize a given novel furnishes the connections among particulars in any and all the modes of discourse we may use to interpret it.

On the other hand, the thematic variations or fictive arguments connected in modes of discourse render the generically constituted novel communicative. As arrangements of particulars in consequential interrelations, they make particulars, in effect, by giving signification to variables in virtue of the mode of arrangement.

In discussing the reason for his choice of the pentad as "generating principle" for an investigation of motives, Kenneth Burke says: "For, to explain our position, we shall show how it can be applied."[1] Since rhetoric is an art, a way of doing something, its value can be affirmed finally only in the doing. I will try to follow the example of Burke and show how we can use the rhetorical criticism developed in this essay, which I began by calling attention to the difficulties readers have experienced in understanding and appreciating novels written in the twentieth century. Therefore, although the rhetorical perspective dictates that all discourse is contemporary with its audience, I am going to take my material from the twentieth-century "worlds" of Günter Grass, John Fowles, Robert Coover, and Flannery O'Connor.

SIX

NOVELS—CONJECTURAL AND DEFINITIVE

To begin with the conjectural novel and follow with a treatment of the definitive novel is appropriate not only because these are the first two of Cicero's issues, and the conjectural novel is the novel of beginning; it is appropriate, too, because these two organizations have something important in common: they are principles of organization in which parts are prior to the wholes they constitute. Moreover, the principles inevitably generate pluralities. Beginning, in terms of which conjectural wholes are organized, is arbitrary and permits endless continuations of whatever is generated. Beginning, middle, and end, which govern the definitive whole, are a plural principle to begin with; and beginning and end are a commonplace within which we find a plurality of middles or accounts which alter the terms of the commonplace and thus can accommodate different beginnings and ends. That is why, as we have seen, definitive wholes seem endlessly expandable in both directions. We will start the discussion, then, with conjectural organization and a named text by Günter Grass.

Let me begin on what must be, by now, a most familiar note. I can organize a novel by Günter Grass in any one of the four ways formally open to me, for there is no formal imperative dictating the choice of one genre rather than another. In chapter 5 I illustrated the organization of conjectural and translative novels using *The Tin Drum*. Moreover, rhetoric is an art of invention, and within the formal limits imposed by the temporality of discourse, I am free to choose. Nevertheless, lest I seem to be begging an important question, I will lay my cards on the table and try to explain the considerations that move me to make a choice that is, rhetorically, arbitrary, a matter of invention.[1]

One organizes a novel, after all, in the way that seems best suited to articulate one's felt experience. My most vivid, persistent impression of the discursive world of Günter Grass is of passionate feeling (most often anger and indignation), and of words—not as fashioned carefully or calmly or judiciously, but rather as overflowing, obsessively pouring forth uncontrolled. This account of my experience tells me nothing about the author and what he was or was not doing. Given this felt experience, however, it seems to me worthwhile to organize a novel that will be unified, and will gain its coherence from the emotions, the desires and passions of agents, functioning as principles of organization. Thus, as a first step toward interpretation, I am going to organize *Dog Years*[2] in terms of beginning, as a conjectural novel of style and manners.

The novel will be unified, then, by the arbitrary doings, feelings, and speech aroused in agents by desire. The principle of unconditioned beginning prevailing throughout the novel, connecting persons, events, situations, has several important implications. The "telling" of the conjectural novel is the quintessential act, first of all. Agents do and say throughout, and because they want to; and the *first* thing done or said will discriminate the orientation of the novel, make it *this* rather than another conjectural novel. We locate this identification at the temporal beginning because in a conjectural novel the beginning in principle and the temporal beginning obviously coincide. When we organize in this genre, then, we will expect to stress narrating, since "telling" is the initial unconditioned action of a conjectural novel. However, this has nothing to do with the question of point of view, a concept extrinsic to the critical vocabulary of this essay. When in chapter 5 I organized *The Tin Drum* as a conjectural novel, Oskar's story and what he said about it figured largely; in the translative organization I borrowed from Friedrichsmeyer, Oskar as teller and how he feels about telling were of no importance. Also, as I noted in chapter 5, the conjectural novel is not what is called picaresque because its unity stems from saying, doing, and feeling, not from an agent.

Dog Years will help us clarify these points. It begins not with a story to be told about someone, or personal memories to be recorded; it does not merge tale with teller or discriminate the teller from his tale. Rather, it discriminates among tellers by asking which of these tellers should begin and implies, therefore, that the telling goes beyond what one teller could encompass. This is reinforced by the immediate introduction of the Vistula: "One of us has to begin: You or he or you or I. . . . Many many sunsets ago, long before we existed, the Vistula flowed day in day out without reflecting us, and emptied forever and ever" (p. 11).

There are three books and three narrators in *Dog Years*; Brauxel, narrator of the first book, is Eddi Amsel, a protagonist, and it is he who has commissioned and who pays the second and third narrators, Harry Liebenau and Walter Matern, to write their books. Liebenau addresses the second book, a series of letters, to his cousin, Tulla. Brauxel says Liebenau applied for the job (p. 119), and Liebenau says that he tells his story "incurably" to himself (p. 125). Matern insists that he has no memory and everyone is trying to give him one, and that Brauxel wants "Matern to shoot the shit about those days" (p. 365).

Liebenau, then, writes because he wants to recall Tulla, whom he loved, Matern because he must do something with himself and has reached an impasse beyond which Brauxel's commission may move him. Only toward the end of Matern's book, the third, does Brauxel-Amsel, now called Goldmouth, articulate his compulsion to tell his part of the tale and to enjoin the other two to collaborate. Smoking and drinking as a fire rages around him and Matern in a Berlin tavern, Amsel cries out: "More stories. More stories. Keep going! As long as we're telling stories, we're alive . . . . as long as stories have power to entertain us, no hell can take us in . . . . Tell stories as long as you love your life" (p. 536).

To ask about narrators or someone called a narrator is to ask the wrong question. If the novel is unified by emotions generating activities and speech, *narration* is the spontaneous, creative act of the beginning; it is a verbal act and, in this case, a passionate verbal act. In *Dog Years* this creative action is initiated by a being who seems to defy identification, much less, as we shall see, characterization. Book 1, "Morning Shifts," opens with the first morning shift consisting of alternate paragraphs concerning the writing of the novel and the "history" and legends of the Vistula. The teller obviously tells what he feels the desire to tell. Who is he? Sometimes he refers to himself in the first person, sometimes the third: "The present writer usually writes Brauksel in the form of Castrop-Rauxel and occasionally of Häksel. When he's in the mood, Brauxel writes his name as Weichsel, the river which the Romans called the Vistula" (p. 11). So much for the beginning. Eddi Amsel disappears after a vicious beating by nine masked S.A. men and reappears later as the impressario Haseloff and then as Brauxel, the mine owner (of a mine in which no mining is done), the "present writer" who is later also Goldmouth, presumably because the teeth knocked out in the beating were replaced by gold teeth.

In fact, it makes no sense to speak about the narrator or narrators as somehow existing prior to the narration. In the conjectural novel, telling or words are also modes of doing and feeling and therefore principles, unifying and generative simultaneously. Consequently, we cannot speak of agents at all as independent of speech and action. The act of narrating generates the characters of the novel, the words generate the whole world of the novel.

It may be said, of course, that this is true of all novels; without words there is no discursive object, and in the other three genres character and personality, identity in effect, are certainly fashioned of words. However, made of words though they may be, they may be made such that they *seem* to develop, or unfold, or build. In the conjectural novel we envision a unity through spontaneous doing, saying, and feeling that contradicts any continuity of character implied by the notion of identity. This blurring of identity is present in the beginning of *Dog Years* in the uncertainty as to who will begin to "tell," in the use of first and third person pronouns by the teller, and in the variety of names attributed to him.

This ambiguity is quite persistent once it has been discriminated in the beginning, "in principle." Names are signs of identity, and we have already mentioned Amsel, Brauxel, and other variants. But, one says, aren't they the same person? Not really. The agents are generated anew throughout. One example should suffice: Amsel and Jenny Brunies undergo a genuine passion, in the sense of suffering. On the same snowy day, Amsel is beaten mercilessly and left buried completely in snow by the S.A. men who dislike scarecrows he has made and dressed in S.A. uniforms, while Jenny is forced, some distance away, to dance before an iron statue of Gutenberg of which children are afraid. When Jenny collapses, Tulla rolls her in the snow into a snowman (pp. 218–29).

At this time Amsel is a corpulent young man and Jenny a very chubby child. Amsel emerges from the snow, mouth bloody, but body slim: "The young man in Amsel's garden... had... Amsel's red hair... broad shoulders, narrow hips. Who had given him such ideal proportions?" (p. 226). At the same time Jenny emerges. "There in the slushy, porous gray snow stood no Jenny Brunies, no frozen roly-poly, no ice dumpling, no pudding on legs, there stood a frail line, on which Jenny's yellowish fluffy coat hung loose, as though shrunk after improper washing. And the line had a tiny doll-like face, just as Jenny's face had been doll-like. But there stood a very different doll, thin, so thin you could easily have looked past her, and didn't budge" (p. 224). If discontinuity is suggested by the ambiguous naming, it is shouted in this episode. I quoted the passage at length to leave no room for doubt that the "thin line" called Jenny is a new agent generated there and then. The thin young man retains a bloody mouth and disappears; as the passages indicated, he is not even called Amsel. He will reappear later as Haseloff, the impressario, and then Goldmouth.

Of course, the matter is a good deal more subtle than that. Discontinuity is meaningless without its contradictory, continuity; they are commonplaces which reciprocally imply one another. The continuity is there in a special sense characteristic of the genre. The name changes often in the case of Amsel, and the body itself changes once. But the bloody, toothless mouth remains to link the thin man with Amsel and later Goldmouth with Amsel. The Brauxel-Goldmouth who owns a mine in which scarecrows are made is linked to the Amsel who made scarecrows in childhood and youth. Jenny's body changes, but not her name or the fact that she dances or the person with whom she lives, Dr. Brunies, who found her abandoned by gypsies and adopted her.

The character of this kind of continuity, however, in its tenuousness, paradoxically reinforces the discontinuity as if it were insisting, over and over again, that everyone is someone new at any moment; there is no stable body, mind, activity. Amsel is an artist who creates scarecrows, a singer, an impressario, a mine owner, an author, and a literary entrepreneur. Matern is in the S.A., is an actor, a self-appointed instrument of revenge against Nazis, an athletic director, a writer of Materniads, the third book of the novel. Identity and the character and personality it implies is never fixed; the characters of the novel are not revealed, but generated throughout by the telling itself. In new lives, generated by new actions and desires, they are, in effect, new characters.

The world of the novel, insofar as we may consider it separately from the persons, is also generated by the telling, and in a manner characteristic of a conjectural novel. Places—Danzig and Kashubian Poland— and the time are brought into being genetically, in terms of beginnings. The novel abounds in histories, legends, and genealogies. Matern and Amsel are about ten years older than Harry, Tulla, and Jenny. The first book ends with the adoption of Jenny; however, in the "last morning shift," the head of the writers' consortium, Brauxel, deciding that a transition to the book of love letters must be devised, recounts his criterion for choosing the author of the letters. This turns out to be a demonstrable knowledge of the city of Danzig and its history. The transition Brauxel contrives is again characteristic: Harry will write to Tulla about the history of their family, but Brauxel now makes the whole world in which she will be said to begin. Beginning with "Tulla Pokriefke was born on June 11, 1927," it continues thereafter for two pages of statements each of which begins with the phrase "when Tulla was born." The doings and sayings and feelings of men make this natural world of weather and vegetation and animals hang together.

> When Tulla was born, the weather was variable, mostly cloudy, with a possibility of showers. Light gyratory winds fluttered the chestnut trees in Kleinhammer Park.
>
> When Tulla was born, Lindbergh, the transatlantic flier, boarded the cruiser *Memphis*.
>
> When Tulla was born, the book *Being and Time* had not yet appeared, but had been written and announced.
>
> When Tulla was born, Harras, her uncle's watchdog, was one year and two months old. (pp. 120–21)

The ending of the novel is the end of a sequence of words, deeds, and feelings, an ending in the mine where the telling began. In the conjectural novel, unified as it is, ending is no different from beginning, in the sense that nothing is resolved, nothing really changed. Then, too, the conjectural novel is the genre that epitomizes organization for its own sake. When we organize a whole conjecturally, in terms of beginning, we are almost forced by the principle itself to be acutely aware of continuous, spontaneous, arbitrary invention. The means of invention are the words, but the discontinuity between one "invention" and the next is a result of the mode of organization we chose. Since links and connections are obliterated in this mode to bring invention into relief, the means, the words and phrases, are especially vivid. Language and its tones, manners of speech, are crucial. I shall return to this shortly.

If the ending is not different from the beginning because there is no development, but rather a gathering up, a multiplication of invented perspectives, of beginnings, how can a conjectural novel end? The answer is quite simple. To organize a novel conjecturally is to call attention to the purely linguistic character of novels, to throw into relief the words qua words. Obviously, then, a conjectural novel has no characters at all in the beginning; it can be said to end when characters have been somehow identified: "And this man and that man—who now will call them Brauxel and Matern?—I and he, we stride with doused lamps to the changehouse . . . . For me and him bathtubs have been filled. I hear Eddi splashing next door. Now I too step into my bath. The water soaks me clean. Eddi whistles something indeterminate. I try to whistle something similar. But it's difficult. We're both naked. Each of us bathes by himself" (p. 569).

Here we have characters finally reduced or refined to genuine identity. Brauxel and Matern are names, of course, but who are they? They are "I and he." Naked and alone, Matern, the I, speaks of "Eddi" and in doing so identifies Brauxel-Goldmouth as the Eddi Amsel who disappeared; and by calling him Eddi, Matern identifies himself as the Walter Matern who once protected that Eddi Amsel. All perspectives taken together have been unified by this identifying of characters who have made this world: Matern, the S.A. man, the Nazi who qua Nazi made the world of before and during the war, and Eddi, the victim who survived by making new identities and who has made the postwar world, and both, who have together made the terminal boundaries of the discursive world, the first and last books of the novel. It is a perfect coming together of before and after the war precisely because the maker of the Nazi world, Matern, tells in the last book of the novel only of the postwar world he himself did not make, whereas Eddi, in the first book of the novel, tells the tale of the prewar world he himself did not make. It should be clear, then, why the conjectural novel is above all a novel of style and manners; for the words and style create manner of speech, and the latter makes communication possible in a genre which lacks fixed characters until the end. As we shall see when we trace themes in *Dog Years*, the words of the generic organization are uninterpreted, but they do have tone and characteristic manner, and these provide continuity and coherence in the absence of character.

The title, because it names the whole, must be considered before we turn from genre to theme. "Dog years" names the novel and therefore names the world of the novel in principle. There are three books, in each of which a dog figures significantly. The identity of the dogs is as ambiguous as that of the human agents and in the same way. First of all, just as the Jewish origin of Amsel's father is ambiguous and the origin of Jenny is ambiguous, so too is that of the dogs: their genealogy extends back to a Lithuanian or Russian or Polish she-wolf. Perkun, a black shepherd, was brought to the miller, Matern, by Pawel, his assistant, from Lithuania: "And Perkun sired Senta; and Senta whelped Harras; and Harras sired Prinz; and Prinz made history" (pp. 23–24).

The dogs' characters are not really fixed either. Harras is dominated and demoralized, turned eventually into a vicious attacker of whomever Tulla wishes to terrorize. Prinz, presented as a birthday gift to the Führer by the Gauleiter of Danzig, flees the bunker prior to the final catastrophe in Berlin and becomes Pluto, the wandering companion of Matern, Pluto who runs with preternatural speed at a remarkably advanced age.

Perkun in book one, as companion of Lorchen, the miller's sister, is surrogate for her lover, Pawel, who never returned from the First World War (p. 24). Harras in the second book attacks viciously as does his human companion, Tulla. Prinz-Pluto is installed at the end of the third book as guardian of the scarecrow mine. In a sense the title names the actual time of the novel (as opposed to the time including that of the genetic accounts) since each book ranges approximately over the life span of a dog.

It seems to me, however, that it also judges the constantly changing world of the novel by asserting, in effect, that the desires and activities which generate it are more bestial than human, and it does this not by means of a maxim or proposition but one word—*Hundejahre*. A stunted woman clings to her lover's dog; Tulla lives for days in Harras's kennel, eating dog food on her hands and knees like a dog (pp. 148–58); and the Führer, well-nigh "unspeakable," is almost totally ignored in favor of an inflated account of the attempt to retrieve his dog, an account couched in a parody of the language of Heidegger, the great philosopher of the period. Amplification of dogs, diminution of the actions and passions of men, crowned by a title, the reductiveness of which constitutes an impassioned judgment of a whole. And the dog, too, is identified at the end; since Prinz-Pluto is installed and identified as guardian of the scarecrow-mine-hell, the novel called *Dog Years* is a novel about a hellish world. Only the novel, or its very existence, affirms the value of the creative action of telling: "As long as we're telling stories we're alive," says Amsel, in the speech that seems to me to state the principle of *Dog Years* as a conjectural novel.

In organizing this conjectural novel, I have seemed, perhaps, to point to particulars, contradicting in fact the concept of genre and its functions, since particulars are made by fictive arguments linked in modes of discourse. What I have done, however, is different, and I will try to be very precise in explaining it. I have used the same process of organizing to construct the exemplary novels of the preceding chapter. In order to organize a specific novel, in a single mode, we must mention specific names, events, scenes, episodes, and so on, so that we discriminate *this* conjectural novel from other novels we might organize as conjectural. But what we point to are really uninterpreted variables, singled out to show that the sayings, doings, and feelings of agents make the world, and that this principle is present in all parts. In the present instance we show that "beginningness" governs the conjectural novel.

Further, titles, appellative of the complexity of a novel, are always reductive considered prior to thematic interpretation, and in the light of the "eternity" of genre. Pride and prejudice, or sound and fury, or the name of a whale are also reductive judgments the full significance of which must be interpreted by means of fictive argument. Nevertheless, to comment on them may seem to be interpretation. To say that *Dog Years* is about a hellish world, however, is not to interpret but to formulate openly what may be said to be barely concealed by the title *taken together with* the incidents I have chosen to point to in organizing *this* book as a conjectural novel: a dog named Pluto guarding a realm under earth in which objects are made at the behest of realms above earth implies hell. But what "hell" implies is another matter altogether. If, on the basis of that information, one were asked to say what hell means, one could not. The "hellish novel" remains to be interpreted. We do, then, require that distinction between organizing a novel and interpreting by arranging variables to make particulars. We require it because we make novels of a given kind by organizing, and we cannot interpret a novel unless we make one to interpret.

We might as well begin with the related temporal variation on eternity, that is, with a reading in the hypothetical mode of argument: If agents act, each from the perspective of his own desires, and encounter and must cope with obstacles presented by the differing perspectives of other agents and their desires and actions, and if these obstacles finally block further action, then agents will continue to assert their own perspectives in speech and writing. Now we can interpret the variables to which we pointed earlier when they served to indicate a disposition of parts in the whole, all existing simultaneously.

Let us take Amsel-Brauxel as agent. With Walter Matern to protect him in childhood from children who attack him because he is fat, he expresses his creative impulses by making scarecrows. When Tulla has already taunted him with being Jewish, and the S.A., including his protector Matern, endangers his life, he alters his identity and disappears. No longer fat, Jewish, creator of offensive scarecrows, Amsel, he survives as the impressario Haseloff. After the war he manufactures for children toy spectacles which reveal the truth about their parents, the Nazi generation. When protest forces these off the market, he acquires an abandoned potash mine and returns to making scarecrows, which exemplify the impulses and passions of men. Finally, he organizes the author's consortium to write the account of how everything began and came to be as it is.

We can construct this kind of account for the other two narrators as well. Harry, who has loved and desired Tulla since childhood, is the one man denied her sexual favors. His account is of action to achieve the object of his desire, action blocked by her actions and by a war which separates them, until he can no longer do anything but tell the tale. Matern wants to be like his apparent ancestor, the resourceful, dashing bandit, Materna; his career in the S.A. is aborted, and his career as an actor cut short. After the war he wanders through West Germany to find and punish Nazi companions he feels deceived him. These agents, encountered, frustrate his desires. He is fleeing to East Germany when he hears a woman on the train chattering about "over here" and "over there" and realizes that East Germany will be no different from West Germany. He returns with Amsel to the mine and will write his account of past action since there is no longer anything else he desires to do.

That agents move in this way, making their worlds by saying and doing in the face of opposing orientations, and telling what was done—this is the mode of discourse of argument. The principle of the novel validates it because it asserts that saying, doing, and feeling make the world and hold its particulars together, connect them to one another. Value is a matter of principle, and the supremely valuable action is asserted by Amsel in the passage I have cited a number of times. The act of narrating is creative even when the tales told are tales of destruction, because action is the principle of life. In principle we could only determine that narration is generative because it is a mode of acting and acting and feeling are the principles of a conjectural novel. The mode of discourse through which I have structured the novel permits us now to interpret that creativity concretely. In the mode of discourse of argument, when nonverbal action is blocked, by absence of desire or an opposing obstacle, agents will then tell their tale—witness the dying Hamlet's injunction to Horatio. Amsel says telling stories will keep them alive. Of course it must! Without acting and feeling and speaking there are no agents, no world, no life, and when consequence tells us that narrating is the one action left to these agents, we know why the value given by principle is in fact so very valuable.

As I have interpreted it in the mode of argument, then, *Dog Years* is Grass's way, his most effective way, of exorcising the evil of the world he grew up in. He cannot undo the Nazi years or alter the postwar developments "Materniads" denounces. But he can deny his world the amnesia it craves by preserving those worlds in the novel. Amsel's words are especially significant then, for not only does he say that telling stories keeps us alive, he also says that as long as they entertain us, i.e., as long as we *pay attention* to them, "no hell can take us in," no hell can deceive us. To deny one's fellows amnesia is to admonish them against succumbing to hell again. If they are entertained, perhaps they may be saved.

We would expect a conjectural organization to sustain a theme in the mode of argument, but it will also sustain other readings, and we must explore them to see what they will reveal. A reading in the causal mode of description, and in terms of agent, briefly, will uncover a "comic" dimension. Amsel grows up, developing naturally; he is fat and un-athletic but artistically gifted. When the contingency of anti-Semitism arises, he has the creative wit to cope with it, remaining nonetheless true to his nature. As a boy he sang and made scarecrows; as Haseloff he creates variant artistic expressions by producing ballets. He survives because he is resourceful enough to shed the physical appearance and name of the half-Jewish Amsel, and talented enough to succeed in a new career (the physical metamorphosis is explicable in terms of the psychology, the nature, of Harry who narrates it). As he achieves success in wartime Germany, so in postwar Germany his natural gifts enable him to triumph over contingencies. He returns to fashioning scarecrows for reanimated worldwide agricultural needs, and organizes the consortium to tell the truth about himself and thus about the nature of the world in which he has managed to survive.

The reality of successive identities of the reading in the mode of argument, real because they are successful deceptions on the part of agents who make their roles, thus themselves and their world, are *simply* deceptions in the descriptive reading—deceptions revealed as the *artifices* of a naturally creative person triumphantly surviving in a hostile world to expose that world for what it is. Why will the man whose development is psychologically healthy, true to his nature, survive in the face of adversity? The conjectural principle tells us that agents act according to desire, the descriptive reading interprets unimpeded desire as natural, thus life-preserving. Not so with Harry and his sick love for Tulla or Matern and his inability to see that he himself is as culpable as the Nazis he wants to punish. Amsel is the lucky contingency that saves them despite themselves by the therapeutic nature of the task he conceives for them. The novel itself, in principle, remains valuable. Now it is valuable because narrating is therapeutic.

In principle, continuous doing, feeling, and saying make for a changing world. A reading in the sequential mode of narration gives us an Amsel whose problem is how, in what direction, the world should change, and how to bring good change about. The virtual conquest of Danzig by national socialism is an evil change. It denies art. Tulla, born in 1927, is a representative figure of this world, and she persecutes Jews in Amsel, artists in Amsel, Jenny, and Jenny's music teacher. It fosters death, not life, in the pile of bones near the crematorium just outside the city, and in Tulla's behavior which leads her to destroy her unborn child. When the war is over, how can one change such a world?

Now we will note still another particular made in this reading, muted in the others. Matern's father, the miller, can answer questions and offer advice by listening to mealworms that infest a sack of flour. Amsel sets him up after the war as a kind of prophet–fortune teller to West German entrepreneurs. His advice seems to be decisive for the recovery of West Germany. This is a false solution to the problem. It makes for the same vulgar, greedy world of the past, a false direction East Germany is eager to take as it tries to gain access to the old man. The attempts to offer insight, through the spectacles, to the younger generation also fails. Amsel's recognition of the way to solve the problem is also an insight into himself and his true creative gift. Only the act of preserving the past, its beginnings in genealogies, founding legends, histories, and an account of the recent past, only narrating in writing can be effective. He shows Matern the world as hell in his mine of scarecrows representing human passions, and chains Prinz-Pluto, the Führer's dog, down there to guard that hell while he and Matern return to write the novel which will alter the circumstances that bear upon change in the future.

Finally, a reading in the holistic mode of exposition will give us the three books as successive levels of transcendence which end with plunges back into the grimy, chaotic world of becoming. Yet each represents a transformation which is a step toward the light of truth. The first book ends with an act of love in Brunies's adoption of the abandoned baby. The transition is now significant in a way we didn't notice before. Following an act of love vis-à-vis an infant, we move to the second book, covering the years of the Third Reich. They begin with a baby and the world as it is at her birth. But

Tulla, stinking of glue, treacherous toward Harry in response to his fidelity to her, Tulla is the epitome of the Nazi era. Unlike Harry, Matern, Amsel, and Jenny, Tulla is devoid of art and stunted even with respect to her physiological creativity. She gives her body to men who do not love her, denies it to the one man who does. Tulla alone accepts the bones, evidence of death, without even needing to pretend they are something else. Her unredeemed viciousness, recalled in his narration, paradoxically prods Harry to an insight into truth and value that he could not achieve earlier.

> A boy, a young man, a uniformed high school student, who venerated the Führer, Ulrich von Hutten, General Rommel, the historian Heinrich von Treitschke, for brief moments Napoleon, the panting movie actor Emil Jannings, for a while Savonarola, then again Luther, and of late the philosopher Martin Heidegger. With the help of these models he succeeded in burying a real mound made of human bones under medieval allegories. The pile of bones, which in reality cried out to high heaven between Troyl and Kaiserhafen, was mentioned in his diary as a place of sacrifice, erected in order that purity might come-to-be in the luminous, which transluminates purity and so fosters light. (p. 318)

The end of the book is a negative transcendence, illuminating the truth of the Third Reich by describing its finale in the bunker in terms of the dog's flight in a parody of Heidegger. Simultaneously, Nazism and what is conceived as its intellectual rationale are exposed as ludicrous and bestial, while the ugliness and incorrigible blindness to truth of the postwar world are foreshadowed:

> Thereupon at-handness takes its leave in the not-noticeableness of the inutilizable, giving rise to top secret message....
> "...Führer's favorite dog Prinz...is Führer's gift to the German people. Acknowledge receipt."
> Whereupon the last radio stations play *Götterdämmerung*.... Whereupon radio silence settles over the government quarter of the Reichcapital. Locus-wholeness, nihilation, open-to-dread, and togetherpiecable. Greatness. Entirety. The madeness of Berlin. Made finite. The end....
>
> All all all see the sun rising in the west and take their bearings from the dog.
>
> Left behind: mounds of bones, mass graves, card files, flagpoles, party books....
>
> All are eager to forget the mounds of bones and the mass graves, the flagpoles and party books, the debts and the guilt.
>
> There was once a dog....

On May 8, 1945, he swam across the Elbe above Magde-
burg almost unseen and went looking for a new master on
the west side of the river. (pp. 356–57, 360–61)

It is important to note that the account of the Third Reich's end in
terms of a dog is in itself a value judgment. The parody of Heidegger's
well-known philosophical locutions constitutes an additional value
judgment compounded with the first. This is achieved through the
peculiar use of words alone, quite independent of content. The principle of a conjectural novel of style and manners thus permeates the
thematic accounts. The emphasis on value is characteristic of the expository mode, the use of a blatant stylistic device to achieve that emphasis derives from the conjectural organization.[3]

The third book plunges into the postwar German world, and all its
chaotic oppositions, the frenzied scrambling foreshadowed in the passage quoted, emerge in the account of Matern's wandering. At the end,
the mine exposes the truth of man's universe mirrored in the scarecrow
hell. This vision of a world made by the acts, desires, and words of
agents has as its final consequent the necessity for engaging in the task
of exposing it in the writing of the novel. The descent into truth leads to
an ascent into the world to try to transform it by telling the truth.

These four fictive arguments linked in modes of discourse are coherently interrelated because of the principle which connects particulars
in all four modes. Each permits us to call into being different particulars. And while each performs the functions of the others—telling the
acts, desires, and speech that invent the world and communicate it *by
communicating it*, describing the nature of the world, narrating the complication and resolution of human problems, and exposing the truth
about the world—all together they permit us to reach a deeper appreciation of the richness of the novel without the sacrifice of coherence, for
the principle has guaranteed coherence in constituting a unified
whole. The variant readings, in turn, enhance the value instantiated by
the generic organization; for they tell us that the conjectural novel is,
because argumentative structure or communication is, life-preserving,
therapeutic, problem-solving, and educative.

To move from the world of Günter Grass to the world of John Fowles
is to step from a teeming, babbling marketplace into the dons' common
room. Yet, after all, that is a bad analogy. Fowles has his own kind of
density, and while I do not experience it as impassioned and obsessed
with words and phrases compulsively repeated, it does seem filled with
curiosity and, paradoxically enough, a detached passion for inclusiveness, and the search for causes. Therefore, I will organize *The French
Lieutenant's Woman*[4] in terms of beginning, middle, and end, as a definitive novel of events and consequences.

The unconditioned character of beginning is, of course, there; an anonymous teller begins to speak. But the beginning serves only to contribute to inclusiveness, since apparently arbitrary events—beginnings—are part of the nature of the universe. End is not like the organizing end of a qualitative novel, in principle necessary. The novel postulates first an ending that is rejected on the basis of the accumulation of evidence, and then two alternate endings, each of which is possible in a world in which chance is possible. Middle is not an englobing principle, assimilating beginning and end to its eternal true idea. Middle is rather the accumulation of elements and facts that the world is made up of.

The universe, and thus this novel, is governed by chance and determinacy, by forces in constant interplay. What we experience as chance may, in fact, be determined. To the extent that we do not know why something is and that it had to be as it is, we attribute it to chance. Perhaps it is chance, perhaps not; we cannot know. Paradoxically, it is the possibility of the unforeseeable that gives life its piquancy, making us curious enough to go on seeking to discover what is really the case.

Chance and determinacy, the real nature of things, and the contingencies of our experience that produce the events that occur and their consequences are adumbrated in epigraphs at the head of each chapter. The novel takes place in Victorian England, but the teller who seeks to describe the reality of the time and place lives, he says, in the twentieth century. The epigraphs are quotations from the biological determinism of Darwin and the economic determinism of Marx as well as the indeterminacy represented by artistic genius in passages from poets of the period. The novel abounds as well in informative essays and footnotes, building a comprehensive picture of the era. Indeed, *The French Lieutenant's Woman* is almost in itself a history of ideas and a social history of Victorian England in which the story of Sarah Woodruff and Charles Smithson, of Mrs. Poulteney and Charles's servant, Sam, is an illustration in the concrete of what it was like to live in such a world.

The narrator's admonitions to the reader to understand the characters in their own terms is part of a total organization set up to show forth the way in which historical contingency conceals the respects in which nothing ever changes. To speak of how the Victorians are unlike us is to implicate the ways in which they are like us. *The French Lieutenant's Woman* is *this* novel, but organized in terms of beginning, middle, and end it contains all the elements necessary for indefinite expansion to a definitive "picture" of the nature of things.

Further, in the case of the definitive organization of a novel, ending is not really distinguishable from the beginning, just as it is not in the conjectural genre. We would expect this since all four genres are governed by invention, which is unequivocally expressed only in the conjectural mode. However, whereas conjectural organizations seem to defy ending because they focus on the unconditioned character of invention—that is, the novel is made up of a multiplicity of beginnings (by definition unconditioned)—definitive organizations seem to defy end and beginning because they focus on the nature of things, which underlies the particularity of finite events and mortal agents. How, then, can a definitive novel end, organized as it is in terms of beginning, middle, and end to encompass all the elements that make up the nature of things?

If we examine the definitive novel rhetorically, we see that its unconditioned beginning is inventive in a sense peculiar to its focus on nature. A "picture" of the nature of things involves the establishment of origins, development, and growth, and these in turn involve the interplay of chance and determinacy. Rhetorical argument, which makes use of example, points to the beginning of a definitive novel as an agent's choice of a particular example by means of which to exhibit the nature of things.[5] The elements of a beginning are shown developing and growing in accordance with nature and in response to chance, wherein natural growth is abetted or impeded. The beginning points to the elements, the middle details their combination and growth. The end comes when all the possibilities of mature growth have been depicted taking into account both the determinacy of nature and the workings of chance. We can read *Mrs. Dalloway* this way and see that all the "natural" possibilities of Clarissa Dalloway have been exhaustively examined with the full account of her party, and then the novel is at an end.

In *The French Lieutenant's Woman* a definitive organization points to what is clearly determined, given the nature of things—Charles's innate difficulty in a relationship with a woman like Sarah, together with his struggle to go beyond convention, his distaste for the crassly commercial, and his blindness to the human motives of a servant—and what depends on unpredictable chance, the decision of a woman like Sarah who is unpredictable and unknowable in the context of her world. Since the end of this process of growth is unknowable, a matter of chance, the novel ends when the *possible* denouements have been suggested. It is characteristic of this kind of organization that only the beginning is in some sense arbitrary. Once the novel unfolds, the maker cannot *choose* arbitrarily one ending over another, no matter how plausibly he can invent it. If more than one ending is plausible given the nature of things, then more than one must be indicated for in the definitive novel the emergence of nature and human nature are the "end" or goal. The example may be arbitrarily chosen, but once chosen it must work out according to nature.

The definitive novel can be said to focus on events and consequences because chance and determinacy *do not* suggest action determined by reflective choice. Agents behave as their nature or their antinatural conditioning move them to behave, given events which occur—both necessary and contingent events, both biologically and culturally determined, for example. Their behavior and that of a complex congery of others give us the consequences of events. What natural and unnatural behavior mean, of course, will depend on the formal themes employed to interpret the novel, i.e., the four modes of discourse.

The title, finally, pointing to the person in whom the story is centered, comments on convention which masks the nature of things, for Sarah is not literally what the epithet implies. And what she *is* can never be fully uncovered. The title names this novel and, by implication, the way things are in a world in which nature and convention clash.

Let us begin with a causal descriptive argument, varying the generic theme in terms of agent. Charles Smithson does not develop in accordance with his nature; he is impeded by Victorian mores and social conventions which lead him to dissociate stable, lasting love from sexual desire. As a result, first of all, he becomes engaged to Ernestina, a sweet, conventional, acceptable bride. Contingency throws Sarah, the disgraced woman, the socially inferior ex-governess, in his path. Overcome by desire, he permits her to seduce him because he believes her to be a fallen woman in any case. He is horrified to discover that she is in fact a virgin, but despite his sense of honor, he cannot bring himself to insist that she accept his proposal of marriage and leaves her. Sitting alone in a church, he undergoes a profound inner conflict between his natural feeling for Sarah and the conventions that bind him. At length, he decides to marry her:

> He seemed as he stood there to see all his age, its tumultu-
> ous life, its iron certainties and rigid conventions, its re-
> pressed emotion and facetious humor, its cautious science
> and incautious religion, its corrupt politics and immutable
> castes, as the great hidden enemy of all his deepest yearn-
> ings.... This is clearly not the moment to bring in a compari-
> son with St. Paul on the road to Damascus. But... there was a
> kind of radiance in his face.... I hope you will believe that
> Sarah on his arm in the Uffizi did stand, however banally, for
> the pure essence of cruel but necessary (if we are to survive—
> and yes, still today) freedom. (pp. 285, 287)

However, the upper-class mid-Victorian Charles, bound by his time and its conventions, doesn't perceive his servant, Sam, as a fully human, complex being. He takes Sam for granted and, preoccupied by his own emotional upheaval, sends Sam to Sarah with a brooch and a letter asking her to marry him. Sam is not content to be a servant (he's told Charles, who has not, literally, paid attention) and wants Charles to give him the money to open a shop. Realizing that Charles will have little money should he marry Sarah rather than the heiress, Ernestina, Sam fails to deliver the message, takes the brooch in lieu of cash, and when Charles returns to see Sarah, she is gone. He assumes she has rejected him.

In effect, then, when he realizes what is naturally right for him to do, it would seem to be too late. By the time Charles's heartbreaking search for Sarah succeeds, she has made a new life for herself. Whether she will finally marry him or refuse depends on factors beyond his control. The alternate endings can be seen as affirming in principle the great complexity in individual lives of the interaction of chance and determinacy; for the determinacy governing one individual functions as chance with respect to his fellows.

In this descriptive argument Sarah, unlike Charles, is seen to have been true to her nature, refusing to permit convention to limit her in terms of class or sexual satisfaction. By pretending to have had an affair with the French lieutenant, she has effectively made herself a pariah, outside any class. She has also become more sexually attractive in her world where governesses are ignored by true gentlemen, but a fallen woman is a temptress. She determines to seduce Charles Smithson in order to experience sexual love with a man she can admire. Knowing that his sense of honor would keep him from yielding to temptation if he knew she was still a virgin, she conceals this from him. Believing he has rejected her, she goes to London, finds an artistic milieu in which she and her illegitimate child are welcome, and is contented. Either ending, then, is "good" for Sarah. She will be happy if she remains as she is; should she choose to be reunited with Charles, to marry him, she would also be happy.

Integrated with this reading is the picture of the Victorian world in terms of which we can understand nature and convention, chance and determinacy. All of the elements that make the world explain why the particulars I have made ought to be connected this way to lead to these consequences.

The novel can be interpreted by means of the hypothetical mode of argument, of agents acting, making their worlds and themselves by doing and saying, each from his own perspective, and encountering other agents and their orientations, which must, in turn, be dealt with. In this light, the insistence of the novelist-narrator that often his characters do as they please against his wishes is neither obscure nor disingenuous. Having "made" Sarah and Charles, he cannot always control the consequences of his invention; the inventions, once invented as this rather than that, have imperatives of their own unforeseen by the maker. The novelist-narrator cannot determine whether Sarah and Charles can finally come together. He offers three endings: Charles will return to Ernestina after his encounter with Sarah. He rejects this on the grounds that Charles as invented would no longer be able to do that or wish to. Charles will, having found Sarah, persuade her to marry him, or, finally, he will fail to persuade her. With these two alternatives he ends his account. The ambiguous ending is as consonant with this sequence as is the inclusion of essays and footnotes.

In the reading in the mode of argument, Charles flounders against the orientation of Sarah, although it is useful to him in making his life anew, saving himself from entanglement with Mr. Freeman, Ernestina's father, and with a commercial success which he loathes. Sarah desires freedom and achieves it in the only way she can, given the orientation of Victorian society. She engages in deceptions so that she may choose her social status freely, however painful a status it might be; and for a similar reason, to gain freedom, Sam deceives Charles. In this mode, however, deception is reality for reality is what agents make it. Sarah is effectively, in society's attitude toward her, a fallen woman; and she is that because she said she was.

Chance and determinacy, the arbitrary and the necessary, all the elements that make up the whole of this novel explain thoroughly the connection among particulars in the mode of argument, for the "deceptions" and contrasting perspectives which confront one another are the natural elements, the ultimate realities and sometime contingencies of the definitive whole. These principles will validate a reading in the holistic expository mode as well, a reading in which we see oppositions successfully dissolved in the light of knowledge, the narrator-novelist achieving finally that level of knowledge which denies him the option of determining an ending; for reality transcends fixed particularity. "The river of life, of mysterious laws and mysterious choice.... Life ... is not one riddle and one failure to guess it, is not to inhabit one face alone or to be given up after one losing throw of the dice; but is to be, however inadequately, emptily, hopelessly into the city's iron heart, endured. And out again, upon the unplumb'd, salt, estranging sea" (p. 366). And throughout the novel Charles and Sarah are transformed by the knowledge achieved through the struggle of their relationship, as the opposition between desire and convention is transcended and transformed by love. The novel can be said to move from knowledge of a place and time to a knowledge of men and women in all places and times, the elements of this definitive novel providing the exemplar for all places and times.

A focus, finally, on the complex problem of the narrator-novelist will give us a reading in the sequential mode of narration. The novelist-narrator, a man living in the mid-twentieth century, must tell a story about mid-Victorians without attributing to them anachronistic motives, feelings, or behavior. He would render them as they really were, as no novelist contemporary with them could have known them to be.

He proceeds to amass exhaustive information on the social, political, economic, ideological, intellectual, and religious facts of the time. He brings these resources to bear in inventing characters and events and offering explanatory notes and admonitory essays. In the process he gains insight not only into the world he would recreate but also into his own limitations, realizing that he cannot determine what would have had to happen, given his inventions, but only what might have happened to resolve the complications of character, thought, and action. He sees this insight as simultaneously an insight into human affairs generally, and his indeterminate resolution has produced changed circumstances in which new problems for narrator-novelists may now emerge. And of course we will recognize that such an indeterminate resolution is itself necessary given the elements which compose this world and connect the particulars in this mode.

All four discursive sequences in all four modes interrelate coherently by virtue of the unity of genre. The elements that compose the definitive novel are explanatory in all four modes, providing the natural substructure and the conventions contingent to it in the descriptive argument, the clashing perspectives of the mode of argument as the natural desires of agents conflict; they provide the natural individual and social facts relevant to resolving complication in a narrative reading, and the oppositions that are dissolved in light of knowledge of truth, which transforms them in the expository reading.

Nature is ubiquitous in these formulations because of the principle. In the modes of discourse in isolation from a discursive object, nature figures prominently only in the descriptive mode. The nature that is present because of the principle is an *uninterpreted concept* in itself. Its signification depends on the mode of connection. In our reading of *The French Lieutenant's Woman* in the mode of argument, the desire that initiates action is natural but the "natures" of agents will differ. In a narrative reading, Charles's nature is a product of his Victorian world and his human biological nature. In the descriptive reading, however, his Victorian attempt to suppress sexual passion is unnatural. In the expository reading neither biological sexual desire nor conventional suppression is permitted to prevail; both must be transcended and transformed in light of a knowledge of love. Each of these readings brings to light a different dimension of meaning in the novel, yet these meanings are mutually enhancing because of the principle which unifies them and guarantees their value.

SEVEN

NOVELS—QUALITATIVE

Robert Coover's first novel, *The Origin of the Brunists*,[1] begins with a prologue in which the Brunists are shown to be a well-established, thriving sect; since the title suggests that the novel will be concerned with events which occurred prior to the emergence of the Brunists as a viable religious movement, the novel may be seen as beginning with the end. Therefore, I am going to organize it in terms of end as a qualitative novel of action and civility. It goes without saying that it might be organized otherwise. For example, the anonymous writer who composed the text for the dust jacket of the 1978 edition says, in part: "Coover took a specific phenomenon of contemporary American life and used it to probe and explore the collective soul: grass-roots evangelism, which, when married to the American predilection for circus-like magnification, offers an astonishing... view of the American religious experience." The statement presupposes a definitive novel of events and circumstances, an account of the nature of things with respect to an important part of American social reality, and it is a legitimate view of Coover's book. On the other hand, the qualitative organization will enable us to call attention to aspects of the novel which might seem to disappear in the definitive.

First of all I should like to examine the prologue with some care. It is entitled "The Sacrifice," which refers to the death of Marcella Bruno, sister of the man from whom the Brunists take their name. The narration of the prologue is in the third person and limited to the consciousness of Hiram Clegg, "—who was to become Bishop Clegg of Randolph Junction, the first President of the International Council of Brunist Bishops, the man to nominate Mrs. Clara Collins as their first Evangelical Leader and Organizer, and who would be, some years later, the Bishop of the State of Florida—" (p. 24). This essentially parenthetic material (the only intrusion in the prologue of a narrative voice in its own right) attests to the growth and stability of the Brunists, so that throughout the account of their early trials the outcome is never in doubt. Thus, if "end" means goal, for example, and the Brunists as fully established sect are the goal, then the end not only determines the beginning, it *is* literally the beginning, and between them there is no middle and thus no novel. We need to consider, then, whether the prologue and title taken together are not somehow misleading. A careful look at Hiram Clegg's memories of the night Marcella Bruno was killed by an automobile, the content of the prologue, is rewarding. The death occurs the day before the Brunists are to gather on a hill to await the end of the world, and Clegg's memories introduce the principal Brunists of the novel with the exception of Tiger Miller, the newspaper editor and publisher of West Condon, who is both on the inside of the movement and opposed to it. Furthermore, Hiram Clegg himself, as it turns out, *is not* an important character at all, having nothing to do with the events that constitute the origin of the Brunists.

Let me propose that the choice of a Brunist bishop as the narrative point of view which opens the novel establishes the fact that a thriving sect exists, the origins of which merit attention. At the same time the choice of Bishop Clegg offers the perspective of a Brunist who is nonetheless not at all implicated in the evolution of the sect until its climactic events. Now the complexities and ambiguities of that evolution are just barely hinted at in the last paragraph of the prologue, and only by implication.

> Some seemed to remember a luminous white bird. . . . Others spoke in later years of a heart-shaped bloodstain. . . . Many vouched that a priest had passed among them. . . . The most persistent legend in later years—and the only one which Hiram knew to be false—was that the girl, in the last throes of death, had pointed to the heavens, and then, miraculously, maintained this gesture forever after. . . . The painters never failed to exploit this legend of the heavenward gesture. . . . Which was, of course, as it should be. (pp. 24–25)

Clegg himself will be seen to be both innocent and ignorant of some of the questionable antecedents of the Brunists; more substantively questionable indeed than the symbolic liberties mentioned in the quoted passage. These antecedents are about to unfold when the prologue closes. Thus the choice of Clegg as narrative voice of the very beginning, which sets up the parameters of what will follow, also establishes for the Brunists as fully developed sect a kind of moral authority, a legitimacy that is being tacitly asserted in the face of any ambiguity in the sect's origins.

We must ask next why Tiger Miller is omitted, a major agent in the novel and involved in the final events; technically, because Clegg's memories are confined to events which do not include Miller. I suggest, however, that his absence may be said to imply that although he is part of the origin of the Brunists as a full-fledged sect, he is also, or rather, his personal story is of equal importance with theirs in the thought of the novel. Therefore, he is not introduced as simply part of the origin of the Brunists because he will occupy the rhetorically necessary place of fully treated anti-Brunist. Since the "end" of the novel, literally, "quantitatively," will concern Miller, we can see how the beginning is determined by it. If we ask how Miller comes to be as he is at the end, we discover that the existing sect of Brunists must be explored, for in their origin lies the beginning of Miller's reversal and recognition. Thus the "end" of the Brunists is the beginning of the novel in a complicated double sense of end.

Following the prologue the novel unfolds chronologically. It is divided into four parts preceded by a prologue and followed by an epilogue. (In our discussion of the qualitative novel in chapter 5 we noted that the "parts" are not the plot, character, thought, etc., of poetic criticism, which also organizes in terms of end, but are quantitative parts in rhetorical criticism.) Part 1, "The White Bird," gives an account of a mine disaster in West Condon, in which Ely Collins, miner and Nazarene sect preacher, dies heroically, leaving an ambiguous message for his wife, and from which Giovanni Bruno, befriended by Ely and harassed and ridiculed by other miners, escapes, apparently miraculously. How he could have escaped death, given his location in the mine, is never really understood by anyone, including the reader. He remains unconscious in the hospital until the end of part 1 when Marcella Bruno telephones Miller to tell him that "Giovanni had been visited in the mine by the Virgin, a vision, so to speak. Yes, he could publish that. She had come to him in the form of a white bird" (p. 116).

Part 1 also traces the effects of the disaster on other members of the West Condon community, including Abner Baxter, a miner and preacher, who will set himself up in opposition to Collins's widow, Clara; Eleanor Norton, a spiritualist of some obscure kind, who sees the disaster and Bruno's survival as a sign; Clara Collins, who feels compelled to see Ely's death as meaningful and tells Miller that Ely had had visions of a white bird from time to time. When Marcella's news appears in Miller's paper, Clara visits the Italian Catholic Bruno, bringing her note from Ely with her. Barely legible and obviously uncompleted, it reads:

> Dear Clara and All:
>
> I dissobayed and I know I must Die. Listen allways to the Holy Spirit in your Harts Abide in Grace. We will stand Together befor Our Lord the 8th of (p. 96)

Giovanni Bruno's vision and survival, Ely's note (which, interpreted, suggests a date for the end of the world), and Eleanor Norton's calculations and visions form the seeds of the Brunist movement. The publicity given Bruno and the note in Justin ("Tiger") Miller's newspaper draws attention from outside of West Condon. Miller's emotional involvement with Marcella Bruno, in turn, gives him entree to the group which enables him to continue publicizing the millenarian movement growing around Bruno. However, city officials and leading citizens who fear the town will appear ridiculous, encourage the out-of-work miners—disaffected and resentful of the elevation of their butt, Bruno, to quasi-sainthood—to unite in opposition to the infant movement. By the end of part 2, "The Sign," these forces have grown in number and intensity. With the help of Ralph Himebaugh, a city official who has been secretly engaged in numerical calculations to determine the advent of the end of the world, Mrs. Norton and Clara Collins have fixed on a date which interprets Ely's ambiguous prophecy, and opposition to the group has resulted in the burning down of Clara's house.

Part 3, "The Passage," tells of Mrs. Norton's efforts to destroy Miller's relationship with Marcella, since Mrs. Norton has from the outset realized that Miller is in fact a hostile force among them. Miller meets Marcella in the newspaper office and makes love to her, telling her he is leaving the cult and wants her to come with him and showing her his story, already in type, publicizing the date, April 19, fixed upon as the time of the final judgment. Since the small group of believers, harassed and threatened by forces both Christian and secular, have decided, as Miller knows, to suppress this information and await the end quietly, his story spread across the front page of the *Chronicle* and sent to wire services across the country is a clear betrayal and brands him an enemy. Marcella puts her clothes on and leaves him, never to see him again. His Brunist special is published on Wednesday of Holy Week, April 8, and the remainder of this section follows the many principals through the next ten days until April 19. During this time, we learn, Marcella Bruno has been fasting, since her flight from Miller on the night of the seventh of April.

Part 4, "The Mount," is the climax, and for the Brunists it is the beginning of a double reversal which affords them insight into the true nature of their communal effort and alters radically the character of their activities. They travel to the "mount," the hill on which the destroyed mine is located, in happy anticipation of the following day, the nineteenth, when the last judgment will be upon them. Groups from the town come after them, and to avoid violence they retreat. The weakened Marcella, left behind at home, follows them later and is killed by the fleeing automobile of Abner Baxter, who had come to the mine site to harass the Brunists. Her death provides a martyr for the Brunists, and Clara Collins's protection of him from the wrath of the community converts Abner Baxter to their cause.

He stood by the dead child in the midst of that mantling hysteria and execration and waited—for what? Perhaps: to be slain. . . . "No, friends! We're *all* murderers!" From a quarter least expected: it was Sister Clara Collins, ennobled, it would seem, by her own great griefs, and thus less undone by this present one, who now spoke forth boldly: "We *all* killed her with our hate and with our fear!" And he recognized the magnitude of it, the greatness of spirit, and he was stirred in the soul and much amazed. . . . "this awful thing is a judgment on us—Please! Join hands with us now and pray!"

And he reached across and accepted Clara's hand, and as he did so, a great warmth surged through him.[2]

Marcella's death also moves Miller to go to the mount on the following day. The anticipated chaos and violence ensue and, of course, the second reversal as well: the first has united the Brunists with a powerful enemy, the union a tangible fruit of the very real and terrible loss of Marcella. The second is negative; the world doesn't come to an end after all. We are then told what happens to the principal Brunists.

The first result of the fiasco on April 19 is the excommunication of Bruno himself from the Roman Catholic Church, and his commitment to a mental institution by the town authorities. His old mother is taken, too. Neither can take care of the other, and Marcella's death has furnished an excuse for committing Bruno to custodial care, presumably in the hope that his absence will dampen the zeal of his followers. The loss of Bruno, however, like that of Marcella, is only an apparent reversal, for it raises the largely silent and essentially symbolic Bruno to martyrdom as well.

The failure of their hopes leads the Brunist remnant to recalculate the date of the "Redemption"; when this new date, too, is proved incorrect, the reversal is complete, and recognition is expressed explicitly by Clara Collins in company with Hiram Clegg and a conference of Bishops: "*God willing,*" she shouted out, "*we will go out and win the souls of the whole wide world!*"[3] thus subtly echoing the conclusions of the synoptic Gospels. The reversals suffered by the Brunists throughout, brought about by their actions and those of their opponents, have built up the community of Brunists. The reversals suffered in the loss of the saintly Marcella to death and of the mysterious Bruno to the "ungodly" forces of the secular community, have strengthened the Brunists with powerful, unifying symbols. The major reversal, the failure of the prophecy, has afforded the insight which forges a new civility, a new concept of themselves as a community united for action in a nonapocalyptic future.

Since we are unifying quantitative parts, however, we must take into account the epilogue, entitled "Return," which ends the book qua book. It concerns Tiger Miller and his return from near-death. The reversal of the Brunists occurred on their "Mount of Redemption," on Sunday, April 19, when the world didn't end. This is what did happen: rain fell, curious onlookers mocked them, crowds turned violent. In this context, Miller, learning of Marcella's death, goes to the vigil to which the Brunists have borne her dead body. He tries to reach it, to protect it from the rain and the mob. The Brunists see him, their treacherous enemy who insinuated himself among them, gained Marcella's love, and then betrayed them, publicizing their intentions and thus bringing down upon them a hostile mob. Perhaps maddened by grief and disappointment, perhaps misinterpreting his intentions toward the martyr's body, they attack him and beat him senseless. The intervention of Clara Collins prevents a last, fatal blow with an ax. The end of chapter 5 of part 4, "The Mount"—two more chapters follow—is, however, ambiguous.

> And it was done, the act was over. Through the web of pain, skies away, he recognized the tall broad-shouldered priestess with the gold medallion. She issued commands and he floated free. Rain washed over him. He seemed to be moving. The priestess was gone. And then there was a fall. Trees. Muddy cleft and a splash of water when he arrived. At which point, Tiger Miller departed from this world, passing on to his reward. (p. 410)

The epilogue reveals that Miller's occasional mistress, a nurse known to him and to us as Happy Bottom, followed him to the hill, found his bleeding body and had him taken to the hospital in time to save his life. The brief epilogue describes his return from unconsciousness and his gradual physical recovery. More important, the trauma of the loss of Marcella and his severe physical trauma have been a crucial reversal for him, just as his earlier love for Marcella was a reversal of all his previous attitudes toward women. He has learned to hate West Condon in the months following the mine explosion. He cannot believe the Brunist message; yet he despises the townspeople who persecute them. We can see that in order to understand Miller's exemplary story we must go back to the origin of the Brunists, just as we must in order to understand them.

Miller despises both himself and the community he was born in and works in; its attitude toward the Brunists increases his alienation from it. His love for Marcella attaches him to the Brunists, but their community is equally alien. Miller undergoes an emotional and physical agony on "the day of redemption," ironically enough for a nonbeliever, precisely because the world doesn't end. Thus the Brunists' reversal is his, too. When he emerges, he has learned to appreciate Happy emotionally and intellectually as well as physically. His newspaper has been shut down and then vandalized by a town that resented his publicizing of the Brunists as much as the Brunists did, and Happy is ready to leave West Condon with him as soon as he is well enough. Meanwhile, he has learned that Abner Baxter, characteristically at odds with his fellow Brunists on points of doctrine, is the only Brunist leader who hasn't fled in the aftermath of the Brunist debacle. He fantasizes about running Baxter for mayor. Then the banker, Ted Cavanaugh, and the "respectable" town clergyman, Wes Edwards, come to visit him with an offer to buy the newspaper:

> The chat with Cavanaugh went poorly from the start. Ted was talking about West Condon's troubles and "the best thing for all of us," Miller was talking about Peter who, hearing the cock crow thrice, got to like the music of it, and Edwards was speaking nervously about friends he had up in the city who might find something for Justin more suitable for his talents. "Where things are livelier," the preacher was saying, and Ted's words were "shoulder to the wheel" and "a tough ball game," while Miller, speaking of money changers and pigeon-sellers and getting nowhere, finally interrupted and said, "I'm not going." Cavanaugh stood. "Why not?" Miller sighed. "Necessity is laid upon me," he said.
> (p. 439)

Miller's reversal has led to a new civility—not a reconciliation with people he despises, but a sense of responsibility for and interest in the community as a whole, a desire to try to influence if not transform it. Miller's thinking of Baxter at this point reinforces the importance of the Brunist phenomenon for his own transformation. The newspaperman, quintessential communicator, is resolved on the forming of a new community. Thus the title can be seen to name the novel correctly.

We saw in chapter 5, in the discussion of *A Portrait of the Artist as a Young Man*, that the qualitative novel of action and civility has more than one end, that the notion of end is ambiguous. Stephen recognizes the "end that he had been born to serve" toward the end of part four of a five-part book.[4] The end of the novel comes only when he leaves Ireland because, if his "end" is to create works of art, he can only do so if he can perceive the beautiful, and this discovery or insight is the reversal which brings the necessary departure from Ireland. He has rejected the communities of family, church and country, one after the other. He must act to place himself in a new community, one formed by artists and their communications, a civility impossible to find under the censorship of Ireland.

Thus, the qualitative novel of action and civility is organized, in fact, in terms of more than one end, for end is ambiguous, since the end present at the beginning is modified by the discoveries and reversals that lead to that end. The novel can be concluded only when the beginning is seen to account for the ends. The initial obsession with words of *Portrait of the Artist* is congruent with the "end" Stephen discovers and the end his action brings about in fact, one end corresponding to discovery and one corresponding to reversal.

The mine explosion—Ely's death and message; Bruno's survival; the very explosion itself qua disaster for Eleanor Norton and Ralph Himebaugh, who have theories about disasters as signs; the explosion as an event which invites extended newspaper coverage—this mine explosion, then, is an appropriate antecedent for the Brunists and the happier, more productive Justin Miller of the end. We end with Miller because he is the principal non-Brunist agent, and his reversal exhausts the potentiality of the beginning. It is end which qualifies beginning in the qualitative novel. A transformed millenarian sect and a completely transformed cynic can be brought into being only by a sufficiently "explosive" event. In other words, the relation between end and beginning is reflexive, they are mutually implicative, and the novel is complete when that reflexivity has been fully communicated because it has been fully expressed.[5]

Finally, the multiple ends—there are others that I have omitted since the novel can be organized as a whole without them—are not like the perspectives that end a definitive novel such as the one we organized for *The French Lieutenant's Woman*. Rather than perspectives, they are a series—greater or lesser—of discoveries and their concomitant reversals which determine the coherence of quantitative parts.

"The Origin of the Brunists" names the novel correctly because that origin is equally the origin of the "returned," almost resurrected, new Tiger Miller. Let me begin to interpret this qualitative novel by reading it in the sequential mode of narration, the thematic variant of the qualitative genre, taking the journalist, Miller, as agent. He begins by doing his job, acting in effect as a bridge between one community—the group gathered around Bruno and concerned with Ely Collins's message—and the community of West Condon. He becomes, through Marcella Bruno's efforts, a quasi member of the community, and now his activities as journalist alter not only the lives of people in West Condon, but also the group itself, to which he lends cohesion by naming them Brunists. Eventually, in publishing the date of the supposed judgment day, he breaks his affiliation not only with the Brunists but with the community of West Condon as well; for his press is vandalized and the *Chronicle* discontinued while he lies between life and death in a hospital bed.

However, Miller's initial problem seems commonplace enough: how can he milk the mine disaster for a great many news stories, including dispatches to larger city papers? He solves this problem by interviewing miners who escaped relatively unscathed, the families of dead miners, the representatives of the operators, and so on. This quest for news stories leads him to Bruno, who is still unconscious and may have sustained permanent brain damage as a result of carbon monoxide poisoning; however, Miller is able to interview Bruno's sister Marcella, and the resolution of his initial problem generates what will grow into his crucial problem: how to "rescue" Marcella from her commitment to the growing religious cult. It is a delicate and difficult problem since he must win her to himself first while continuing to do his reportorial job, which, if done honestly according to his lights, may alienate her. The problem grows gradually, imperceptibly. Her innocent, awed admiration for the one-time basketball hero Tiger Miller captivates him. His concentration on the horrors of the disaster depress him.

> The mine disaster had touched off something latently restless in him, and now he could not be satisfied. Miller felt rotten, edgy all the time.... Stained and stung, daily abused, Miller sought relief—even a redemption of sorts—in the company of Marcella Bruno. At first... he saw her almost daily on one pretense or another, almost always in connection with her brother.... what he saw there was the browbeaten child turned egocentered adult psychopath, now upstaging it with his sudden splash of glory—a waste of time. But he made good copy, and Miller sold some of it nationally. With Marcella, it was another story. For one thing, she flattered the hell out of him, the way she looked at him.... But, finally, there was something that got between them.... It was her child's view of the plenum—until she accepted it as the mad scatter it was, they could never get beyond banalities and sex play. Did he *want* to get beyond? Apparently, though it surprised him, he did.[6]

Miller realizes that "Collins, to be popular, must surely have touched more than once on the never-dead chiliastic expectations of the lower-class Christians" (p. 141), and that the events surrounding his death "now made these people... wonder if something disastrous, perhaps worldwide in scope, might not be in the air" (ibid.). Amused, Miller

> printed everything he thought might help them along, might seem relevant to them, amateur space theories, enigmatic Biblical texts, filler tripe on peculiar practices and inexplicable happenings elsewhere, as well as everything they wished to give him. Once the emotions had settled down and the widows themselves had established new affairs or found mind-busying work, their eccentric interests of the moment would be forgotten, of course. Which, in its way, was too bad. As games went, it was a game, and there was

some promise in it. Games were what kept Miller going. (ibid.)

Marcella, however, assumes that he is sympathetic, and his first discovery is the realization that his game playing has placed him in an impossible situation: his love for her makes him ashamed of his cynical use of the Brunists, as he has himself named them, and moves him to want to rescue her, "convert" her from her folly. He decides therefore to print the date fixed for the end of the world, knowing it will attract West Condon bullies, the news media and curiosity seekers, but believing that he will be far away with Marcella safe from dangerous crowds and inevitable humiliation. By printing the news, Miller will free himself at last from his false position with the Brunists, will defy the civic "leaders" of West Condon whom he despises, will nonetheless save the woman he loves from harm, and, finally, will keep his self-respect by meeting his professional obligation to print what is clearly news. "He would show her the night's edition, ask her to leave with him.... He recognized that it might not be easy, but he believed, once the choice was clear to her, that her commitment to him would outweigh any other—Miller had that much faith in the gonads' clutch upon what folks called reason" (p. 299). But Marcella, though passionately in love with him, cannot understand or accept his revelation that he is leaving the cult and wants her to join him. She puts on her clothes and runs from him.

This reversal is, however, indeterminate. Miller is distressed, angry, puzzled, but without insight. A Brunist, Betty Wilson, comes to visit him during the ensuing week, and he learns that the Brunists are making the best of the publicity and openly seeking last-moment converts. He also learns, to his distress, that Marcella "hasn't eaten a bite or said a word for nigh on a week now, and she seems, well, a bit strange" (p. 348). He tells himself that she is mad, that "it was she, staking too much on a thin fantasy, who broke herself; he was little more than the accidental instrument" (p. 349). He doesn't yet recognize, however, that his perception of women is severely flawed. That her loving him was not a simple matter of "gonads" doesn't really strike him. Yet he feels depressed and guilty. The night of Marcella's death Miller spends with Happy; when he awakens, it is two o'clock in the afternoon of the next day, the television news is showing the march to the "Mount of Redemption," and Miller sees Marcella's body. In a daze he tells Happy to get dressed and come with him, but she says she will come later. When Miller reaches the site, he sees the body.

Miller just couldn't attach her to this brittle blue corpse that rocked on the road before him. The run here had weakened him, had made him sweat.... Marcella. He saw her name on

> his desk blotter, heard her gay laughter, smelled her body on his, saw the intricate turn of a lightly tanned wrist, tasted the newness of her mouth. . . . Was it something in her he had loved—or something in himself he had hated? He felt old. (p. 400)

Then a young reporter whom he has never seen tells him that "the word is she got banged by the guy who grinds out the local scandal sheet. He was a big cat in the club, but he cut out on them and got into her. She went off her nut and, so they say, finally knocked herself off" (ibid.).

In the light of this sequence of events, the near-death of Miller can be interpreted: it is an expiation of guilt. Deliberately putting himself in the way of the frustrated, humiliated Brunists who are now tasting the results of his treachery in the jeering, curious crowds his newspaper in effect summoned, Miller is asking to be punished. Miller becomes involved with Marcella initially innocent of what their relationship will mean to her; but in his arrogant refusal to see beyond "the gonads' clutch"—and that refusal is not altogether innocent given *his own* experience of the contrast between his feelings for Happy and his feelings for Marcella—he drives her to her death. He will never understand Marcella, but he does tacitly acknowledge his guilt, and he suffers for his part in her death and emerges to a new kind of life with Happy.

As is the case with a rhetorical rather than a poetic reading, the paradoxical or contradictory dimensions of human experience—and artistic expression and impression are human experiences—are rendered especially vivid and emphatic. Miller's discovery is and is not discovery. He discovers *that* he is guilty of destroying someone, he discovers *how* he must live his life, just as he simultaneously discovers that his initial problem with respect to Marcella was completely misconceived, or, if one prefers, that he has failed to solve that initial problem. On the other hand, he never discovers what it was that Marcella meant to him, or he to her. He can reach love through sexuality with Happy—perhaps he owes that achievement to Marcella—but he never understands how some people can live and love and feel intensely beyond sexuality. He undergoes a reversal in losing Marcella, a tragic reversal; yet the final "reversal" is that only in the sense that the direction of his life is radically altered. It is not after all a genuinely tragic reversal. Nevertheless, the sufferings and losses are very real; and not only the loss of Marcella herself but the loss of an opportunity to experience life with an intensity he can only guess at.

The rhetorical reading in the narrative mode, like all rhetorical readings, preserves for the "reader," because it forces the reader to be always aware of, the simultaneity of opposing meanings. Thus, discovery is never absolute insight, reversal never completely tragic reversal or completely comic reversal. The way in which it works, structurally, is fairly simple: discovery and reversal are the tools by means of which the contrary perspectives are preserved. If there is a final tragic reversal, we "qualify" the tragedy by noting that the "knowing" which rendered the reversal inevitable mitigates it. Here discovery, or knowing, qualifies reversal. A reading of *Oedipus* in the narrative mode would do this. That's how an audience finds tragedy bearable. On the other hand, Miller's recognition that he has destroyed Marcella and lost forever the enlightenment she represents is qualified by the reversal of his way of life because the tragic recognition of loss makes the "good" reversal possible. Obviously, rhetorically reversal and discovery are both synonymous and different in meaning. We can treat them either way or both in succession to enhance our appreciation of a complex text.

The principle of organization validates this way of *connecting* particulars and thus making them because it says that action and interaction produce civility, and the action and civility of *this* whole affirm this narrative reading of the Brunist community and Miller's return to human involvement, both personal and communal, after the cynicism of his recent past. The principle as statement of value affirms the value of wholeness, the community achieved when problematic, discordant situations are resolved. The community or civility of the generic organization is uninterpreted; the reading in the narrative mode has interpreted that civility as the forging of individual persons, through their self-determined actions, into viable communities: the Brunists after great struggle, uncertainty, and travail; Miller and Happy after equally great struggle, uncertainty, and travail.

The qualitative organization will support a causal, descriptive reading as well, a reading which fashions and brings into focus some new particulars.[7] With Miller as agent, we begin with a man who, for a long time, has cultivated one part of his nature, the physical, to the neglect of emotional and intellectual needs. A high school basketball star with uneventful university and military careers, he became a wire service reporter and then purchased his home town paper, the West Condon *Chronicle.* "He'd always wanted his own newspaper, had a lot of untried ideas for one, and here it was, a good buy and everyone anxious to make it easy for him, a working knowledge of the town, even his folks' old house to live in. Why not? And so here he was, years later, the prince become a frog, living grimly ever after, drowned in debt, sick to death of the disenchanted forest, and knowing no way out" (p. 69).

His sex life is equally dismal, but sexual need is persistent; he comments on a woman seen for the first time at the site of the mine explosion.

She was the disconcerting epilogue to all his high school eroticism here, his fatuous taste then for the dumb poppy

141

that ran to seed with the first tentative wound.... The conquest was always a come-down—in the end, they laid for
want of imagination....

It disgusted him, yet in spite of himself, he started picking
up messages from below, and there was a stirring there. She
was too obvious and there was a cheap-soapiness about
her, but he was oddly agitated.... He tried to put his principles in order and found, in short, he had none. He felt
overworked and unrewarded, tired of the game he played,
the masks he wore. West Condon, community of Christians
and coalminers, and he its chronicler: if they were mad, how
much more so was he? So, screw them; when in hell, do as
the damned do. (pp. 70, 71–72)

His first encounter with Happy Bottom at the hospital seems equally
sordid, but Happy has humor and intelligence as well as a robust sexual
appetite, and she is a contingency, a chance involvement the end of
which cannot be easily predicted. Miller's infatuation with Marcella
Bruno is simultaneous with his first serious revulsion from casual sex,
and as such is moderately therapeutic since he begins for the first time
to feel something more for a woman than uncomplicated lust. However,
the moral and mental activity of covering the Brunists is unsatisfying.
Marcella has seriously eroded his unalloyed cynicism, yet only from
purely cynical and self-aggrandizing motives can his coverage of the
Brunists be justified. The town "notables" begin by wanting the publicity for Bruno's miraculous survival to offset the bad press resulting
from the disaster, and Miller isn't pleased to satisfy them. Eventually he
publicizes the Brunists against the banker, Ted Cavanaugh's wishes,
and then against theirs. By that time, having insinuated himself among
them to get news and having remained to be near Marcella, Miller is
hopelessly compromised morally.

In addition, the restraint required of him with Marcella begins to be
unhealthy, too. She is anticipating the end of the world, and sex, even
in marriage, seems absurd and irrelevant to her; Miller had "even
hinted at marriage and she had laughed, supposing he must be joking"
(p. 298). Until her fortuitous death, Miller is hopelessly entangled. It is
in fact a resurgence of psychological and moral strength that precipitates the end of their relationship. Miller could wait until the
apocalypse disappoints the Brunists to seriously propose marriage to
Marcella. However, his decision to publish the date the Brunists have
fixed upon places Marcella in danger given the forces that publication
will provoke, and Miller wants to be in a position to protect her.
Furthermore, the cult might fail to collapse, and he would have to reveal
his real feelings about it in any case. Thus, too late for Marcella's well-
being, Miller makes his attempt at honesty and is rejected.

Marcella's death is a traumatic contingency; it frees him from her, but at great cost to himself, literally, since he is moved to go to the vigil to see her body. The Brunists almost kill him, and this physical experience, a terrible trauma in every way, saves his life in almost taking it. In the hospital, when he has finally regained consciousness, Miller speaks to Happy.

> "Why did you bother, Happy?" he asked. He expected her to make some crack, but instead she only smiled and said, "I don't know. I guess because I like the way you laugh."
>
> Yes, there was that. Not the void within and ahead, but the immediate living space between two. (p. 435)

Then come "a lot of feelers from radio and television, but all they offered him was a job and he didn't want a job" (ibid.). After many years lived in a psychological imbalance, an unnatural denial of dependency needs and the need to nurture and care for someone, Miller goes to the other extreme in his relationship with Happy. He is at last made whole by a woman who satisfies a natural sexual need and the others as well. She has allowed herself to become pregnant, and it is clear that Miller's uncommitted life is over. At the same time he decides to remain in West Condon and run his paper seriously at last. For Miller the descriptive reading is a "comic" reading in which a personality in danger of dissolution is reintegrated and love and sex are therapeutic. The principle of a novel organized qualitatively validates the reading because it provides the structure which affirms such a formulation. The action which leads to civility, to the personality integrated in itself and interrelated with others, is natural action in the descriptive reading. To live in productive interrelation with one's fellows and in heterosexual passion and loving mutual dependence with a fellow being is to live according to nature and thus to live in civility. That is the thought of the whole, the value judgment rendered by this descriptive reading of the novel organized qualitatively, that is, according to end.

The descriptive reading is suggestive with respect to Coover's use of sex. The importance of sex in Miller's story seems paradigmatic for several less extensive accounts in the novel. Marcella, to begin with, can be seen as part of a rhetorical commonplace she shares with Miller. Miller begins by exemplifying sex without love, Marcella love without sex (if we can agree to let love mean responsibility, protectiveness, emotional attachment aside from the overtly sexual.) He moves toward correcting the imbalance in wanting to marry her and in not attempting to seduce her until he's sure he does want a permanent relationship with her. She desires him physically, but when she discovers that he has lied and doesn't share her beliefs, she rejects him totally. I should like to be very clear about what I think is implicit here. Miller has grave doubts about her, given her orientation to the world. "Marcella's mind was complex and delicate, contained sweeping world-views that made cosmic events out of a casual gesture or a cloud's idle passage, and, in such a mind, the commonplaces he liked to use were not common at all and refuted nothing." (p. 298). But his feeling for her makes it worth trying to overcome the difficulties of communication between them.[8] She, on the other hand, is too rigid to be able to tolerate disagreement with him, to love him enough to even try to understand his apparent betrayal or the imperative of his physical need for her. Her development has been hopelessly unnatural and is beyond the reach of therapy in the guise of love. The first traumatic contingency she encounters destroys her. She starves herself to kill feeling and ends by, in effect, killing herself, since she is hardly aware of the approaching automobiles and too weak in any case to avoid them.

The subtle affinities between religious enthusiasm and sexual stimulus are adumbrated throughout the novel when we read it descriptively. Ralph Himebaugh, eccentric keeper of cats and calculator of cosmic forces, is protectively devoted to Marcella. He watches over her after her break with Miller at the beginning of her silent fast.

> He turns his head, watches her bare feet pad wearily across the wooden floor. Poor dear child! She is very weak.... She arrives at the bed, pauses. She has forgotten to turn out the light. An urge to kiss her small toes—just a foot from his face—leaps to his lips, but he overmasters it. Discipline is his greatest virtue. She curls a toe. Oh God! He starts to cry, clamps his hand between his teeth, bites down with all his strength. (p. 358)

She goes back to the door, turns out the light and returns to her bed.

> At last, she enters the bed. The mattress hardly sinks beneath her weight now, so thin is she. He reaches up, strokes the gentle depression. Calm returns. He waits for her to sleep. The perfect man is the motionless cause. (ibid.)

Himebaugh is found dead under her bed in the deserted house a few weeks after the debacle on the "Mount of Redemption." Himebaugh's pathetic chaste and furtive devotion is only one strand of the sexual thread that runs through the formation of the Brunists. To give one more illustration, on the day of judgment, in the rain on the "Mount" Elaine Collins, Ely's and Clara's young daughter, engages in a strange, sadomasochistic ritual with Abner Baxter's son in which they beat one another furiously with a whip.

The important Brunists who survive their disappointment and develop a viable sect from the seeds of a cult in shambles are Clara Collins and Eleanor Norton, hearer of voices and believer in occult powers. It is instructive to note that both women might well be considered atypical in some respects at least—the first in her exercise of Christian charity under extraordinary circumstances, the second in her very unconventional beliefs. Eleanor Norton is obviously highly eccentric; although she is a high school teacher, her true "vocation" lies in her contact with the powers of the universe, especially one Domiron, who comes to her in visions and through automatic writing. Indeed, her absorption in her version of the supernatural is such that it cannot be contained, and she invites her more sensitive, receptive students to share in her system of beliefs, thus rendering herself vulnerable to the wrath of concerned parents. Her position at West Condon high school is precarious, and after her open involvement with the Brunists she is finally dismissed, the last in a long series of dismissals which only stop short of the traditional tar and feathers.

Eleanor Norton is saved by natural strengths which sustain her, and these are of three sorts: hers is not a rigid fanaticism; emotionally, she can adapt her beliefs to an evangelical Christian vocabulary; and she has the requisite intelligence to translate her "messages" into a language acceptable to the dominant group. She also has an ability to empathize with others and act in cooperation with them, and a natural cleverness that enables her to do so without loss of what we might call doctrinal integrity; she assumes that others will misinterpret a cosmic event but does not require that they accept her version of it, only that they recognize that such an event has occurred. "All arrowed upon the same incredible event, long foretold, but terrifying in its realization: Giovanni Bruno's body had been invaded by a higher being! . . .So far as she knew, she was the only person alive who realized it, the entire burden of keeping the connection alive was on her shoulders." (p. 132) But Eleanor Norton is also a woman, living with a husband in harmony and mutual respect and affection. She is an important example of the stubborn survival in the novel of those who function well in heterosexual relationships.

Clara Collins is another. The widow of Ely Collins, beloved preacher, admired by his fellow miners regardless of denomination, she is shattered by his death. Like Ely, she has been wholly absorbed by religion, unread except in the Bible, unnaturally obsessed with one facet of human experience; and when he dies, she cannot understand why God should have taken so saintly a man. Her obsession with his note, and her interest in the alien, Italian Bruno, his companion who survived, seem to be motivated by a need to come to terms with Ely's death, to justify God's inexplicable cruelty by hypothesizing a swift reunion.

Yet Clara Collins, too, has characteristics recognizable as natural strengths in a descriptive reading. For the principle with which we have organized *The Origin of the Brunists*, the qualitative organization in terms of end, gives us action and civility as the terms in which our "world" makes sense and is of value; and in a descriptive reading these uninterpreted variables are taken to be the nature of things. Thus, acting to promote the harmonious interrelation of one's fellow men *is* acting according to one's nature. Clara Collins acts decisively twice to express natural civility, the harmonious interrelation among human beings: she forgives her enemy, Abner Baxter, for running down Marcella—thus saving him from the Brunists—and she prevents a Brunist mob from killing Tiger Miller. Both acts help to forge a strong community—the former absorbing a powerful enemy into the group, harnessing his powers to enhance the community, the latter saving the group from a poisonous burden of guilt.

However, Clara Collins's religious commitment does not involve self-denying chastity, a value which the otherworldly Marcella Bruno may have absorbed from her Roman Catholic background.[9] Contrary to common, perhaps stereotypic notions about evangelical or pentecostal religious leaders, Collins is not at all a hell-fire and damnation preacher, as is his counterpart, Baxter. It is said of Ely Collins:

> If they heard him once, they always came back. He stood tall and calm and his clear steady voice spoke assuredly of salvation from our sins through Christ Jesus; in every sermon, he always said, "Grace is not something you die to get, it's something you get to live!" (p. 48)

Clara's grief at losing him is profound; he is unquestionably someone she loved.

> "He was a good man, Mr. Miller!" she cried in sudden protest. "He done no wrong! He didn't deserve to git killt like that!" Swallowed sobs shook her. Miller felt her grief, but was helpless. . . . The woman, clutching her husband's note, slumped from the couch to her knees on the floor. She wept so huskily, so brokenly, that Miller was certain that, though perhaps she prayed often, she wept seldom. (p. 88)

But proof of the quality of their relationship is given in action rather than words, for when the Brunists at last recognize that they must go on living in this world, they do so supporting one another, naturally drawn to one another because of the great and terrible events they have experienced together. Rather than remaining isolated in widowhood, Clara Collins marries Ben Wosznik, a strong, gentle, farmer, brother of a dead miner, and himself a devoted Brunist.

Eleanor Norton does not move through any alterations in her orientation to sex, but she does move through intellectual and emotional traumas relative to her beliefs, and throughout these she is never alone but is supported by her devoted husband, the simple, earthbound veterinarian. Clara Collins lives through the early days after Ely's death sustained by her belief that his death is meaningful and then, specifically, that it points to their reunion; religion absorbs both the emotional energies she has always given to it and the emotional resources used up and renewed in the marital relationship. When the millenarian hope is finally relinquished, she marries again.

It is not natural sex activity per se that marks the *successful* survivors of mine disaster and cosmic disappointment and their many consequences; it is rather responsible, committed heterosexual relationships. And it is certainly the case, conversely, that those who lack them are lost: Ralph Himebaugh, whose theories are as eccentric as Eleanor Norton's; Marcella, who cannot live even until her longed-for day of judgment; and Giovanni Bruno, who seems to go unprotesting into permanent passivity in a mental institution.

However, a persistent interest in sex, however imperfect its natural development, does mark survivors that we might not call successful. The miner, Vincent Bonali, survivor of the explosion, is a good example. In the descriptive picture of the world that gave birth to the Brunists, Vince Bonali is the important representative or exemplar of a part of West Condon that demands a fairly detailed portrayal. The educated, moneyed, WASP superstructure of the town is delineated in brief vignettes throughout, of the mayor, the banker, and the Presbyterian minister. Their characteristics and motives, a product at least partially of status and environment, are fairly obvious, and their initial excited attention to Bruno, their fuss over him, is as predictable as their later distaste for the Brunists, what the group represents and what consequences its growth will have for the town.

On the other hand, the major Brunists and Miller, the ambivalent, ambiguous link with both worlds, require and get extensive treatment. The question that needs to be addressed is simple: we can see why the Brunists attract uneducated miners, religious and superstitious, terrified of the future if they are miners, burdened with grief if they are widows and relations of the dead. We can understand Miller's role and the motives of educated eccentric occultists like Mrs. Norton and Ralph Himebaugh. But why are there equally uneducated, superstitious bereaved miners who fiercely oppose the Brunists? It is important to understand this because from this group come those who express in physical violence the verbal "upper-class" opposition to the Brunists.

Vince Bonali is the most fully and sympathetically treated representative of this group, and he, too, is marked by a complicated, if banal, sex life. Further, sex is not "used" in any way by Mrs. Norton or Clara Collins, for whom it is by implication simply a natural part of life; and Miller makes conscious choices with respect to sex which are not healthy and must be and are radically altered eventually. Bonali, however, exemplifies yet a different orientation; and he survives, his life, however, seriously crippled by environmental forces he could not control and by his own sick behavior.

He is significantly representative of his part of West Condon because, like the other Italian miners, he resents and is embarrassed by Giovanni Bruno. Before the explosion Bruno is ridiculed by the miners who discover in his pocket a poem written to his mother; they push him around and subject him to humiliating physical jocosity. The morose, dreamy Bruno is not really one of them, and survivors like Bonali who have lost close friends in the disaster resent the publicity given Bruno as a miraculous survivor. When news of his cult role reaches them, they are ashamed because he is Italian. When Cavanaugh, the banker, calls on Bonali for help in persuading fellow miners and their families to eschew the cult, Bonali is flattered and eager to comply. More is involved, however, than simple flattery. The explosion has closed the mine for an indefinite period; although Bonali doesn't seem to feel this financially at the beginning, he becomes increasingly worried and restless. At first he reacts with bravado and insists he'll never work in a mine again. Then he begins to brood, afraid that he cannot find other work at his age in the limited economy of West Condon; and it turns out that he can't. Because he has no job his sense of manhood suffers, and he begins to visit Wanda, the widow of a miner, a thin woman to whom he can make love as he cannot to his obese wife, Etta. After Clara Collins's house burns down, Cavanaugh comes to enlist Vince's help in suppressing the Brunist phenomenon which seems clearly to be leading to trouble. Interestingly enough, Cavanaugh has long pondered a way of uniting the community to revitalize West Condon, too dependent on coal for the wealth of its economy. This clearly negative means of creating a civility, by uniting against, attempting to exclude, has struck Cavanaugh as his answer, and it proves a bad one for everyone involved, especially Bonali.

Bonali is eager because he needs something to make him feel wanted and useful. But the need is material as well as psychological; he believes that Cavanaugh will reward him in some way with a political career to make up for his current joblessness. The fantasy of himself as a VIP carries him through public meetings and private visits to Brunists with whom he is acquainted and potential Brunist sympathizers. The latter task, the private, moves him to involve some of his cronies as support and help. His success at a public meeting cures his impotence with Etta with respect to whom manhood is associated with livelihood as well as sex, as it is not with Wanda.

At the height of his euphoria, Bonali permits his friends to persuade him to disguise himself and go with them to frighten Ralph

Himebaugh, who has recently treated their anti-Brunist efforts with obvious contempt. They fail to move Himebaugh; however, Vince has had to get drunk in order even to embark on the enterprise, and, thoroughly drunk now, he forces himself on Wanda, who rejects him, confessing her conversion to the Brunists. His friends break in on them and try to rape her. She eludes them and calls the police. Vince and his friends are seen being taken to the police station, and when they leave a newspaper photographer is waiting for them.

> Shit. [Bonali thinks.] Felt like the number-one all-star ass of all time. And it was bound to get worse. All those cameras. And he knew better than to think Johnson could keep his fat mouth shut. . . .
> Four A.M. Staggered from the bed. Reached the bathroom door and up it came. . . . Sat on the side of the tub, head in hands. Sick. Not just in the gut. Sick in the heart, too. Fucked it up. End of the world. It was all over. (p. 383)

Vince, penitent and miserable, his hopes destroyed, attends Sunday mass on April 19th; when Baxter and a group of Brunists invade the church, hurling epithets at the priest, Bonali and friends destroy the Nazarene church. Then they head for the "Mount." Bonali encounters Cavanaugh and the mayor, but they have seen newspapers and witnessed his disgrace on the television news, and they snub him. Heartbroken and raging, he returns to town with friends to seek out Himebaugh, a target for his rage. They don't find him at his home, and fall asleep drunk in the rain where the police later pick them up.

Vincent Bonali falls ill with influenza and recovers, but he can't really recover from his disgrace. One day he goes for a walk and passes the church he helped to destroy, and he is appalled: "'What do we do it for, God?' he asked aloud, and wouldn't have been too surprised to get an answer. 'Do You understand what makes it happen? Can You forgive it?'" (p. 480). He wanders through the empty Bruno house looking for something "by which to remember . . . the whole Brunist story" (ibid.), and hearing ambulances, and terrified of being found there and suffering more public humiliation, he hides under the bed which conceals the body of the long dead Himebaugh. He rushes out into a closet, overcome with horror.

> He lay curled up there in a corner of the closet, bawling like a newborn baby. "Don't leave me again!" he sobbed. "Without You, God, it's horrible!" He had to still his sobs from time to time, because others, curious, came up to look, to shudder, to shrink away. . . . When finally the tears had stopped, when he felt like all the horror had washed out of him and he could stand alone again, he stood and walked

out, walked down.... But it could be worse. And, walking out of the home of the prophet Giovanni Bruno on that lush night in May, Vince Bonali . . . looked up at the magnitude and care of the universe and thanked God that, if no one else had, he at least had come at last to his Redemption. (p. 421)

Vince Bonali's is the account of a man buffeted and bruised in the struggle to satisfy the needs of the body. Food, clothing, and shelter as well as sex are the imperatives with which nature goads him. His manhood, his pride are severely threatened by the loss of livelihood, and he turns to extramarital sex to repair the psychological damage inflicted by the impairment of his natural functions as breadwinner. But sexual satisfaction cannot substitute for the requirements met by a job, and it fails psychologically as well. Its failure to restore pride is attested to by the destructive near-rape of Wanda. His behavior is demeaning and really unlike himself, and it leads to humiliation and the loss of whatever opportunities Cavanaugh might have offered.

Bonali, the epitome of the "natural" man, does survive, however, and his survival and peculiar "redemption" attest to the resilience of the natural man even when the contingency of a disaster has wrenched him out of his normal way of life and led him to violate his own natural instincts. Bonali experiences a therapeutic return to his own natural community, the Roman Catholic church (his devotion to which has been hitherto somewhat lukewarm). In his case, as in that of the more sophisticated Miller, the redemptive experience, albeit profoundly spiritual and moral, is rooted in the physical and psychological: Miller is beaten almost to death; Bonali achieves his nearly experiential awareness of death and his appreciation of life as lived in his own religious community by encountering death in its full physical horror, touching, lying beside, a decaying human body.

The expository dimension of *The Origin of the Brunists* gives us Miller, the Brunists, and Bonali moving through conflicts toward knowledge of the truth. We have seen that in a narrative reading variables are arranged relative to problems to be solved or conflicts resolved, and the movement toward resolution involves gradual discovery of information, increase of understanding, and, in short, whatever is relevant to resolution and the consequent new directions for action. Then, variables were arranged as elements composed into a whole in the descriptive reading; Miller, Clara Collins, Vince Bonali, the Brunists as a group finally emerge as viable "wholes," persons and a group who have been "well" constructed having survived their contact with highly dangerous contingencies. As agents they have constructed themselves well enough, and although some contingencies have seriously threatened them, some others have been therapeutic: Happy, for example, in Miller's case, the Brunist community itself in the cases of Eleanor

150

Norton and Clara Collins, for Bonali his heretofore neglected religious faith; of course, Marcella cannot survive, having denied the natural bent in so many ways.

In an expository reading the variables are arranged hierarchically, leading to the assimilation of conflicts on higher and higher levels of action and insight. I would interpret the novel in this mode by focusing for the most part on Justin Miller and the Brunists as a group. First of all, Miller can be said to be at the outset in a state of ignorance and ennui. He is dissatisfied with his life without really knowing why. However, he does his job well when the mine explodes. The disaster is depressing and painful for him. For days he must witness the gradual unearthing of bodies, and interview survivors and kin of the ninety-eight dead. When he goes to the hospital to interview Marcella, he has already seen her briefly and has been curiously touched. On his way he formulates "questions, but images of her fragmented them . . . . The hospital, usually a dead white inside, was today somehow blurred and hopeful. . . . Uncommonly, neither the blood of birth nor the knock of death jolted his mind this afternoon as he entered, but rather a flush of pleasure in visible human progress warmed him. We move on. Things can be better" (p. 107).

At this point, before there is any Brunist cult, we learn his attitude toward religion. He almost runs into the Presbyterian minister, Wesley Edwards, and he's pleased that Edwards doesn't see him.

> Actually, the man Edwards, while unimaginative and soft-souled, was no worse than the rest of the West Condoners—no, what rankled was his goddamn presumption. All his breed galled Miller, but especially the complacently doubtful types like Edwards—he blanked out this town's small mind with his codified hand-me-down messages, and when you pushed him he would slyly hint he didn't believe it himself, goddamn ethical parable or some crap of the sort. Well, you're still the old fundamentalist at heart, Miller accused himself. (ibid.)

This attitude will move him to an initial sympathy for the Brunists, and it explains that he supports them by giving them the publicity they want partly in defiance of an "establishment" which treats them with contempt. Miller's ennui and his lack of commitment to or genuine interest in anything are gradually transformed by love for Marcella. His generalized hostility to people like Edwards is turned into a positive effort to help the Brunists. This serious moral level of action in turn generates new conflicts hitherto impossible; he cannot pretend indefinitely to believe in the Brunist message, and his professional ethical imperatives impel him to publish what is news no matter who is hurt or thinks he will be hurt as a result. His loss of Marcella forces him to face the truth about their relationship and its hopelessness. From the point of his arrival at the Mount of Redemption, where he sees what his rejection of the Brunists has led to for Marcella and what his publicizing of the date has led to for the Brunists and West Condon as a whole, another transformation begins. Miller is trying to stop his employee Jones from photographing Marcella's body when some Brunists catch sight of him, and Eleanor Norton screams in rage that he is Marcella's murderer. The chapter ends with the curiously ambiguous "curtain line" to the murderous attack on him: "At which point, Tiger Miller departed from this world, passing on to his reward" (p. 410). Two chapters intervene before the epilogue, which begins: "The West Condon Tiger *rose from the dead.*"[10] What follows emphasizes by means of additional heavily allusive words and phrases the translation of Miller to a new plane of existence. He feels "nailed fast to his torment," and "an Angel of Light—*the* Angel of Light—appeared."[11] Next, he sees Marcella in various postures and loses consciousness again, after being described as "crosshung" and feeling that something "knocked against his cross" (p. 432).

Happy, the Angel of Light, of course, converses with him briefly, explaining that Clara saved him. He relaxes and plunges into unconsciousness without fear, for "the nails in his palms" are basketballs now (p. 433). He dreams he is Judas betraying the prophet whom he knows to be ineffectual, betrayal for the same reasons, ultimately, that moved him to begin writing about the Brunists. "He [Judas] looked up toward where the prophet knelt, saw that the man was watching him. He'd expected that, but felt a shudder just the same. He stared out on the hard dry hills, stared ahead at the days succeeding days, the endless wearisome motions, all prospects sickened to habit, stared out on the hopeless generative and digestive processes of unnumbered generations, and thought: Well, anyway, it's something different. And he went down into the town" (ibid.).

Later, awake, he jokes with Happy about starting a cult, says "anyway, it'd be something different," and Happy, agreeing, begins to caress his belly: " 'And on this rock . . .' she said, and they both watched the church grow" (p. 434).

Having heard what happened to some of the others who gathered for the abortive apocalypse, Miller becomes deeply depressed. Two nurses are giving him an enema, and he asks Happy why she saved him. Her reply cheers him, and when the enema is removed, "the despair, a lot of it anyway, flooded out of him with a soft gurgle. 'My message to the world,' he said" (p. 435). He thinks about job offers he doesn't want: "Dear Mr. Christ: In view of your experience in personnel management..." (ibid.). His arms immobilized, he thinks of himself: "Crucifixion was a proper end for insurgents: it dehumanized them.

Man only felt like man when he could bring his hands together" (p. 436).

At the end, having decided to keep and revitalize his paper, Miller suggests that they remain in West Condon until November, but Happy counters with January, telling him she is pregnant. For some time she has been inventing satirical accounts of the last judgment and sending them to him at the *Chronicle*. After the sequel to her news, the novel ends with her final piece on the last judgment. Following is the brief conversation between Miller and Happy and the last part of Happy's tale with which the novel ends:

> "I'm talking about *tigers*, man," she said, and patted her belly.
> "Hey! You mean it? But when—?"
> She shrugged, grinned. "Sons of Noah . . ."
> "Aha! sign of the covenant!"
> So they quickly signed a pact, exchanged gifts, broke a chamberpot, bought Ascension Day airline tickets for the Caribbean, and, nailed to the old tree of life and knowledge that night, she murmured in his ear one last *Last Judgement* . . .
>
> . . . *the whole affair bogged down entirely in bureaucracy and the impenetrable paradoxes of behavior, language, and jurisdiction, until at last one day it occurred to someone (most likely not a child, in spite of the overwhelming tradition) to ask why the whole thing was being perpetrated in the first place, and the Divine Judge found Himself hard put to provide an answer that satisfied even Himself, having to confess that He was less amused by it than He had thought He would be. It was therefore agreed to drop it, and the various Divine Substances took their leave. The only trouble was that by that time the enormity of the support organization and the goal hunger of the participants were such that the absented Divine Substances were never missed. The proceedings, indulging the everlasting lust for perpetuity and stage directions, dragged on happily through the centuries, the only consolation for those who might have guessed the true state of affairs being that which the risen Jesus centuries ago offered to his appalled disciples . . . .*
> "Come and have breakfast."[12]

I hope these brief quotations will help to make clear the way in which Miller's transformation can be interpreted in the mode of exposition. His role must be seen as ambiguous, as he himself sees it. He is both Judas and Christ. He *has* undergone a resurrection. How are we to understand the paradox? Judas as a figure of worship has a long tradition, of course, the premise of which is simply that without his betrayal the redemptive death of Jesus would be impossible. The son of God could not commit suicide, obviously; he had to *freely accept* (the specific phrase is from the canon of the Mass) the death imposed by others. Judas or someone like him was needed to perform the essential function of making Jesus accessible to his enemies. Miller is, then, a betrayer without whose treacherous publicity the Brunists would have failed to win converts and become a viable religious communion.

However, what is more interesting is Miller as Christ figure. The passages I have cited suggest that the role is, in characteristic rhetorical fashion, fortuitous rather than intrinsic or substantive. In other words, Miller is Christlike because he was almost killed and he was subjected to intense physical suffering by a hostile group of people; and that he returned from near-death seems little short of miraculous, a resurrection in effect. *He did not suffer this trauma because he was Christlike to begin with.* Rhetorically, reality is made by actors acting.

Has Miller been transformed and redeemed by his experience? In fact he has achieved a much closer approximation to knowledge of the truth than he had to begin with. Throughout his confinement to the hospital he struggles to make sense of his life. He ends knowing that leaving West Condon will not do because other places aren't really any better; that he has *to make* his life meaningful by action, personal and professional.

The Christian vocabulary of much of the epilogue is parody if taken in conjunction with what is being presented. At one point Miller, trying to articulate his new, "resurrected" feelings about his life and future, recalls his fellow basketball star, Oxford Clemens, killed in the mine explosion. Ox had scandalized an entire stadium of fans and players when, after a brilliant play, "face dripping sweat and eyes closed, hand on a hard-on that not even a jockstrap could hold back, he gasped, '*Oh Jesus! I jist wanna jack off!*' . . . Miller had remembered Ox's mystical moment, and he was thinking about it now."[13] Ox Clemens's masturbatory orgasm is what mysticism is all about; Miller's message to the world, expressed after a joyous instant of insight into love, is the defecation induced by an enema; the "cult" of Happy and Miller, their personal church, is also built on a rock sometimes called peter, Miller's erect penis. Yet none of this communicates as contempt for religion. Curiously enough, it is rather that the vocabulary of Christian allusion conveys a persistent appreciation for, an honoring of, the very fragile physical base—funny, vulgar, painful, satisfying—upon which the human communal enterprise is raised. Miller suffers and is resurrected in the body, but he goes beyond the body to union in love with a woman, and to a rejoining of a community for which he can perform essential services which help to sustain a civility.

The knowledge achieved by the Brunists in their rise through Becoming to a state closer to Being is different from Miller's.[14] We can see the movement best by focusing on the sections of the novel and how each begins and ends. The prologue begins in uncertainty and some chaos; Hiram Clegg, summoned to await the end of the world, didn't expect to find himself "watching a young girl die." It ends with that death having risen beyond its concrete particularity to the status of "sacrifice," a "theme for religious art," a symbol containing a higher truth than the simple facts of its source. For the paintings always show the girl pointing to heaven—as she did not in fact—, and they omit the bubble of blood on her lips which was indeed there.

Part 1, "The White Bird," begins with a plunge back into the world of ignorance and flux. It treats a bewildering complex of persons and events, before, during, and after the mine explosion. The section ends with a kind of epiphany; the miraculously alive Bruno has regained consciousness and lifts the disastrous events to their first level of possible meaning by telling his sister that he was visited in the mine by the Virgin, who came in the form of a dove.

Part 2, "The Sign," begins back again in the complex, ambiguous world of becoming, with Eleanor Norton reviewing all her astral messages to try to understand the disaster. Part 2 takes up the slow, painful clarification of the cult's cosmic idea. Mrs. Norton hears of the dove, to her a symbol of the soul, the "volatile principle" (p. 129), and visits Bruno as does Ralph Himebaugh, for whom the universe is evil and the disaster a sign of an impending end. Mrs. Collins comes because of Ely's relation to Bruno. Miller visits to get stories and see Marcella. Ely's note provokes calculations of the date for the end of the world. Oppositions arise as well; Abner Baxter takes over Ely's church and preaches against the still fragile cult. At the end of part 2 the Brunists have settled on a tentative date and visit the hill, the site of the closed mine. They have quarreled among themselves and have been harassed by others, and Clara Collins's house burns down as the result of arson. But disasters are to be expected in the last days, and a final disaster at the end will bring them together.

Part 3, "Passage," is quite short, as the word suggests. The activities of the anti-Brunists intensify with Miller's special edition, and the Brunists begin seriously to proselytize. The section ends with sexual encounters, the first two realized, the third projected: Elaine Collins with Carl Dean, a young Brunist; the Reverend Wesley Edwards with his wife; and Ben Wosznik wondering whether Clara Collins will marry him if the world doesn't end. This third section marks the "passage" of Marcella Bruno from loving a man to being exclusively dedicated to an idea, of the Brunists from terrified, circumspect, harassed believers to aggressive religious cult.

The final transformation occurs at the end of part 4, "The Mount," which begins with the town itself and touches directly on all the important persons for the last time, except for Miller, whose epilogue we have already considered. The section ends with Clara Collins Wosznik's cry, which echoes the Gospels, and the community has been transformed from a cult into a sect that knows the truth it must embody. Clara says of it: "A body visited by Grace must *live* by Grace!"[15] The last section ends with the naming of the sect: "Everybody stood up and clapped and cheered and cried and said she'd have to give that speech on television, surely no one could resist, and then Bishop Clegg led them all in fervent prayer. They had been calling themselves the Reformed Nazarene Followers of Giovanni Bruno, but that night they decided to go back to the name Mr. Miller had given them: the Brunists" (p. 430).

Miller called them Brunists in an offhand way because Giovanni Bruno was at the center of their melange of beliefs. Now they call themselves Brunists because they "know" at last what Ely's and Bruno's ambiguous messages meant. And in knowing they have been transformed—they are a religion, generated in darkness and united at last in truth.

The expository reading calls attention in a new way to Marcella Bruno. The "unhealthy," "unnatural" Marcella of the descriptive reading is not contradicted but, rather, simply disappears. Her death *is*, it exists in the beginning because of the prologue; for the reader this stark, simple fact surrounds and enriches her every appearance with special import. That import varies, of course, depending upon the mode in which the text is read. The descriptive mode impels us to see how very inadequate are Marcella's natural resources for coping with the world, with sexual, emotional involvement, with the extraordinary situation in which the disaster has placed her. It does so because in the mode of description death is the natural end when the living organism has lost whatever is necessary to maintain life.[16] Knowing Marcella will die, we are peculiarly sensitive to symptoms of impending, of probable, death. That doesn't mean such symptoms are manifested unambiguously. It means that we interpret ambiguous variables in that way rather than another because the prologue tells of her death, and we are reading descriptively.

The import that death in the prologue lends to subsequent encounters with Marcella is quite different in an expository reading. It places her as a special symbol of transcendence, of the ascent from the changing ambiguities of phenomenal experience to the stable clarity of truth. In her we see some of the conflicts above which all the Brunists will have to rise, but we pay more careful attention to them knowing that for Marcella the world will literally come to an end even if it will not for anyone else. Finally, all of Marcella's appearances in which her consciousness is presented are italicized, a visual reinforcement of her importance as a Brunist symbol in any mode of interpretation, an importance unequivocally communicated by the prologue and its title, "The Sacrifice."

Marcella's first appearance in an inside view occurs at the beginning of chapter 5 in part 1, as she is still awaiting the removal of bodies on Sunday morning, the third day since the explosion on Thursday night. She feels sick, blows her nose.

> *It is as though once-disparate things are fusing, coalescing into a new whole, a whole that requires her sickness no less than the explosion that set the parts in motion. A puzzle oddly revolving into its own solution . . . . all of it–each pain, each cry, each gesture–is somehow conjoined to describe a dream she has already dreamt. She knows first the curse, then hears the passing miner utter it; recognizes the platinum disc of the emerging sun behind the watertower, then observes it there. If one among the present looks over at her, it is clearly a look of recognition–not of her, but of* what is happening. . . . *she feels her hand write an arc through the air, like a word without letters, yet for that all the more real–feels suddenly wrenched apart from herself, staring down, observing that act, that arc, that bold single sign in an otherwise stark and motionless tableau.*[17]

When someone comes to tell her that her brother has been brought out alive, she says that she knows. In the hospital, sedated by the doctor and lying in a room next to Giovanni's, Marcella awakens and goes to see him. She thinks *"he is . . . somehow . . . changed: yes, a new brother must come of it."*[18] Later her old, feeble mother comes and they pray together. She loves her brother; he is not a strange object of ridicule to her as he is to the miners. He is *"the tall boy whose shy protective love has brought her safely to womanhood."*[19]

Two persons are instrumental in bringing her to a new stage of development, a new understanding of the wholeness she had barely perceived at the beginning. With her brother a focus of intense interest, she is brought into contact with Miller whom she begins to love and Mrs. Norton who is a mother surrogate and who explains to Marcella aspects of her experience. Below is a very important passage in full:

> *She heard them as a child, a voiced flutter of angels at her bedstead. Marcella, frail and often ill, watched for them, and they sustained her. . . . Growing, she rediscovered them at the altar and in nature. No longer words, but whole sensations were what they brought her. An indivisibility to life, an essential sympathy: then, everything mattered. Giovanni heard them too. In truth, perhaps they were his, not hers. Of age, she lost them, seeking them. They fled from being*

understood. "It is grasped whole, Marcella, but never learned."
Thus, with tenderness and patience, Eleanor leads her back to her
abandoned voices. [20]

This history of mystical experiences, suggestive of psychological disorder in a descriptive reading, points in the expository mode to a long
preparation for a symbolic role not yet perceived; and in a manner quite
different from Miller's, she too will, through her active choices, come to
enact a role which contributes substantively to the creation of the
Brunist civility. Her death is *called* a sacrifice, and she becomes a
powerful, unifying symbol; thus, like Miller's resurrection, Marcella's
death is, in effect, Christlike.

Mystical experiences like Marcella's are traditionally held to be free
gifts of God. For Mrs. Norton, they come from the "universal forces,"
they can be sought after and achieved with genuine effort. Eleanor
Norton returns Marcella to the activity of seeking them out. Further,
mystical experiences in the Catholic tradition are associated with
single-minded, exclusive love of God, shutting out human entangle-
ments of any but a detached nature. Marcella's love for Miller is not
detached, however; although she seems unaware of its full implications, it is intense, this-worldly heterosexual love. Marcella's in-
cipient conflict is resolved when Miller's sympathetic association with
the fledgling group reassures her that they can face the apocalyptic
future together, that their love is good and in harmony with her visions;
in effect, too, Eleanor Norton's involvement with her has removed Marcella and her visions from the Catholic ambience of her childhood. She
is the happiest of the group, feels no dread at what awaits them.

The coming of light! Do none of them perceive it so well as she?
So plain! . . . Do not their morrows flash with promise? Is not this
very room bursting with light? Are they blind? Are they all so
old? Need they their terrors? Must they distort it? [21]

Sitting in her garden one day, alone, Marcella

laughs. The fact is, Marcella doesn't exactly believe in the cata-
clysm. At first, she had some doubts about her brother even, for
she had never confused love with worship. But she has grown
greatly in these few weeks, has discovered the true solidity of
truths she previously only suspected, or thought might just be
creatures of her own inturned foolishness. For example: that Jesus
is not salvation, but only a single path among many . . . . She has
been greatly helped by them all . . . . And most of all by Justin.
Though silent, apart, calm, singular, he is yet at the heart of the
Plan . . . aloof from the human frailties of the group. Justin is—in a
sense—their priest . . . . God is terrible, but as beauty is terrible,
not horror. [22]

158

On the other hand, Marcella's peace is disturbed by Mrs. Norton's suspicions of Justin; she is troubled, too, by the difficulties the others experience in determining what awaits them and when it will come. The uneasy peace she has achieved between apocalypse and love growing in time is shattered when she discovers Justin's betrayal. The Brunists are shaken by it too, but, as we have seen, they respond by using the unwanted publicity to gather converts; and Justin's treachery, like Judas's, is a paradoxical instrument for good, enabling the Brunists to become a religious movement rather than a failed cult.

For Marcella, however, the betrayal is the destruction of her original synthesis wherein her understanding of the "universal pattern" was congruent with her personal love for a man. Her commitment to her vision of reality is irrevocable,[23] and she rises in anguish to a new understanding. We learn only from others that she is fasting, that she has given up speech. The Brunists agree to pose for photographers, and Miller seeing her in a group picture "hardly recognized her.... Those eyes that had so captivated him now stared vapidly out past the camera, too large for this face, all their bright glitter gone" (p. 385). The night before the final gathering on the Mount of Redemption, the Brunists go up to the site and leave the weakened Marcella behind, asleep. She awakens to find them gone, and believing that the time has come and they have forgotten her, she tries to follow them. Running along the road to the hill she sees light and feels it behind her.

> She sees her shadow as the light sweeps down on her from behind. She tries to enclose herself in its sweep. She spreads wide her arms to hold it back. Suddenly: lights spring up before her! out of nowhere! lights on all sides! flooding the world! she in its center! It comes! she cries. God is here! she laughs. And she spins whirls embraces light leaps heaving her bathing in light her washes and as she flows laughs His Presence light! stars burst sky burns with absolute laugh light! and [24]

The passage is given from Marcella's point of view; what has happened is, of course, obvious. There are cars chasing the Brunists up to the hill in order to harass them. These are behind Marcella, going in the same direction. Then, the Brunists having decided to leave the hill to avoid their persecutors, cars are coming toward her from the hill. Thus the sudden light behind her and before her.

However, for Marcella the cars provide the perfect death and a necessary death. A life on the plane of the ordinary, the inevitable return to the world of becoming that must follow the achievement of any new synthesis, is the fate of the Brunists, and one they gladly accept since they face it with new knowledge and new purpose. But for Marcella such a life in the "new" church without Miller would be meaningless.

She has gone through conflict and pain to the acceptance of a pattern of meaning, and her death is right when it occurs. She has achieved the knowledge, the love, and the union with a universal meaning which makes ordinary human life no longer valuable. And to the Brunists her death contributes much more than her continued life possibly could.

This expository reading casts still more light on Miller, too, for each can be seen to play a decisive role in the achievement of knowledge and meaning for the other, and each plays such a role precisely because the other is totally ignorant of the truth about him. Marcella can finally slough off this world because of Miller's betrayal, since he alone attaches her to it; and Miller learns to love because of Marcella.

Finally, the expository reading, because it moves dialectically, will reveal a double ladder, a twofold hierarchical arrangement of variables—one is a ladder of love, the other of knowledge. Because exposition is assimilative, love and knowledge are not in truth separate; rather, love and knowledge truly achieved will be seen to be identical. But in process they can be distinguished. Miller seeks love; we know that because he is looking for something that can enable him to care, to feel that life is not pointless. Marcella seeks knowledge; she begins with love for her brother and ends, despite Miller, with a cosmic love. But because of him she achieves knowledge of the way the world is, and what she learns forces her to reject the world's love, just as what she learns from Eleanor Norton leads her to embrace assimilation to the cosmic forces which are speaking through the Brunists. Miller achieves love, and it gives him knowledge of life's meaning for him.

A reading of *The Origin of the Brunists* in the mode of argument will afford the reader a view of the multiple perspectives that give the novel its remarkably rich texture. In the hypothetical mode of argument, agents act, make the world and the self by doing and saying, and when the orientations of other agents interfere, adjustments are made; if doing is blocked they resort to speech as action, if speech is blocked to thinking as action. We can read the novel in this mode taking any one of the principals as agent or the Brunists as a whole. However, I would like to interpret the novel in the mode of argument through an agent we haven't discussed yet at all: the teller or maker. This program may seem to present some difficulty, however. In *Dog Years,* for example, the three principals are also the three narrators, and to interpret in terms of agent is to interpret in terms of the narrator simultaneously. The telling of *The French Lieutenant's Woman* is conducted by a narrator who identifies himself as "the novelist," the creator of the named text. He is a simple enough agent through which to arrange variables into interpretive accounts. In both cases, however, the novels were organized in terms of principles which are equally valid for the organization of the entire universe as a single whole. The conjectural organization makes a whole out of the desires, i.e., the speech and actions, of men. A philosophical orientation of that kind would suppose the universe itself to be what spontaneous speech and action make it. The definitive organization composes the world out of elements, and any given whole could be theoretically expanded to encompass the universe.

Only the principle of the qualitative novel postulates a universe made up of many different structured wholes, no one of which can be said to mirror, to be expandable to, or to exemplify the entire universe. The structured whole which is said to be a given qualitative novel, then, is a different kind of context for the four modes of discourse than are the other generic modes, and when we turn to reading it in the mode of argument, we can use this agent-oriented mode to explore the making of the whole by a single maker, as well as the making of their several stories by the protagonists of the novel. Whereas these makings are identical in conjectural and definitive organizations wherein a protagonist making his world is making the novel, they can be separated here because the protagonist making his world is different from someone making a novel—which is only a part of the world.

The agent of our reading in the mode of argument will be, then, "Robert Coover," whom we may call, with Wayne Booth, the implied author. We will have to infer his intentions or desires from what he does and says because the telling of *The Origin of the Brunists* is effected by a nameless teller who comes as close to objective presentation as is likely to be feasible in discourse. As we would expect, then, the telling is presented in the third person and is managed by constantly shifting points of view, so that comment and continuity must be achieved through the many agents presented, and there is no overall comment by a narrating voice; and between one agent's "scene" and another's there is oftentimes no continuity at all. This means that we must infer the teller from the juxtaposition of episodes and from his choice of beginning. Having done that—after all, "someone" placed one episode after another and began where he did—we can arrange the variables in the mode of argument, taking the teller as agent, and trying to determine the meaning of his activity as we have suggested the meaning of the activities of other agents in the other modes of discourse.

Coover begins by doing what he wishes to do, as do all agents in the mode of argument. Apparently he wishes to tell of the existence of the Brunists, an established religious sect, and he does so through the recollections of Hiram Clegg who joined them at the climactic moment of their coming-to-be. The consequences of this arbitrary choice of beginning are several: the events Clegg recounts are dramatic and intriguing, but Clegg cannot satisfy curiosity about the origins of the Brunists since he was not present at their formation. Second, Clegg's account, of events remembered because they were indeed memorable, offers information about the death of Marcella Bruno and what the principal Brunists felt for her, information which the teller clearly wishes us to have. Why? Certainly ignorance of her death which occurs late in the novel would deflect attention from events and persons unrelated to her and focus interest and suspense on her relations with Miller. Presenting her death at the outset also lends a dimension of tragic irony to scenes involving both Marcella and Miller. Finally, the narrator's separate voice occurs twice in the prologue; and the second occurrence is somewhat ambiguous. Toward the end of the prologue a parenthetical phrase indicates that Clegg would later become a Brunist bishop, and although the entire prologue is in the third person limited manner, one might argue that Clegg would know this at the time of recollecting the past. However, the first intrusion, occurring at the beginning, is quite clearly unambiguous. It reads: "He had been prepared, *as only a man of great and simple faith can be prepared*" (italics mine). That is clearly a narrator's intrusion rather than an inside view. Why does the narrator intrude, probably twice? Again, we infer his motives from what he does and says and their consequences. The comment *on* Clegg establishes reliable testimony to his character; ergo, we believe his account and believe that the Brunists are a religious sect that merits serious consideration because a man of great faith has risen—the second passage—to a high place in it.

In effect, Coover has chosen a source of information, and just enough information, to seduce the reader into following him as he makes his world. He begins part 1 by describing West Condon in terms of how it looks and what its inhabitants—children, businessmen, miners, etc.—are doing, thinking, and feeling. If the first five paragraphs seem to contain commentary, it is inextricably part of the creation of a locale and a community prior to bringing in specific persons. The comments, in the absence of specific agents to whom they can be attributed, nonetheless do seem to reflect the inhabitants' feelings about their world.

> Business is in its usual post-Christmas slump. Inventories are underway. Taxes must be figured. Dull stuff. Time gets on, seems to run and drag at the same time. People put their minds on supper and the ball game, and talk, talk about anything, talk and listen to talk.... West Condon, West Condoners—mostly that: West Condoners, what's wrong with them, what dumb things they've done, what they've been talking about, what's wrong with the way they talk, who's putting out, jokes they've told, why they're not happy, what's wrong with their homelife. (p. 30)

The miners are treated in detail next, named and described, in nine pages devoted to their trip to the mine and what they are doing before and at the moment of the explosion. Except for a miner's memories of the past, all the inside views and narrative portions are written in the historical present. Here is an example from the end of the first chapter, a second before the explosion occurs:

> Rosselli hesitates, looks around, his headlamp slicing through the unfamiliar blackness, bringing timbers and tunnels and strange equipment into momentary view. He accepts a cigarette, fits it in his mouth. . . . The mine is silent except for the distant scrape of machinery and voices, and what seems to be a sound nearby somewhat like that of bees.
> (p. 40)

In the next chapter the miners are followed as they struggle to escape or to resign themselves, as does Ely Collins, to die. Those outside the mine are depicted just prior to and following news of the disaster—the basketball players at the local high school, mine managers, miners' families, young people related to miners or important townspeople. Except for the glimpses of the basketball game, the accounts are presented in the normal past tense.

In the first five chapters all the protagonists, major and minor, have been introduced and the narrative technique established. The telling will be scenic, episodic, sometimes with and sometimes without connection between one episode and another. Coover begins chapter 5, for example, with a one-page-long interior monolog, an inside view of Marcella Bruno. Immediately following is an episode following Tiger Miller as he awakens in his apartment and then goes to the mine. It ends with his noticing Marcella, then moves to her thoughts, then back to Miller. No transitional stylistic devices are used, but rather mechanical ones which silently imply the author. There are two mechanical devices and one inherent in reasoned discourse that facilitate transitions. The latter is simply continuity of subject matter, a kind of simple free-association on the part of the teller. For example, in the third chapter of part 2, a section in which Abner Baxter thinks resentfully of the special homecoming celebration for Bruno is followed by an inside view of the banker, Ted Cavanaugh, whose idea the celebration was. The mechanical device of extra spacing between episodes is used as well in that instance, as it is used between episodes that have no intrinsic link explaining their juxtaposition. The second mechanical device is the use of italics for all of Marcella Bruno's solo appearances, all inside views of her consciousness, and for Happy's "Last Judgment" pieces, both those written and those delivered to Miller orally.

The teller, then, presents a world in which agents act according to their own desires, each from his own perspective; actions so motivated lead to consequences, and these in turn clash with others, and the agents must adjust and readjust themselves in order to continue to speak and act. Coover postulates a situation in which a miner lights a cigarette in an area filled with volatile gases and causes an explosion—the perfect, arbitrary act to lead to consequences for many agents. Miller does what he wishes to do as a newspaperman—he interviews miners and miners' families and publishes what he learns in the *Chronicle.* Thus Eleanor Norton learns of the miraculous escape of Bruno, and a woman far removed from the miners professionally, socially, educationally, seeks out Bruno and eventually decides that his body is occupied by one of her "higher powers." She must adjust her language to the Christian orientation of Clara Collins, and she does, but she never alters her own beliefs, and she gradually converts Marcella to them.

Through these complex encounters the Brunists will be born—a result of many agents, each contributing some part of the message which, in its entirety, will be conveyed to a wide audience because of Miller's desire to do his job and to "play the game," as he calls it. Miller's involvement is a form of game playing, of amusing himself; but it too will lead to consequences he must eventually come to terms with. At the end, Marcella is an agent who has been blocked from action and speech by encountering at last the real orientation of Miller, a trauma that weakens her, and by encountering the anti-Brunist action of Abner Baxter quite literally, being killed by his automobile.

We ought to note at this point what happens to the uninterpreted variable, civility, of the qualitative principle with which we have organized *The Origin of the Brunists:* in the narrative reading it became the several communities formed by the resolution of problematic situations; in the descriptive reading it became the natural communities developed by healthy reactions to contingencies and by therapeutic contingencies acting on unhealthy developments; in the expository reading, civility became the harmonious wholeness of love and knowledge.

Civility in the mode of argument is the audience made by the actions of the various agents following the explosion and channeled through the speech or words of the newspaper. One example should help to show what is involved concretely. Abner Baxter's joining the Brunists can be interpreted as a transcendance of conflict brought about through Clara's Christian love and his own consequent knowledge of Christian love. But in the mode of argument Baxter is as spontaneous and "willful" as any other agent, and in this mode we are looking at spontaneity, arbitrary action and its consequences—not the gathering-up, the assimilations, of an idea-dominated mode but the chaotic activity of a mode dominated by agents and their desires. Chasing the Brunists, intent on destroying their movement which rivals his own Nazarene Church, Baxter kills Marcella—an unforeseen consequence of his action, the result of a direct confrontation with another agent's desire, the latter quite unpredictable. He must cope with this unforeseen happening on a number of levels: practically, he will have to defend himself if the death is reported, and the town establishment is as hostile to him as the Brunists are. Emotionally, he must deal with feelings of guilt, since he isn't a murderer and is horrified at his unwitting act of killing. Clara Collins's offer of forgiveness is a way out, a new direction which will save him practically and still leave an avenue open for religious action, and all in the name of Christian love which he can openly accept without loss of face.

This is how the audience for the Brunist message grows through acting and speaking, and that audience grows simultaneously with the message itself. A rhetorical message is made at the same time that its audience is made; there is no preexisting message or audience. Himebaugh and Norton and Collins contribute to the message that will be Brunism as does Bruno under questioning from Eleanor Norton, at the same time that they are all being constituted an audience for that message. This is true of Ben Wosznik, who becomes audience and maker of Brunism in the songs he writes which are broadcast on radio.

> *March on! march on, ye Brunists!*
> *March on and fear no loss!*
> *March on beneath thy banner,*
> *The Circle and the Cross!*
> *In spite of all adversity,*
> *March out upon that mine!*
> *The Cross within the Circle*
> *Will make the vict'ry thine!*
>
> *March on! march on, ye Brunists!*
> *Forever shall we live!*
> *The Cross within the Circle*
> *Will us God's Glory give!*
> *So know ye are the chosen,*
> *The gold among the dross!*
> *March on beneath thy banner,*
> *The Circle and the Cross!*[25]

Miller himself is audience for the Brunist message while his formulation of Brunism for the *Chronicle,* as it grows, contributes to that message even as it promulgates it, making an audience of adherents and opponents. In this reading Miller's position in the middle stands out vividly. He is vulnerable to, has sympathy for, the apocalyptic vision—he realizes that he is an "old fundamentalist at heart" (p. 107), at the age of thirteen "had read Revelations and never quite got over it" (p. 141), knew that "it wasn't sex that whipped him, whipped them all, it was the spook behind sex, that thing that designed him, reshaped him, waked him, churned him, thought for him even: Jesus, when was the last time he'd committed a wholly rational act! . . . Wesley Edwards had once chided him for his "romantic attachment to rationalism." Rationalism indeed! Christ! Old Edwards would laugh his ass off if he knew!" (p. 156).

Given his love for Marcella, then, why does he reject the Brunist vision, why does the Brunist "argument" finally fail to win him? This reading in the mode of argument raises to prominence and, indeed, makes particulars which do not emerge in the other readings or play a minor role in the interpretation. This is the case in part because the mode of argument features the narrator as an agent, and whatever he does may be taken into account since the reader is aware of it even though the protagonists of the novel may not be. A case in point is Happy, whose "Last Judgments" create no audience save Miller and the reader. Happy's continuing parody does not affect the Brunists directly, but only in its effect on Miller. We must look to Happy for Miller's rejection of the Brunist message, a rejection which can never seem other than inexplicable or simply wicked to Marcella and Eleanor, who don't know Happy and her parody.

Marcella as woman loved, but never sexually enjoyed, is a powerful argument together with his own feelings for the fundamentalist position. Opposed to these is Happy, physically loved and enjoyed, who offers an intellectual (as opposed to the spiritual in Marcella) dimension in the last judgment pieces, a dimension seriously lacking in Marcella. Happy has won the debate on the intellectual level by the time Miller proposes marriage to Marcella; but Marcella will not leave the Brunists, and Happy has won on all counts.

The internality of *The Origin of the Brunists* is filled with debates and with opposing "pairs" of agents in this reading. Marcella and Happy, the spiritual, fragile, dependent woman and the strong, intelligent, sensual woman; Giovanni Bruno, the sensitive, strange, alienated Italian miner, attached to the Blessed Virgin but not to the Church, paradoxically the fountainhead of a protestant, millenarian sect. Contrasted with him is Vince Bonali, also an Italian miner, and initially indifferent to the Church, a sensual, earthy man. Bonali will move through his clashes with the Brunists to greater sensitivity and devotion to the Church, remaining sensual and earthy. Wesley Edwards, rationalist Presbyterian, forms one kind of contrast with Brunists. Ely Collins, Nazarene preacher, represents Christian love, kindness, mildness; Abner Baxter, Nazarene preacher, represents Christian hell fire and damnation. Himebaugh and Eleanor Norton are both occultists of a sort; but Eleanor believes in powers of light, whereas Himebaugh's universal powers are universally horrible.

All of these voices will be preserved throughout. The contributors to "Brunism" never relinquish their own beliefs for a common synthesis; rather, the common Brunist experience is interpreted in several ways, and the embattled community is not greatly concerned with doctrinal consistencies. Furthermore, during the greater part of the novel they are awaiting the end of the world at which time all things will be clear, and the "imminent end" seems to be the one belief they all share. Among the Brunists, Baxter and Norton and Collins will persist and endure, gathering an audience far beyond West Condon, an audience represented within the novel by Hiram Clegg. Because they can no longer "make" the world end through their calculations, they will instead preach the word of God according to Ely Collins and, by extension, Giovanni Bruno.

The town and Edwards and Bonali—these orientations also persist. And Miller will persist as well, prepared at the end to continue his debate with the town from the orientation of Happy, who has won him.

If we examine, finally, the orientation of Coover, we can see that he too has made an audience, and we need to look more closely at the message reaching that audience, for the message is what makes the audience. I pointed earlier in this discussion in the mode of argument to stylistic devices, modes of presentation which can be attributed only to the narrator, i.e., to the agent we call Robert Coover. He can be said to make an audience separate from those made in the novel by the sayings and doings of the protagonists.

What kind of argument is implied (1) by the absence of overall, reliable commentary, (2) by the episodic presentation reinforced by the mechanical use of increased spacing between episodes, (3) by the use of italics to emphasize Marcella's inner thoughts and Happy's "Last Judgments," and, finally, (4) by the inclusion of two items, one very brief, almost casual, the other in episodes, but both addressed almost exclusively to the external (Coover's) and hidden throughout from the internal audience? To begin with four, the first item is mentioned only once and then nothing is made of it. Only two of the protagonists are aware of it, and they do not really understand what it means, if anything. The Brunists never learn about it. Here is the relevant passage:

> Of course, the greatest story would have to remain untold. Happy's description of Giovanni's abdominal scars had rung some kind of bell in his [Miller's] mind. She'd said they were all horizontal or vertical, but, though intricate, had no apparent design to them. It made him think of cracked wood and that made him think of the wooden statue of Saint Stephen in the local Catholic Church—its patron. He'd first noticed it at

> Antonio Bruno's funeral a month ago.... It was [Antonio
> Bruno's] very artificiality, oddly giving life to the statues in
> the Cathedral, that had drawn Miller's attention to the
> boyish Stephen. Torso writhing, eyes turned inward to con-
> front death, arms twisted up over his head, the boy was
> naked but for the usual loincloth... yes, the belly was that
> abstract fretwork of tiny scars she had described. (p. 300)

We will return to the scars presently. The second item concerns the
sudden epidemic of vandalism in West Condon culminating in the
burning down of Clara Collins's house. The vandals sometimes defecate
in boxes and leave these to be found and opened by their victims, and
they strangle cats and poison dogs. They refer to themselves as the Black
Hand, and the Black Peter, and later the Black Piggy, but they leave only
an ink drawing of the black hand behind them. Prior to the burning of
Clara's house, with which the strange epidemic terminates, someone
defecates behind Abner Baxter's church pulpit, leaving him in a tow-
ering rage and the police in consternation.

The police chief, Dee Romano, is very troubled, fearing a revival of
the famous Black Hand. "Opinions vary. Italians... fear the revival of
old blood enmities, of old extortions and death by night, but, strangely,
few Italians are struck. Some blame out-of-towners, even rival cities.
Others the Klan. A maniac. Communists. The mayor recognizes the
adolescent style: some high school prankster (p. 215).

Coover's external audience alone, the reader, is privy to the truth, so
that the epidemic remains a mysterious horror appropriate to the "last
days" for the millenarians and further proof for their opponents that the
Brunist phenomenon is constantly breeding discord. The perpetrators
and their motives are revealed to the reader in a few episodes which
remove all mystery. Abner Baxter's son, Nathan, was different from his
father, for

> while his father believed in the eventual redistribution of all
> property equally to all people (or anyway all saints), no mat-
> ter how it had to be accomplished, and as Jesus Christ, he
> preached, had intended, Nat Baxter recognized no property
> rights at all. "Whatever the eye sees and covets, let the hand
> grasp it." At the high school gymnasium the Sunday of the
> mine disaster, Nat's eye saw and coveted a beautifully
> gnarled black hand that lay, carbonized and unattached,
> among the bodies and other refuse, and, covertly, his hand
> grasped it, stuffed it in a paper sack. (p. 163)

Having grown weary of playing Batman and Robin with his little
brother, Paulie, Nat terrifies Paulie with the hand, then allows him to
be Black Peter since Paulie had just "got his peter whopped by their
father's razor strop" (p. 164). Later they initiate their sister Amanda,

who is unhappy when they torture and beat smaller children, and to punish her they beat her mercilessly. In order to avoid a beating she anticipates, Amanda resolves to do the bravest deed of all, and alone, unbidden by her brothers, she sets fire to Clara Collins's house since their father doesn't "like Widow Collins anymore." Throughout, their activities are described in Nathan's and Amanda's thoughts in an echo of their father's words when he preaches and when he punishes them. They bring their adventures to an end largely because their older sister has guessed that they are behind the Black Hand outbreak, and they fear she will tell Abner.

It seems to me important that although the explanation for the Black Hand outrages remains unknown to the principals of the novel, the town's explanation—that the Brunists have bred violence and discord of all kinds—and the Brunists'—that these are times of mysterious providence-directed upheaval—in no way contradict each other or the account presented to the reader, who is left to infer the causes of the children's behavior for himself. Certainly we are not surprised that the children of Abner Baxter, who are frequently and brutally beaten, should act out a fantasy life in which they inflict righteous cruelty on others. The cruelty is always at secondhand in the case of adults, who could hurt them or, worse, betray them to their father. But it also involves children younger and weaker than themselves, who are whipped as their father whips them. The phenomenon does not seem to require the Brunists or a mine disaster to provoke it. Yet the circumstances are what they are, and no one can say that Nathan and Paulie would or would not behave as they do at any other time and without the stimulus of the dead hand. I stress this because we must decide why Coover withholds the explanation for this frightening social disruption from the protagonists of the novel while revealing it to the reader.

The obvious conclusion is that the reader is meant to be able to judge how inaccurately both the Brunists and the town interpret events. But the fact that all three explanations are not mutually contradictory ought to remind us that more than one position can be legitimately defended in debate; and, after all, there is a sense in which all three make sense. The reader's position is self-evident with respect to the Baxter children and their obvious psychological motives. But the town, ignorant of the vandals' identity, is right to the extent that Baxter's quarrel with the Brunists leads Amanda to burn the Collins house. On the other hand, a mine disaster is a profound upheaval for a community, and if the "end of the world" is not literally imminent, the disaster has led to the end of the world as they have known it for a good many people, indeed for West Condon as a whole. Thus the Brunists, who attribute the Black Hand phenomenon to the ambience of such times, are figuratively right; they are literally right insofar as the hand itself is a direct result of the explosion. I would suggest, then, that Coover is not asking the reader to judge the folly of cultists or the malice of a town; rather, he asks the reader to see how ambiguous human experience really is, how many are the modalities of truth.

Let us consider now the scars on Giovanni Bruno's abdomen. They are and remain mysterious. The Brunists cannot make use of their symbolism—assuming they could be said to be symbolic—because they are ignorant of the scars. Miller cannot publicize them lest Happy be accused of a breach of ethics. What do they symbolize? Nothing we know of. The scars on the statue of the martyred St. Stephen are the result of cracked paint! The scars on the living man would seem to be stigmata of a sort, but if they are they lack traditional provenance. Saints who showed stigmata had bleeding foreheads or sides or hands, their stigmata "imitations" of the wounds of Christ. Bruno, the lapsed Catholic whose vision of the Virgin comes to him in the form of Protestant Ely Collins's white bird, has unique stigmata. It should be noted that the white bird vision, often mentioned by Ely and familiar to his fellow miners, has, with respect to Bruno, the same curious ambiguity as do the stigmata. Stigmata are in the Catholic tradition but not Bruno's; the white bird recalls the dove, the traditional symbol of the Holy Spirit but never a form in which the Blessed Virgin manifests herself.

However, the scars are there and inexplicable. Their message is not meant for the Brunists or the townspeople, neither of whom can receive it, and it cannot be meant for Miller and Happy, who dismiss it finally. Therefore it is meant for us. It comes through Miller because it cannot be presented objectively in words other than the words of a story teller, and Coover tells by putting together and speaking through other agents. Thus are we given notice that Bruno is in some way extraordinary. It is the only way we can learn, in fact, that he really is, since his survival may be a fluke, his vision hallucinatory, and his pronouncements meaningless until interpreted by Eleanor Norton, who is not a reliable teller.

The absence of reliable commentary, the first point I suggested as one of Coover's means of communicating with his reader, emerges at this point as a way of insisting that *The Origins of the Brunists* is an account of the inception and growth of a religion; it is not an argument for truth or falsity. The complex perspectives which together contribute to this growth are thus presented episodically, for they seem disconnected relative to one another, representing as they do the spontaneous activities of agents acting according to desire and without any *necessary* interrelation with one another. The Black Hand incident and the way it is handled reinforces the sense that the origins are complex both because they are *many* and because all are capable of multiple interpretation. Certainly Bruno's stigmata leave permanently open the questions of spiritual reality, and prevent the external audience from assuming that Coover is muckraking on the American religious scene.

Before we turn to the italicized passages, Marcella's consciousness and Happy's running account of the last judgment, we should examine briefly Coover's use of the present tense, scattered throughout the novel, since the interior views of Marcella, both narration and monologue, are all presented in the present indicative. At the beginning, the events involving miners and leading up to the explosion are narrated in the present tense (except when a particular miner is thinking of the past), as are the brief episodes on the basketball court.

I want to suggest that this grammatical device points up the importance of the mine for the town, the importance of the miners themselves and the disaster. That is, before the explosion occurs, we cannot read the account of the ordinary events that precede it—miners going to work—and the introduction of the ordinary persons involved as a relatively unimportant setting of scene. We cannot because the present tense in discourse calls attention to itself, and in the absence of narrative commentary it serves as a spotlight, heightens interest and suspense as we wonder why it is being used at all, especially since other interspersed episodes are presented in the conventional past tense. However, the present tense also suggests immediacy and tension, and events couched in it take on a kind of eternal dimension, so that the grammar itself, independent of content, becomes symbolic and the events are in a sense said to be always present, never past; thus we see that the mine disaster is permanent, existing always in its far-reaching consequences. What occurs simultaneously with the explosion takes on this quality as well, as long as it is a singular, self-contained event. That is, whereas the boy and girl petting in a car will develop their relationship later on, *this* basketball game will forever be the game in progress while men suffered and died. The game is a happy event, a beautiful exercise and celebration of the human body employing and enjoying its physical capacities for their own sake. It will be forever linked with horror because of an accident of time, and because the gymnasium will shortly house not young, beautiful, living bodies but the charred corpses of dead miners. The rhetorical contrasts thus displayed by the agent's choices, Coover's, make a point about life and death without the use of words but rather by means of nonverbal commonplaces—the life of the game, the death of the mine—expressed through a formal grammatical device.

Later in the novel, selected episodes preceding crises on the "Mount of Redemption" are narrated in the present indicative, and it lends the same qualities of timeless significance and heightened expectancy to them that characterize the passages preceding the explosion.[26]

In the present indicative Coover presents the feeling life of his world when its inhabitants, principals, and minor figures are keyed up, uncertain, worried—above all, feeling, doing, wondering, waiting, rather than thinking out or engaging in any deliberation, internally or with others; reasoned discourse is waiting on an event in these passages. A passage may concern a single protagonist or several, their varied activities and locations at a single moment noted. The effect in either case is of acceleration *and* stasis, the paradox of increased movement and breathless anticipation which gives the reader the sense of a peopled world, rich in variety, on the verge of an awesome event.

The immediacy and tension suggested by the present tense are communicated in the inside views of Marcella. However, the context modifies the effect and consequently the meaning. Although Marcella's past is faintly suggested, she is never realized with the density of some other agents. She seems to live in an eternal present, the only one of the Brunists completely at home in the prelude to apocalypse. It is not so much that her past is hazy, but that the contradictions of the present do not seem to touch her. If "Brunism" seems a mélange of Protestant, Catholic, and occult elements, Marcella is untroubled by that fact although the others must make an effort to adjust to one another. Miller's background, clearly secular, does not disturb her with foreboding. In short, she is not troubled by the possible consequences of the present; in effect it is not a sense of the past that we miss in her but a sense of the future. The everlasting present through which we enter her mind does much to furnish the tone which reinforces the impression conveyed by the content of her mind.

The italics, however, tell us something else, that she is an essential figure, perhaps even more important than Giovanni Bruno. Marcella is the ultimate link between Miller and the Brunists, and as a newspaper man he is one of the most important aspects of their origin (Judas though he may be, he is the first to spread the gospel according to . . .). The "contradictory" of the Brunists is Miller, and *The Origin of the Brunists* as a whole depends on the interplay of the commonplace. Marcella, then, is *the link* from the perspective of individual human relations, and *the symbol* of the Brunists, as one extreme of a commonplace; for she symbolizes the eternal, non-rational present, the mysterious openness to a consciousness of signs and portents, a feeling for some cosmic imperative beyond logic and a materialistic view of sense data. Thus Eleanor Norton tells Miller, "Not think, Mr. Miller! This kind of insight is never achieved by thinking" (p. 200).

Miller is torn between love for Marcella and his secret sympathy for the Brunists, and an educated skepticism he cannot give up. These are further complicated by the newsman's instinct for a great story and the gratifying sense of power that his control of communications gives him.

From the point of view of idea, then, Miller is not a good symbol of a pure, antiapocalyptic stance. What is required is a protagonist whose motives and desires are less complicated than Miller's, but whose relationship with him is as strong, as gripping as Marcella's. Happy, the nurse he encounters at the hospital when he first visits Marcella, is that person. She is Marcella's opposite sexually: Happy enjoys sex without complication or guilt, whereas Marcella is chaste, a virgin. Miller is easily turned from her by Marcella, but he never breaks the connection to which he is held by sexual need. But these facts make Happy the likely person, a woman to contrast with Marcella. She is also intelligent and witty and provides the intellectual contradictory to the millenarian Brunism symbolized by Marcella and her voices, in a series of running accounts of the "Last Judgment," parodies which reduce the mysteries of divine judgment to mundane, slightly chaotic, bureaucratic politics. These she shares only with Miller, and they exemplify the secular orientation in a pure form as Miller cannot because Coover has made him too complicated for purity.

Happy serves this function because Coover has conceived her with great subtlety. She is even more lacking in past than is Marcella, who has a brother and parents, is said to have gone to high school, and remembers her brother and herself when they were younger. Happy's surname and given name are unknown; she appears only with Miller or in his mind, and his mind, the only "narrator" who mentions her, never thinks of her as anyone else but "Happy." There are no inside views of Happy; she never furnishes a perspective for "telling." She is author of the pieces Miller receives in the mail after the Brunist belief about the imminent end of the world is widely known. Here are some excerpts from Happy's "Last Judgments":

> Bankers and businessmen, as the whole world could have predicted, were, without exception, condemned. Go directly to hell, the Divine Judge would roar upon being confronted by one of them; do not pass Go, do not collect $200. The egalitarians were also sent to hell, of course, but they were allowed to collect the money. Sometimes, even the Divine Mind is scrutable...

> A poet, seeking favors at the Judgment, composed a brilliant ode to Divine Justice, and presented it. It was so enthusiastically received that the poet was proclaimed Judge of the Day and granted Supreme Authority for twenty-four hours. So ingenuous and sweet-natured was the fellow, however, that he unhesitatingly absolved everyone who appeared before him. God finally had to call an end to the poet's franchise for fear of being laughed at...

The next supplicant, a virgin . . . was brought before the Judge. . . .
—And why do you wish to be admitted to Heaven?
—What is Heaven?
—Why, Heaven is where I am.
—And where are you?
—I have said.
—And so have I.
The judge smiled and because, to tell the truth, there had never
been a Heaven before, the Judge and the virgin forthwith created
one and had a Hell of a good time doing it. . . .[27]

Clearly the italicized passages pertaining to Marcella and Happy's "Judgments" just quoted, each epitomizing one of the women in Miller's life and also two contradictory perspectives on the notion of the millennium, must serve an important purpose for the agent and teller, Coover, since he has called them so vividly to the attention of his readers; and we must remember, too, that aside from Miller's reading of the "Last Judgments," they and the inside views of Marcella are known only to the reader.

They are, first of all, a way of embodying, in order to express, the thought of the whole. There are these two perspectives on the universe, and each is fully achieved, fully realized—the apocalyptic by Marcella in the choice she makes and the death she embraces; the secular expressed in Happy's "Last Judgments" and lived out in her rescue of Miller, and his emergence to a life of continuing action and, above all, speech addressed to an audience made by the communications of his *Chronicle*. However, they are also a means of unification in this reading. A reading in the mode of argument does not ordinarily address questions of unity. Protagonists do and say; in consequence they clash with agents acting and speaking from different perspectives. They adapt or change course, and if, eventually, they cannot continue to act as they wish, they will turn to speaking or writing. Such a reading is thematically adequate in the context of a conjectural or definitive generic organization, regardless of whether or not the agent we use to contrive our reading is a protagonist or the maker of the whole.

When we have organized a qualitative novel, however, that context modifies the reading since, as we have seen, the qualitative is the only organization in which the whole is a self-contained object among other objects and does not exemplify or mirror the cosmos and cannot be said to be infinitely expandable to contain all of the nature of things. Thus, the qualitative principle which validates the arrangement of particulars in this reading permeates the formal thematic structure. We have seen that the undefined terms of the principle—action and civility—are interpreted in this reading as doing and saying spontaneously, and thereby generating an audience. The self-instantiating form of the qualitative whole must also be sustained in this reading from the perspective of the inventive agent—Coover—whose desire was to do and say what he must to make a separate, identifiable whole, a *kind* of artificial object, to borrow that term for the sake of clarity.

The form, then, is organized in this mode around Miller and in terms of two aspects, or two loves which influence him and consequently influence the origin and growth of the Brunists, whose journey to identity is inextricably bound up with communication. Miller's love for Marcella and hers for him influence him profoundly, but he doesn't really understand how or why: an explanation of what and who she truly is cannot come to us from him, then. But the italicized views of her transcendental perspective illuminate for the reader the ways in which her kind of love can motivate a man to action. The witty, clever judgments of Happy offer better insights into the real nature of the love between Happy and Miller than does the simple fact of their mutual sexual pleasure. Together, these are two contrary modes of love: one innocent, trusting, barely sensual; the other earthy, cynical, intelligent, and matter-of-fact; together they organize a novel in the mode of argument which, without them as focal, would contain too many different, unrelated perspectives to sustain the integral wholeness of the qualitative genre. The death of Marcella and his own experience of the violence of others mark the end of Miller's action in relation to the Brunists. Happy's verbal apocalypse marks the beginning of his new dedication to "saying" in the *Chronicle*. Thus we have a reading in the mode of argument perfectly integrated with the organization of the novel as qualitative.

Let me conclude this discussion of *The Origin of the Brunists* by recalling that there are three other ways of organizing the text as a novel, a whole. These would in turn modify the readings according to the modes of discourse. Then, too, each of the formal themes can be further varied by different choices of agent, idea, circumstance, or problematic situation in terms of which to devise the thematic accounts. And these thematic accounts, finally, will be valid readings of a novel organized as conjectural, definitive, qualitative, or translative, for prior to organization as one of these kinds there is no novel but only a text of some sort.

I am certain that other readings would further illuminate Coover's text, since it seems to me rich enough to sustain a variety of interpretations. Given the critical, rhetorical resources at my disposal, I hope I have been able to show that Coover's novel communicates a thought—a thought of the whole—and not by any means simplistically.

The four thematic readings permit us to appreciate its complexity because each offers a different perspective on experiencing the novel. Taken together they tell us that problematic situations are aspects of the nature of things, for individuals and communities, and that the nature of things which includes problematic situations also embodies the values and the human preoccupation with search for the values of truth, goodness, and beauty. And, finally, all of these are simultaneously the result of agents doing and saying what they want to do and say.

Our rhetorical analysis enables us to be especially sensitive to perspective, then, and this has consequences that do not derive solely from the practice of tracing multiple themes. Our thematic readings merged the forms of the modes of discourse with the matter these called into existence as the arranging of variables transformed the latter into particulars. However, the formal choice we made of the qualitative genre enabled us to see Coover communicating an inclusive design, which sets the artificial object apart from other objects and also embodies a pluralistic perspective: the double "end" presented in the internal, apocalyptic thoughts of Marcella and in the external, satirical "Last Judgments" of Happy. This formal, double nexus of unification is balanced by a double material nexus: for the ambiguous stigmata of Bruno are a material variation on the vision of Marcella, while the defecatory parodies of evangelical religion shown in the Baxter children are a material variation of Happy's secular, verbal "Judgments."

What the novel says, then, is complex indeed and cannot be reduced to a single statement. But what we have uncovered by means of a rhetorical critical method is, I hope, a partial insight into the thought of the whole; and the latter, as opposed to the thought of protagonists within a novel, is the proper end envisioned by and achievable by a rhetorical criticism.

EIGHT

NOVELS—TRANSLATIVE
A Discussion of Comparative Analysis

We turn now to the organization of a novel in terms of middle, the last of the modes available to us for organizing a discursive whole. *Beginning* gave us the conjectural genre, the novel of style and manners; *beginning, middle, and end* the definitive genre, the novel of events and consequences; *end* the qualitative genre, the novel of action and civility. Now, the englobing middle, the "always present" principle of *middle*, doubly defying the finite because it is without beginning or end, will give us the translative genre, the novel of ideas and feeling. However, for the conclusion of this essay in rhetorical criticism, I should like to illustrate the way in which rhetorical criticism enables us to formulate a context for the comparative analysis of two or more separate named texts, and provides the method for carrying out comparative analysis.

Before we begin, it seems best to examine briefly what we mean by comparative analysis. It is, of course, a very common critical activity, sometimes engaged in as literary history, but often directly concerned with comparing literary works for reasons other than the tracing of some kind of progression in time. University departments of comparative literature study literatures in different languages to note what they have in common and how they differ. No matter what is "compared," however, a context is perceived as essential since "comparison and contrast," one of the famous techniques of exposition as presented by the "rhetoric" texts, implies some common ground without which nothing meaningful can be said. It is as we noted at the outset of this discussion: unless there is connection of some kind, there is no "meaning."

It is beyond the purpose of this essay to discuss in detail the critical implications of the concept of "comparative literature";[1] it is enough to point out that in addition to context there must be method, and it seems to me clear that rhetoric is the best method of comparative analysis. To recapitulate my earlier argument briefly, both grammatical criticisms with their literary objects made of natural parts and poetic criticisms with their artificial objects rest on firm premises which regard a text as absolutely unique. Even when genre is invoked it serves primarily to help the critic focus his own attention and his readers' on criteria relevant to the analysis. Although a critic may find that his wide reading of "lyric poems" helps him to deal with *this* poem, no comparisons are made. To leave this point as unambiguous as possible, let me suggest that the poetic or grammatical critic's use of genre as context is like the physician's use of contexts of age, sex, and so on for diagnostic purposes. The individual person must nonetheless be examined in himself as unique, the contexts serving only to focus attention on relevant areas of consideration.

On the other hand, dialectical critics may be said to focus primarily on context, the individual text having its identity only when its context has been perceived within it. If comparisons are made, they are comparisons of the structures or myths that constitute the context of literature; and if individual texts are cited in such discussions, they are cited only as embodiments of that context. As a result, grammatical, poetic, and dialectical criticisms lack methodological resources for comparative analysis, and when critics do serious comparative analysis, whatever their theoretical commitments may be, they are mutatis mutandis doing rhetorical criticism. For rhetoric, concerned with the thought of the whole, is the one mode of criticism methodologically adequate to the task of comparing one text with another. In themselves, texts are not unambiguously related to one another; but as they exist in the experience of an audience they are.

Whatever the context chosen—form or content in their myriad manifestations—the formal requirements remain the same: to "make" the context, the "world" within which the "parts" will be related to one another, and to do the comparing, the relating of those parts. This is obviously an enterprise very much like the one we have been engaged in throughout part 2 of this essay. We can organize a context as we organize a novel; there is no formal difference between them. It is the case, however, that the organization in terms of middle, which gives us the translative novel, is especially good for this purpose, resembling as it does dialectical criticism, which itself features context. The conjectural and definitive organizations will accommodate whole texts as their acts and words, and natural elements, respectively, only with some difficulty; and the qualitative organization, already assuming a world of separate wholes, would also require a complicated adjustment to a series of whole texts as the quantitative parts of one of those wholes. Nonetheless, all three organizations of context are certainly feasible.

Finally, we should keep in mind the fact that the translative context is not uncommon, although it isn't recognized as such. "The Romantic Movement" is a translative context, as is "The Enlightenment." They are fashioned out of ideas and feelings which seem to dominate the expressed thoughts of the historical periods involved. The context in which Ian Watt compares Fielding and Richardson, for a contrary example, is a grammatical context composed of circumstantial elements.[2] The controversy which surrounds such formulations results from the discrepancy between the claim they make and the large number of disparate texts and circumstantial elements that must be accommodated to them once they are made from their original sources, usually smaller in number.

This difficulty disappears if the rhetorical character of such formulations is recognized. That is, instead of taking the concepts which structure an epoch as substantive, the "nature" and "convention" that characterize some formulations of Romanticism, for example, they can be taken rather as terms of a rhetorical commonplace. From that point of view, we see immediately that what *seems* natural from one perspective ("natural" is one of Samuel Johnson's favorite critical terms) *seems* conventional from another (that of the "Romantics," who rejected Augustan notions of what poetry ought to be). From this rhetorical standpoint, "Romanticism" needn't be proved to be an existing quality that characterizes every work or most works of an epoch in order for it to be an illuminating, productive critical concept.

The translative organization, then, in which—as in its dialectical relation—the parts are always seen as embodiments in small of the entire whole, seems the most promising mode of formulating a context for a comparative analysis. The named texts I propose to examine are two stories by Flannery O'Connor, and therefore the context I require is simple enough to provide a helpful illustration of the formal operation of making a context.[3] In examining several texts by O'Connor we can avoid the inevitable difficulties attending larger views because, although our first formal act, too, will be to make a context, we shall do so on the basis of a finite, limited number of texts and a single author, and thus our claim must be modest in scope and susceptible of checking against the sources which evoked it and—the important point—*only* against those.

We can begin, then, by recalling what must be done and what assumed in order to organize a translative novel. Excluding as it does both beginning and end, the translative organization locates the unity and coherence of a whole in the intelligible structure of the universe, which the whole is said to embody and reflect. Obviously, the context of the universe to which the text has been translated from the universe of discourse must be thought to be intelligible prior to and beyond any of its particular manifestations—*this* society, *this* novel. In our earlier discussion of Kazantzakis in chapter 5, we saw that in this organization a story is paradigmatic (in the manner of the myths of Plato, for example).

Thus we determine the intellectual structure of the story and postulate it as the intelligible structure of the universe of which the text is an instance. To be as clear as possible, let me repeat this in another way. To organize translatively is to say that a text implies that the universe is organized in a given way such that the text is simply a concrete manifestation of its structure. This is to say that the structure concretely manifested is itself not concrete, but rather an intelligible structure of ideas variously embodied in the concrete.

The translative context, whether a novel or a context for comparative studies, is structured by means of the englobing middle as principle, and thus the principle is infinite and timeless. Also, a two-termed polarity, like the thesis and antithesis of dialectic, organizes the translative whole. The persistence of the two-termed structure is apparent if we look at "Romanticism," for example, for however complex the variations become, the dichotomies of "head" and "heart" or "tradition" and "spontaneity" prevail in formulations of it. Can we, then, find in the writings of Flannery O'Connor a structural formulation which we can translate to the universe and attribute to it as its intelligible structure? If we examine the short stories collected in *A Good Man is Hard to Find* and *Everything That Rises Must Converge*, and the two longer texts, *Wise Blood* and *The Violent Bear It Away*,[4] of course we can, since we can organize any text or texts translatively. I repeat yet again the essential caveat: neither the individually named texts nor any discursive "worlds" of O'Connor are being said *to be* translative texts or worlds. The "world" will be, and will be what the reader makes it, when he makes it—and it might just as well be said to be a conjectural, definitive, or qualitative world; that is the perspective, the subjunctive vocabulary of the critical stance of this essay. With this in mind, to avoid the awkwardness of repeated qualifications, I shall begin the discussion of Flannery O'Connor in a conventional propositional vocabulary.

The discursive world of O'Connor is interesting in many ways, and the publication in one volume of *The Complete Stories*[5] has facilitated a reconsideration of her work as a whole since it contains all the stories, twelve of which have never before been available in book form. In addition, the stories are printed in chronological order so that comparisons in terms of her literary development can be more easily made. Her early death certainly limited her achievement with respect to quantity, but she has been said to be "narrow" in scope as well.[6]

The twelve stories excluded from the two collections would not really alter this judgment. Four of the twelve were revised for the first novel, *Wise Blood*; one became, revised, the opening chapter of the second novel, *The Violent Bear It Away*. A sixth story, one of the earliest and the first of the six O'Connor submitted as an MA thesis at the University of Iowa,[7] was reworked and appeared as "Judgement Day" in the posthumous collection. Only six remain in which to seek a fresh perspective on O'Connor's achievement, but for that purpose they are disappointing since they concern the milieus and a range of events and persons already familiar from the two collections and the two novels. Only one of the six, "Wildcat," is unique in being her only story exclusively concerned with black people, and with them quite independent of their relation to whites. But the story is different only "racially," so to speak, and race per se doesn't seem to be important to the story in any case.

However, I would like to take the position that any works which communicate in terms of concrete persons and events, feelings and ideas, place and time, are narrow in some sense since they inevitably exclude more than they include. That they communicate with an audience other than the particular one they are thought to mirror seems to me warrant for assuming that they are indeed "wide" enough in any way that matters. What seems to me more interesting than O'Connor's range in the literal sense of limits of milieu and social and psychological type is the extensive reworking of the same material in such a way that the chapters of *Wise Blood* do not in fact render the stories which preceded them somehow obsolete; on the contrary, the stories retain their own interest and artistic integrity, their essential wholeness. This is true, too, of "The Geranium," the original version of "Judgement Day." This kind of reworking doesn't point, it seems to me, to artistic growth; it doesn't suggest improvement of an original. Rather, it points in an entirely different direction to a special concern or fascination with an idea or a character or some combination of the two so that they are repeatedly realized in many variations.

I have mentioned thus far the reworkings duly noted by the editor of the new collection, Robert Giroux, but there is one that seems to me as obvious as those he does mention, and perhaps he omits it because the alterations are in fact considerable. However, because the two—the novel, *The Violent Bear It Away*, and the story, "The Lame Shall Enter First"[8]—are so very much the same and yet so very different, I think they will reward careful examination. Moreover, as the two terms of the principle of *middle*, they will provide a translative context of ideas and feelings, a "World of Flannery O'Connor" at which we can look as an instance of the intelligibility of the universe.

The Violent Bear It Away, first published in 1955, is the earlier work by roughly seven years, "The Lame Shall Enter First" having appeared in *Sewanee Review* in summer 1962. The novel gives an account of an unwilling, apparent recipient of Grace, fleeing the call of God, yet finally caught despite himself. Its ultimate, archetypal source is in the Old Testament, in which three important prophets reject the call of God only to succumb at last to a power greater than themselves. The earliest is Moses, who, in the third chapter of Exodus, is summoned by the voice in the burning bush. He offers a series of excuses which exhaust the possibilities open to him: the Egyptians will not believe his message; the Israelites will reject him as spokesman; and, finally, when God has dealt with these arguments from "audience," he objects that he is "slow of speech." Aaron is then appointed as speaker, and Moses capitulates. The prophet Jeremiah objects, saying that he cannot speak because he is a child; but God literally, so to speak, puts the words into his mouth (Jeremiah 1: 6 and 9). Finally, Jonah flees rather than simply arguing, only to be pursued on sea by a fierce storm and cast into the belly of a big fish; when the Lord rescues him, he agrees to carry the prophetic message.

The "hero" of *The Violent Bear It Away*, Francis Marion Tarwater, shares important characteristics with prophets: like Samuel he has been brought up to be a prophet, and he believes that prophecy may be in his blood because his great-uncle, Mason Tarwater, who raised him, insists that he is himself a prophet. Jeremiah's prophetic provenance, for example, is unquestionably prenatal: "Before I formed thee in the belly I knew thee; and before thou camest forth out of the womb I sanctified thee, *and* ordained thee a prophet unto the nations." (Jeremiah 1: 5). Young Tarwater is also marked by a special sign of election, for the Lord has saved him from contamination by the city and by city schools.

These biblical congruences are important because Tarwater has learned reading, writing, and history with the Bible as his only text; the Bible is, for him, an account of the way things were and are. The narrative of his flight from the Lord is a tale of ambivalence, but not of a conflict between belief and disbelief in God. One flees a danger perceived as genuine, and young Tarwater rarely wavers in his belief in the Lord but, rather, only in his belief in his dead uncle's version of the Lord's will. Moreover, he does not even disbelieve altogether in that version of God's will so much as he dislikes and resents it. The great-uncle, Mason Tarwater, is dead when the text begins, and the simple, phenomenal facts of the death and its immediate aftermath are never in doubt. The very first sentence covers them thoroughly:

> Francis Marion Tarwater's uncle had been dead for only half a day when the boy got too drunk to finish digging his grave and a Negro named Buford Munson, who had come to get a jug filled, had to finish it and drag the body from the breakfast table where it was still sitting and bury it in a decent and Christian way, with the sign of its Saviour at the head of the grave and enough dirt on top to keep the dogs from digging it up.[9]

The circumstances as perceived by Tarwater follow in a matter-of-fact narrative voice which offers no comment of its own. The old man "had rescued him from his only other connection, old Tarwater's nephew, a schoolteacher who had no child of his own at the time and wanted this one of his dead sister's to raise according to his own ideas" (ibid.).

The nephew had taken the old man in for three months once, and old Tarwater was outraged to discover that he had been observed and used as material for a journal article explaining his "delusion" of a call from God as the result of insecurity. Tarwater fled, kidnaping young Tarwater, an infant then, baptizing him and raising him in his home in the woods. When the nephew, Rayber, tried to rescue his sister's child, the old man shot him, damaging the ear that might have heard the "word."

While digging a grave for the old man, young Tarwater recalls these stories heard when he was a child. When the old man told of shooting the schoolteacher Rayber, Tarwater felt free, as if he had "escaped some mysterious prison." But

> Then the child would feel a sullenness creeping over him, a slow warm rising resentment that this freedom had to be connected with Jesus and that Jesus had to be the Lord.
>
> "Jesus is the bread of life," the old man said.
>
> The boy, disconcerted, would look off into the distance. . . . In the darkest, most private part of his soul . . . was the certain, undeniable knowledge that he was not hungry for the bread of life. Had the bush flamed for Moses, the sun stood still for Joshua, the lions turned aside before Daniel only to prophesy the bread of life? Jesus? He felt a terrible disappointment in that conclusion, a dread that it was true. . . .
>
> The boy sensed that this was the heart of his great-uncle's madness, this hunger, and what he was secretly afraid of was that it might be passed down, might be hidden in the blood and might strike some day in him and then he would be torn by hunger like the old man, the bottom split out of his stomach so that nothing would heal or fill it but the bread of life. (p. 315)

These passages are the heart of the ambivalence. The old man has adjured the boy to carry out a mission of great importance should the old man die before he is able to do so himself: young Tarwater is to kidnap the mentally retarded son of the schoolteacher and baptize him. This is not young Tarwater's idea of a prophetic call. As he continues to dig in the hot sun he becomes aware of a new voice inside himself, the voice of "a stranger." Initially, he is aware of it as part of himself, a skeptical voice at last free to speak as he is now free of control with the death of the old man. When Buford and his wife find him digging the grave, he runs from them to escape their sympathy and questions, and he settles down with a bottle of the old man's hidden liquor. The voice

becomes more shrill and points out that the old man only wanted someone to bury him.

> Any man, seventy years of age, to bring a baby out into the
> backwoods to raise him right! Suppose he had died when
> you were four years old instead of fourteen? Could you have
> toted mash to the still then and supported yourself? I never
> heard of no four-year-old running a still.
>
> Never did I hear of that, he continued. You weren't any-
> thing to him but something that would grow big enough to
> bury him when the time came and now that he's dead, he's
> shut of you but you got two hundred and fifty pounds of
> him. . . . He said he brought you out here to raise you ac-
> cording to principle and that was the principle: that you
> should be fit when the time came to bury him so he would
> have a cross to mark where he was at. (p. 329)

Gradually, as he becomes more drunk, the voice is "his friend," and
tells him to forget about his "Redemption"; the old man deprived him
of company and knowledge.

> How do you know that two added to two makes four? Four
> added to four makes eight? Maybe other people don't think
> so. How do you know if there was an Adam or if Jesus eased
> your situation any when He redeemed you? Or how do you
> know if He actually done it? Nothing but that old man's word
> and it ought to be obvious to you by now that he was crazy.
> (p. 330)

Buford tries to get him to bury the old man, but he is too drunk.

> His cheekbones protruded, narrow and thin like the arms of
> a cross, and the hollows under them had an ancient look as if
> the child's skeleton beneath were as old as the world. "No-
> body going to bother you," the Negro muttered, pushing
> through the wall of honeysuckle without looking back. "That
> going to be your trouble." (p. 331)

When he awakens, he goes back to the clearing and sets fire to the
shack without looking inside. The act is astonishingly courageous because the old man had always feared that the schoolteacher might have
him cremated, and warned the boy not to permit it. Now young Tarwater believes he is burning the body himself, defying the notion of the
resurrection and all the other notions of his great-uncle. Then he runs
out to the highway and thumbs a ride into the city.

This first part of the text is itself an instance of the second. The second
is different in concrete detail, but the struggle between ideas and feelings is the same. The willful desire to reject one sort of call as unworthy,
the refusal to submit totally to God's will, opens the boy to the danger-

ous voice of the "stranger," "friend," who counsels not rejection but skepticism, and leads the boy to a terrible act, to burning the body and running to the city for refuge. That the city as refuge is a mistake is very economically suggested by the simple device of Tarwater's mistaking the lights of the city that the automobile is approaching for the lights of the fire he has left behind him.

Tarwater is wary of the driver who picks him up; he remembers the old man telling him that his mother, the schoolteacher's sister, was a whore and

> that with the devil having such a heavy role in his beginning, it was little wonder that he should have an eye on the boy.... "You are the kind of boy," the old man said, "that the devil is always going to be offering to assist, to give you a smoke or a drink or a ride, and to ask you your bidnis. You had better mind how you take up with strangers." (pp. 337–38)

He finally reaches his uncle and persuades him that the old man is dead; then he sees Bishop.

> Tarwater clenched his fists. He stood like one condemned, waiting at the spot of execution. Then the revelation came, silent, implacable, direct as a bullet.... He only knew, with a certainty sunk in despair, that he was expected to baptize the child he saw and begin the life his great-uncle had prepared him for. He knew that he was called to be a prophet and that the ways of his prophecy would not be remarkable. His black pupils... reflected... his own stricken image of himself, trudging into the distance in the bleeding stinking mad shadow of Jesus, until at last he received his reward, a broken fish, a multiplied loaf. (p. 357)

Part 1 ends with the call fully revealed and defiantly rejected: "'I won't have anything to do with him!' he shouted and the words were clear and positive and defiant like a challenge hurled in the face of his silent adversary" (p. 359). Part 2 is an account of Rayber's struggle to wean Tarwater from the influence of the old man, a struggle doomed to failure. Rayber wants to make up to the boy for having deserted him when he was a baby, but Tarwater rejects him out of hand. Rayber makes mistakes—talks about school, tries to give the boy an intelligence test, reawakens echoes of the old man's story of being put inside the schoolteacher's head. However, the most important part of this section of the book is the insight it offers into Rayber, who was also once kidnaped by the old man and never forgave the old man for returning him to his parents. He would seem to have rejected everything the old man stood for, but that is misleading.

> The love that would overcome him . . . was love without rea-
> son, love for something futureless, love that appeared to exist
> only to be itself, imperious and all demanding, the kind that
> would cause him to make a fool of himself in an instant. . . . It
> began with Bishop and then like an avalanche covered ev-
> erything his reason hated. He always felt with it a rush of
> longing to have the old man's eyes—insane, fish colored,
> violent   with   their   impossible   vision   of   a   world
> transfigured—turned on him once again. The longing was
> like an undertow in his blood dragging him backwards to
> what he knew to be madness.
>   He knew that he was the stuff of which fanatics and mad-
> men are made and that he had turned his destiny as if with
> his bare will. He kept himself upright on a very narrow line
> between madness and emptiness, and when the time came
> for him to lose his balance, he intended to lurch toward
> emptiness and fall on the side of his choice. (pp. 372–73)

Rayber discovers that Tarwater goes out every night to listen to a child preacher; when Rayber confronts him, Tarwater insists that he goes only "to spit on it" (p. 386). Shortly thereafter, Rayber takes Tarwater and Bishop to a lakeside lodge. Again he makes mistakes. In his exasperation he tells Tarwater " 'I can read you like a book.' The words were out before he could stop them" (p. 406). Then moments later he tells Tarwater that he is just like the old man, that "you have his future before you" (p. 407). Finally they stop quarreling and Tarwater takes Bishop for a ride in a row boat, and Rayber awaits them, asleep at the lodge. When he awakens it is night, and they haven't yet returned:

> What had happened was as plain to him as if he had been in
> the water . . . and the two of them together had taken the
> child and held him under until he ceased to struggle. . . . He
> knew . . . that he [Tarwater] had baptized the child even as he
> drowned him, that he was headed for everything the old man
> had prepared him for, that he moved off now . . . toward a
> violent encounter with his fate. . . . He stood waiting for the
> raging pain, the intolerable hurt that was his due, to begin,
> so that he could ignore it, but he continued to feel nothing.
> He stood light-headed at the window and it was not until he
> realized there would be no pain that he collapsed. (pp.
> 422–23)

Through Rayber, part 2 has shown concretely the life of someone touched with a special sensibility and the price he has paid to deny that sensibility. The very presence of Bishop is enough to make apparent Tarwater's struggle; Rayber's final insight transmits the result of the struggle. Since part 2 is told from Rayber's point of view, it becomes another realization of the paradigm. The terrible ambivalence and the struggle to flee from the burden of an intolerable gift are embodied in Tarwater in part 1 and in Rayber in part 2. The drowning of Bishop at the end of part 2 is ambiguous despite Rayber's certainty that Tarwater has baptized Bishop, i.e., said the ritual phrases. Yet we are certain, whatever the final significance of the drowning, that Tarwater has said the words; we believe Rayber. Why? First of all, in the course of the afternoon at the lodge, Rayber has recalled an earlier occasion there when he tried to drown Bishop and failed (pp. 403 ff.). And Rayber and Tarwater share a family resemblance, a "blood"; but more important is Rayber's own "education" at the hands of the old man. He understands Tarwater because they have been permanently scarred by the same kind of experience. And they are curiously linked further, for to lay down the intolerable burden of his frustrating love, Rayber really *permits* Tarwater to kill Bishop. Bishop's death is somehow the symbol of their common rejection of the old man's legacy. Yet, if killing Bishop is asserting Tarwater's freedom, baptizing Bishop is the opposite. The ambiguity must be resolved or the novel cannot end.

However, since any discernible "part" of a translative structure is a microcosm of the whole, we can ask at this point how part 2 can end when we are left with young Tarwater's ambiguous action and do not yet know the consequences of it for him. In other words, if we take into account only Tarwater, part 2 ought to continue; the novel ought not to be divided into three parts, or at least not here. On the other hand, in a sense our problem is similar to the one we isolated in chapter 5 in discussing Thomas Mann's *Death in Venice* as a translative novel. The leitmotif cannot be apprehended until the whole is made, in effect, in a second reading. Nevertheless, because this concrete translative whole offers two agents, who reflect one another in crucial ways—familial connection, the kidnaping experience in childhood, the early indoctrination in the old man's beliefs—we can ask how the agon is ended for Rayber. The conclusion, quoted at length above, is a perfect illustration of the way in which a translative novel of ideas and feelings must end. Translative novels are not only translations of a text from a context of discourse to that of the universe itself; they are also translations of ideas into occurrences, the embodiment of idea in concrete phenomena. In fact, a series of translations occurs: intellectual structure of the universe into idea expressed in discourse, idea into paradigm, paradigm into concrete phenomenon. We then can arrive at the original intelligible structure of the universe by proceeding in the opposite direction. We read the account of the concrete occurrences, discern the paradigm and the idea it embodies, and finally discern the idea as an expression of that intelligible structure.

Since such a generic organization translates ideas into occurrences, when the feelings evoked by the occurrences can no longer evolve and change, the novel ends. The final passages of part 2 end Rayber's reflection of the whole (i.e., its intelligible structure) because they mark the end of his capacity for feeling. He has suppressed feeling by substituting the one negative feeling of pain for love or joy or any other feeling. That is not, incidentally, an interpretive statement about symbolic import. We are told that he suppressed his desire for the old man's eyes "with their impossible vision of a world transfigured," by a "rigid ascetic discipline"; "he denied his senses unnecessary satisfactions" (pp. 372–73). The irony of the rigorous asceticism associated with deep religious commitment, undergone in the name of antireligion, is a terrible irony indeed. But the way of life of Rayber, ironic as it may be, is literally a cultivating of pain, and for quite obvious psychological reasons (although some interpretive readings may argue for less obvious ones as well). Anyone who has ever had a toothache, a severe headache, or an infected finger can attest to the way in which pain per se absorbs the attention and shuts out all other feelings. When Rayber discovers that Bishop's death does not cause him pain, he collapses. Nothing more occurs in the text to change Rayber's feelings. He has denied love and joy, and now pain is denied him. It is curiously worded. He has been "overwhelmed" by feelings of love and joy in the past and has actively suppressed them and avoided the stimuli that seem to evoke them. On the other hand, he has actively sought pain. Now the pain itself must come from outside, it is "his due," and he would then "ignore it." But he doesn't feel at all, and that pain has been denied him is overwhelming. At the end of part 2, Rayber seems emotionally dead and physically burnt out. Bishop's death removes the principal stimulus of the feelings of love and, unexpectedly, the motive for enduring pain. The source of change for Rayber's feelings is gone. We cannot interpret these variables until we make particulars of them in a thematic account. But we can say that part 2—microcosm of the whole as the whole is microcosm of a still larger whole—is ended.

Part 3 is only twenty pages long and takes us back to Powderhead, his and the old man's home, with young Tarwater. First he rides with a truck driver who needs someone to keep him awake by talking. Tarwater, however, is too preoccupied with his late activities to be of much use, and the trucker abandons him. It seems that Tarwater is determined to go home and live his own life, dismissing the words of baptism as trivial:

> "I'm going back there. I ain't going to leave it again. I'm in full charge there. No voice will be uplifted. I shouldn't never have left it except I had to prove I wasn't no prophet and I've proved it." He paused and jerked the man's sleeve. "I proved it by drowning him. Even if I did baptize him that was only an

accident. Now all I have to do is mind my own bidnis until I die. I don't have to baptize or prophesy." (p. 428)

Now it is clear that part 3 is necessary. Tarwater's fate cannot be finally determined until he *knows* that his great-uncle has been buried, for that is knowledge which might change his feelings once more. In a structure of ideas concretely embodied in occurrences, knowledge is always important. In the city Tarwater apparently learned that he couldn't avoid his fate unless Bishop no longer existed. He is resisting the ironic result of his action. Moreover, in order to learn of, and then to come to terms with, his great-uncle's burial, he must get home. The journey too, then, is important.

In the truck he says he is hungry: "I'm hungry for something to eat here and now. I threw up my dinner and I didn't eat no supper" (p. 429). The driver gives him a wrapped-up sandwich, but he doesn't open and eat it.

> "When I come to eat, I ain't hungry," Tarwater said. "It's like being empty is a thing in my stomach and it don't allow nothing else to come down in there. If I ate it, I would throw it up." (Ibid.)

Then he seems compelled to talk, and we learn his not unastute opinion of Rayber.

> "My other uncle knows everything," the boy said, "but that don't keep him from being a fool. He can't do nothing. All he can do is figure it out. He's got this wired head. There's an electric cord runs into his ear. [Rayber has a hearing aid as a result of the injury sustained when the old man shot him.] He can read your mind. He knows you can't be born again. I know everything he knows, only I can do something about it. I did," he added. (Ibid.)

Tarwater understands that Rayber himself has failed to escape the old man, and this makes comprehensible his rejection of Rayber. He has rejected Rayber emotionally, too, because Rayber failed to rescue him from the old man when he was a baby in Rayber's care (pp. 366–69). When the driver falls asleep, Tarwater recalls himself and Bishop in the boat, and "by his side, standing like a guide in the boat, was his faithful friend, lean, shadow-like, who had counseled him in both country and city" (p. 431). The stranger's voice of the beginning has gradually taken on shape and the identity of an "other." It is night, and in the darkness he sees his "friend's" eyes, "violet-colored, very close and intense, and fixed on him with a peculiar look of hunger and attraction. He turned his head away, unsettled by their attention" (ibid.). The friend tells him one must act in dealing with the dead; no word is enough to say NO (capitals in text). Suddenly, in this half-waking dream, Tarwater feels Bishop climb on his back and pull him down into the water. He becomes violently agitated, struggling to awaken, like "Jonah clinging wildly to the whale's tongue" (p. 432).

The truck driver throws him out at this point, and he proceeds to walk toward home. The sun becomes hotter and hotter and he tells himself again that he has saved himself from the old man's madness and the fate he envisioned when he first looked into Bishop's eyes and saw "himself trudging off into the distance in the bleeding stinking mad shadow of Jesus, lost forever to his own inclinations" (pp. 434–35). He tries to slake his terrible thirst at a well, but "the water had strangely not assuaged his thirst" (p. 436). He tries to buy a soda pop at a store, but the proprietress, who knows him, berates him for failing to bury his uncle (she does not tell him someone else did) and setting the house on fire, and he moves on. Finally, recalling yet again his great-uncle's warnings about strangers, he nonetheless accepts a ride in a lavender- and cream-colored car. The driver has lavender-colored eyes, and Tarwater is uneasy. Vanity leads him to accept a strange-tasting cigarette and drink of a burning, thick whiskey. He loses consciousness, and the narration explains that the stranger takes him into the woods for an hour and returns to his car with Tarwater's corkscrew, given him by Rayber, and his hat.

Tarwater awakens to find the sun above his head and himself naked except for his shoes. His hands are tied with a handkerchief said to have been left in exchange for the hat by the stranger who is referred to as Tarwater's "friend." He sets fire to the place wherever the stranger might have touched it. He then runs toward home, for he is close to Powderhead, although it now looks alien: "He knew that his destiny forced him on to a final revelation. His scorched eyes no longer looked hollow or as if they were meant only to guide him forward. They looked as if, touched with a coal like the lips of the prophet, they would never be used for ordinary sights again."[10]

Tarwater stops at a gap in the wood where the clearing of Powderhead is visible. He recalls his great-uncle's delight in the view, and again the text alludes to "Moses glimpsing the promised land" (p. 443). Tarwater sees the empty clearing, "the sign of a broken covenant" (p. 444), and then feels, senses someone behind him, and hears his friend urge him to take possession of the place and promise him that just as he has been with Tarwater since Tarwater began to dig the grave, he will never leave young Tarwater again. Now Tarwater can smell the presence, and he shakes free of it and burns all the bushes behind him, making a "wall of fire between him and the grinning presence" (ibid.), who is now, at last, perceived as an adversary.

When the boy reaches the clearing, it seems strange to him, "as if there might already be an occupant."[11] "Even the air seemed to belong to another." He is terribly hungry and, seeing Buford on a mule, thinks that he can go home with him and eat. Immediately, he becomes nauseated: "He blanched with the shock of a terrible premonition." He walks forward to meet Buford, the grave between them that Tarwater assumes is half dug. He looks down and sees the freshly mounded grave, at its head a cross, and his "hands opened stiffly as if he were dropping something he had been clutching all his life." The boy hears Buford tell him that he dug the grave and plowed the corn and erected the cross, but the boy doesn't speak, staring only at the cross. Buford senses a "burning in the atmosphere" and leaves abruptly.

Tarwater looks up at the field Buford has crossed, but he sees it peopled with a throng, including his great-uncle, waiting for the multiplied loaves and fishes:

> The boy too leaned forward, aware at last of the object of his hunger, aware that it was the same as the old man's and that nothing on earth would fill him. His hunger was so great that he could have eaten all the loaves and fishes after they were multiplied. . . . He felt his hunger no longer as a pain but as a tide. He felt it rising in himself through time and darkness, rising through the centuries, and he knew that it rose in a line of men whose lives were chosen to sustain it, who would wander in the world, strangers from that violent country where the silence is never broken except to shout the truth. (pp. 446–47)

He sees a red-gold tree of fire rising behind him—perhaps the glow of the fire he himself set. But "he knew that this was the fire that had encircled Daniel, that had raised Elijah from the earth, that had spoken to Moses and would in the instant speak to him. He threw himself to the ground and with his face against the dirt of the grave, he heard the command. GO WARN THE CHILDREN OF GOD OF THE TERRIBLE SPEED OF MERCY" (p. 447). By midnight he is on his way, the burning woods behind him, going toward the city, "where the children of God lay sleeping" (ibid.).

Part 3, then, in a rapidly accelerated account, shows Tarwater "burned clean" by the Lord, what old Tarwater has always claimed is the terrible fate of the prophet. The rape he experiences serves two purposes: it is a *kind of* expiation for his murder of the child and a penultimate necessary experiential insight into the old man's wisdom, an insight which leads to his repudiation of the "friend" whose "violet eyes," remembered in the truck reverie, seem like the lavender eyes of the rapist. But he is no longer free to reject the Lord as well. Already his home feels as if it belongs to someone else. It remains only for him to realize the truth about the hunger and nausea he has felt throughout his

flight home. Part 3 ends when the hunger and thirst have been identified as unchangeable feelings which cannot be assuaged in the
phenomenal universe we inhabit. The ambivalence is resolved and the
fleeing prophet caught at last, ending the novel itself. At the end of part
1, all of the component parts of Tarwater's flight and his ultimate
capitulation are present, for it ends after he has seen Bishop and seen
the significance of Bishop. The conflict and its ultimate outcome are
present in parts 2 and 3. The three parts are different one from the other,
but each in its way mirrors the whole. What is, then, the intellectual formulation of the prophetic paradigm?

For *The Violent Bear It Away*, qua translative whole, the structure of
the universe might be formulated as the interplay of the forces of nature
and supernature, nature and grace. The gifts of grace, of the spirit,
differ, but those gifts are rejected at our peril. Rayber's rejection is very
dear, and the bill is never finally settled. He seems to go on paying over
and over again. Young Tarwater struggles with his own very different
resources against a "gift" that also seems very different from Rayber's.
But Tarwater seems to have less choice, perhaps because he lacks the
sophistication that gives strength to systematic disbelief. The formulation is abstract, certainly, but under it can be subsumed the struggles of
the novel and those of the world as we know it; for men are always
struggling against their own nature-rooted vices and those of others
with whatever moral or spiritual resources they can muster. However,
before we consider further the principle I have tentatively formulated,
we must examine "The Lame Shall Enter First," which constitutes the
second term of the principle we will use to structure our "world of
Flannery O'Connor" and gives us a context for comparative analysis of
her work.

"The Lame Shall Enter First" reinforces at least one of the obvious
observations about short stories as compared with novels: if a story has
what we call characterization, it cannot be a function of circumstantial
detail—there isn't enough time for it (or space, if we prefer to say it that
way). In contrast with *The Violent Bear It Away* specifically, the absence
of detail seems to have resulted in a broader brush stroke—villainy, on
the face of it, and folly as well, seem more unambiguous for the lack of
complicating background and motivation. The story line itself, our primary interest for generic organization, seems easier to summarize.

Sheppard, a social worker who is City Recreational Director, works as
counselor at a reformatory, without pay, to help boys "no one else cared
about." His wife has been dead for over a year, and he has a ten-year-
old son whom he perceives as selfish, dull, and greedy, a boy who will
grow up to be "a banker. No, worse. He would operate a small loan
company."[12] Sheppard is distressed because his son Norton continues

to grieve for his mother, a grief Sheppard considers unhealthy after so long a time.

Sheppard has encountered fourteen-year-old Rufus Johnson in the reformatory, and his interest in Johnson is partly the result of Johnson's obvious intelligence—he has an IQ of 140. Rufus's father is dead, his mother is in the state penitentiary, and he has been raised in a shack by a fanatically religious grandfather who beats him. When he is released from the reformatory, Sheppard schemes to take Rufus in, hoping to rehabilitate him. For, the first time he saw the boy, "the case was clear to Sheppard instantly. His mischief was compensation for the foot" (p. 450), a monstrous club foot. If the boy had food and shelter and could learn the real truth about the world, he would be saved from a hopeless future. Their first exchange exemplifies the very uneasy relationship between them.

> "There are a lot of things about yourself that I think I can explain to you," he said.
> Johnson looked at him stonily. "I ain't asked for no explanation," he said. "I already know why I do what I do."
> "Well good!" Sheppard said. "Suppose you tell me what's made you do the things you've done?"
> A black sheen appeared in the boy's eyes. "Satan," he said. "He has me in his power."
> Sheppard looked at him steadily. There was no indication . . . that he had said this to be funny. The line of his thin mouth was set with pride. Sheppard's eyes hardened. He felt a momentary dull despair. . . . This boy's questions about life had been answered by signs nailed on the pine trees: DOES SATAN HAVE YOU IN HIS POWER? REPENT OR BURN IN HELL. JESUS SAVES. He would know the Bible with or without reading it. His despair gave way to outrage. "Rubbish!" he snorted. "We're living in the space age! You're too smart to give me an answer like that."
> Johnson's mouth twisted slightly. His look was contemptuous but amused. There was a glint of challenge in his eyes. (pp. 450–51)

After leaving the reformatory, Johnson finally uses the key to his house which Sheppard has given him, and the terrified, resentful Norton must make the best of it; for when, swelled with fury, he tells Sheppard that Johnson invaded his mother's room and used her comb, Sheppard ignores him, and Norton's account of Johnson's contemptuous comments on Sheppard himself draws this response: "I'd simply be selfish if I let what Rufus thinks of me interfere with what I can do for Rufus. If I can help a person, all I want is to do it. I'm above and beyond simple pettiness" (p. 458). After Sheppard leaves the room at the end of this speech, " 'God, kid,' Johnson said in a cracked voice, 'how do you stand it?' His face was stiff with outrage. 'He thinks he's Jesus Christ!' " (p. 459).

Sheppard places a telescope in the attic for Johnson, Norton shows no interest in it, and Johnson insists that he himself will not, contrary to Sheppard's prediction, go to the moon one day in his lifetime, and adds that when he dies he will go to hell. This marks the beginning of an argument about heaven and hell which ends with Johnson's promising to tell Norton all about heaven and hell when his father is away. Sheppard has told Norton that his mother doesn't exist anymore, and in the midst of the exchange between Sheppard and Johnson, Norton asks, in great agitation, whether his mother is in hell, and Sheppard repeats his dictum that she simply doesn't exist.

> His lot would have been easier if when his wife died he had told Norton she had gone to heaven and that some day he would see her again, but he could not allow himself to bring him up on a lie.
> Norton's face began to twist. A knot formed in his chin.
> "Listen," Sheppard said quickly and pulled the child to him, "your mother's spirit lives on in other people and it'll live on in you if you're good and generous like she was."
> The child's pale eyes hardened in disbelief.
> Sheppard's pity turned to revulsion. The boy would rather she be in hell than nowhere. (pp. 461–62)

Johnson tells Norton that if she believed in Jesus, his mother is in heaven, and Norton says, ignoring Sheppard's whispered denials, that she did.

Johnson is picked up by the police on a vandalism charge, insisting that he didn't do it. Sheppard allows him to spend a night in jail only to learn the next day that someone else had been caught and charged with the crime. Johnson uses the incident to play on Sheppard's feelings of guilt, and the next time the boy is picked up, Sheppard defends him. Later Johnson refuses to wear a new shoe Sheppard has ordered for the club foot, and he humiliates Sheppard in the shop. Gradually, Sheppard is becoming aware of Johnson's genuine contempt for him, and he finds it more difficult to endure despite his psychological explanations for Johnson's hostile behavior.

Meanwhile, since the discussion about heaven and hell, Norton has spent all his time looking through the telescope. Johnson now quarrels with Sheppard saying that in fact he did commit the crime for which another person was arrested and two others of which he was accused. Sheppard insists that he is going to "save" Johnson who counters with "Nobody can save me but Jesus" (p. 474). Sheppard cannot bring himself to throw Johnson out, but he "longed for the time when there would be no one but himself and Norton in the house, when the child's simple selfishness would be all he had to contend with, and his own loneliness" (p. 475). Norton has been converted to Bible reading. When Johnson says, "If I do repent, I'll be a preacher.... If you're going to do it, it's no sense in doing it halfway." Norton says he is going to be a space man (p. 476). Johnson then tells Sheppard as the exchange becomes increasingly heated, that Sheppard himself is in the power of Satan. Later, Johnson leaves the house, and Sheppard, anxious but relieved, finds Norton at the telescope in the attic and tells him to be in bed in fifteen minutes, ignoring Norton's shout: " 'She's there!' he cried, not turning around from the telescope. 'She waved at me!' " (p. 479).

Shortly thereafter, Johnson is brought back to the house by police, who have caught him in the act of vandalism. He insists that he wanted to be caught:

> "To show up that big tin Jesus!" he hissed and kicked his leg out at Sheppard. "He thinks he's God. I'd rather be in the reformatory than in his house, I'd rather be in the pen! The Devil has him in his power." (p. 480)

When Sheppard tries once more to speak to him, to reach him somehow, Johnson screams:

> "Listen at him! ...I lie and steal because I'm good at it! My foot don't have a thing to do with it! The lame shall enter first! The halt'll be gathered together. When I get ready to be saved, Jesus'll save me, not that lying stinking atheist, not that ..."[13]

Sheppard returns to the house, goes in, and recapitulates to himself all that he has done for Johnson, repeating three times, "I have nothing to reproach myself with" (p. 481). Then, suddenly, he says aloud,

> "I did more for him than I did for my own child." He heard his voice as if it were the voice of his accuser. He repeated the sentence silently....
> His mouth twisted and he closed his eyes against the revelation. Norton's face rose before him, empty, forlorn.... His heart constricted with a repulsion for himself so clear and intense that he gasped for breath. He had stuffed his own emptiness with good works like a glutton. He had ignored his own child to feed his vision of himself. He saw the clear-eyed Devil, the sounder of hearts, leering at him from the eyes of Johnson.... He saw Norton at the telescope.... A rush of agonizing love for the child rushed over him like a transfusion of life... the image of his salvation. (pp. 481–82)

He rushes back up to the attic only to find Norton "hung in the jungle of shadows, just below the beam from which he had launched his flight into space" (p. 482).

The Violent Bear It Away, as we saw, was a concrete embodiment of a prophetic paradigm taken from the Bible, and we were able to generalize the prophet's flight and subsequent capitulation to a universal conflict between nature and grace, human inclination and supernatural intervention. I want to emphasize that the generalization is not, as it may at first seem, reductive. Certainly the novel is rich in ideas, and its interest lies in its concrete and unique version of the paradigm rather than in the paradigm itself. But the paradigm is transparently present, giving unity and coherence to the structure in this translative organization, and we are at this point interested only in the structure of the uninterpreted variables preparatory to engaging in interpretation, arranging the variables in thematic readings.

First, we need to ask how "The Lame Shall Enter First" can be organized translatively, and second, whether and how the two structures of concrete occurrences can in any way be likened to the two terms of the principle of middle which organizes a translative structure. We do know that any translative whole ought to be conceivable equally well as part of another translative whole since it is in any case given its wholeness by virtue of the intelligibility of the universe of which it is an instance. (As noted in chapter 5, a translative novel must be thought of not as a text, but as an instance of intelligibility.) However, treating the two texts as independently reflections or parts of a universal ideational whole is not satisfactory. We want to put them in interrelation with one another and make of them a text, a "world of Flannery O'Connor"; and once having constituted this text and, in effect, named it, we should be able to show that the world of Flannery O'Connor will accommodate any named texts of Flannery O'Connor as parts which can then be compared with one another with respect to ideas embodied in thematic accounts or in single agents or occurrences or milieus and so on. We need to organize with at least two texts because a translative structure of ideas is organized around the interplay of a dichotomy. We know, then, that the texts we have chosen can be treated as parts or wholes without any difficulty as long as we are organizing translatively. Let us then return to "The Lame Shall Enter First" and give it a translative structure; then we can address the second question and try to structure the "world of Flannery O'Connor" using the two translative wholes taken together as parts.

Certainly the prophetic paradigm doesn't apply to the short story. If we refrain for the moment from any comparison with the novel, and any interpretation beyond a noting of essential details taken literally, we must first bear in mind that beginning, middle, and end qua parameters are irrelevant in a translative organization: With respect to a structure of ideas with no beginning or end, whether or when Sheppard encounters Johnson doesn't matter. What matters rather is: What do Sheppard's behavior and thoughts reflect? What do they seem to embody in the concrete? His earliest thoughts and exchanges with Norton are clear. They concentrate on Norton's dullness, greed, and selfishness. Norton has had advantages, Rufus Johnson hasn't—would Norton like having a mother in the penitentiary? "A knot of flesh appeared below the boy's suddenly distorted mouth. His face became a mass of lumps with slits for eyes. 'If she was in the penitentiary,' he began in a kind of racking bellow, 'I could go to seeeeee her.'" (p. 447).

Norton's grief elicits reproach, not pity; Norton's fascination with saving money evokes contempt, his eating habits provoke disgust. Sophisticated psychological theory is invoked to account for Rufus Johnson's hostility and his criminal vandalism; Sheppard doesn't use theories to account for Norton's collecting of money, his apparently compulsive eating, his persistent grief. The contrast is marked. The vocabulary of Sheppard's thoughts about Norton is radically different from that of his thoughts about Johnson. He wanted Norton to be "good," "unselfish" (p. 445), any "fault" is preferable to "selfishness," and Norton is "selfish," "unresponsive," and "greedy"; Sheppard also recalls, suggestively enough, that he never realized that the child was selfish when his mother was alive (p. 446). The "Norton vocabulary" is in fact garden variety moralistic. Finally, the narrator simply presents action in this section, but certain juxtapositions are highly communicative. Norton's eating habits are gross and repel his father, who, as I have said, comments on them aloud or in his thoughts. But Sheppard is presented without comment eating soggy cereal from a cardboard box, oblivious to his own lack of fastidiousness.

The Johnson vocabulary is very different: In their talks Johnson says things "in dissent or senseless contradiction," "for the sake of his pride" (p. 451). Johnson has a "kind of fanatic intelligence" (p. 449), and "nothing excited him [Sheppard] so much as thinking what he could do for such a boy" (pp. 451–52). After Johnson humiliates him at the brace shop where they've gone to fit a new shoe, Sheppard ponders the incident. "He realized that the boy had refused the shoe because he was insecure. Johnson had been frightened by his own gratitude. He didn't know what to make of the new self he was becoming conscious of. He understood that something he had been was threatened and he was facing himself and his possibilities for the first time. He was questioning his identity" (p. 471). In effect, Sheppard considers what can be seen as shortcomings—to say the least—in Johnson by means of a vocabulary of rationalization liberally sprinkled with psychological jargon. He thinks of Norton by means of a pejorative vocabulary.

At the end, of course, Sheppard undergoes a drastic alteration in perception; he sees himself at last in a new way. Leaving Johnson aside for the present, the literal surface of the text presents Sheppard as realizing that he has failed to love his child, that he has been a glutton himself, as selfish himself as he has accused Norton of being. We will have to consider presently what Sheppard *does not* realize and also try to understand why Norton dies at the end. But we can see that one way the story can be structured translatively—on the basis of the text itself, carefully examined—is in terms of love and the absence of love. If one considers Sheppard's words about Norton, one might justly contrast love with hate, which is, after all, simply a stronger term, more positive, than the absence of love or lovelessness. Without love of others, "good works" are sterile and even destructive. Sheppard doesn't pay attention to the reality of Johnson, nor does he "respect" (another *love* word) him enough to take him seriously. Sheppard believes he will experience joy in working with an extremely bright boy and making of him what Sheppard is certain he ought to be. Norton is apparently not bright enough, nor does he show interests Sheppard respects and which would, one suspects, satisfy Sheppard's ego were he to discover them in his child.

Without love, then—in its widest sense—the activities of men are empty and worse, evil, and we can generalize this struggle between loving activity and loveless activity, activity motivated by concern for others and that motivated by concern only for one's own perceived needs; it is in another kind of formulation the contrast between treating people as subjects or treating them as objects. We can translate this struggle to the structure of the universe. It is an overarching, englobing principle in terms of which the universal life of humankind can be understood in all its variety.

We can turn now to our second question: How can these two texts be used as the two terms of a translative dichotomy? We would be involved in what seems to me an empty mechanical exercise were we to argue simply that love and lovelessness can really be assimilated to nature and grace. They can be, since the terms of a rhetorical commonplace are always empty variables until they are given meaning by particularization to a concrete situation. But a context for comparative study should be richly concrete; if it remains abstract formulation it is not very interesting, and comparisons on the abstract level would be obvious and offer little insight.

However, if we look at the problem from the point of view of function, we may be able to show how the two stories, taken together, give us a world of Flannery O'Connor. We begin with the nature of commonplaces, empty, uninterpreted terms until they are used to make a concrete meaningful situation. For example, good and bad mean nothing really until we attribute them. When I speak of good oranges I know that good is a favorable evaluation of taste, texture, ripeness, etc. It is a judgment based on criteria relevant to judging food consumed by humans. The "goodness" of hats and that of ballet performances are again different kinds of goodness.

On the other hand, a commonplace does have meaning of a sort insofar as each of the terms functions to make meaning possible to the other. "Good" would have no meaning even in application to oranges or anything else except in terms of "bad," and the reverse is true as well. The "supernatural" makes sense only if there is a "natural" one contrasts it with. "Natural" is also meaningless except in relation to "super" or "unnatural" or "artificial," and so on (each, together with natural, producing a totally different commonplace).

If we look at the two texts we have organized, they will function as commonplaces do *if each illuminates the other*. Then, just as the terms of commonplaces functioned to make the formulations with which we organized each text into a coherent whole, the two texts should, between them, function to furnish a context of ideas which will give structure to "the world of Flannery O'Connor," a whole within which a great variety of parts can be compared.

The extent to which *The Violent Bear It Away* illuminates "The Lame Shall Enter First," and the converse, is extraordinary; this is certainly the case because of the similarities between them which indeed strike the reader as fairly clear evidence that the short story is a conscious reworking of the novel (since the story is, of course, later). Whether or not Flannery O'Connor did consciously rework the ideas in the novel,[14] a comparison of the two, side by side so to speak, suggests strongly that assuming that she did would yield worthwhile results. The agents of *The Violent Bear It Away* form a triangle that we would recognize in "The Lame Shall Enter First": the fathers, sole parents of unsatisfactory sons, in a decisive conflict with potential surrogate sons who reject the fathers and their values and are responsible for destroying the natural sons. In addition, these surrogate sons share a fundamentalist religious orientation. It is furthermore hard not to recognize the identity of Sheppard with Rayber, of Bishop with Norton, of young Tarwater with Johnson. Moreover, in both stories the father, Sheppard-Rayber, is attempting to uphold and transmit rational secular, humanistic values to a boy, Tarwater-Johnson, steeped in a fundamentalist Bible culture, who sees this attempt as an effort to somehow enslave him; whereas Sheppard-Rayber sees himself as trying to save the boy from a terrible future.

These likenesses are unmistakable; but the differences are more interesting still. We can let the commonplace of doers and what is done organize the comparison, and we realize immediately that the terms of the commonplace, as is characteristic of rhetorical commonplaces, oriented to the perspectives of agents, begin to merge and interpenetrate. Take "what is done," the action. The action of the novel is based formally on the prophetic paradigm, and it concerns Francis Marion Tarwater's struggle to escape his destiny, his prophetic vocation. That the action of the short story seems radically different is immediately apparent. No one is attempting to escape a consciously recognized imperative; certainly not Rufus Johnson, Tarwater's counterpart in our assumption that this is a reworking of the earlier story. The ending is at first glance similar; the rural, fundamentalist adolescent is responsible—directly in the novel, indirectly in the story—for the death of the younger child. In both stories the father is in some way culpable in failing to prevent that death, or in permitting it to occur. But, above all similarities, the difference of action is marked and is inextricable from the difference in the doers, the agents and how they are characterized. That is, *The Violent Bear It Away* is young Tarwater's story; "The Lame Shall Enter First" is Sheppard's story.

The narrative point of view supports that conclusion, if it needs any support other than the reader's immediate experience. The novel is not told exclusively from Tarwater's point of view—for example, a narrator lets the reader know that Buford Munson has buried old Mason Tarwater while the boy is asleep drunk. But most of parts 1 and 3 are inside or observational views of young Tarwater, and the deviations are made only to clarify the action or, as in the burial information of part 1, to make the point that, despite young Tarwater, forces are at work to prevent him from doing anything that would make irrevocable his rejection of what he sees as a demeaning and, also, frightening prophetic call. Part 2 focuses on Rayber as what Tarwater might become if he could break loose from the old man's conditioning by means of secular, scientific educational values. Rayber's recollections, both silent and offered in dialogue with Tarwater, correct and illuminate and frequently verify Tarwater's account in interior monologue of the family past as told him by his great-uncle. We will return to Rayber presently. But clearly the story of the novel is Tarwater's, as the conflict of the novel is his.

In Johnson we sense no conflict at all. Again, an omniscient narrator presents Johnson's encounters with Norton since Norton must be actively won over by the threatening Johnson as an inert, mentally deficient Bishop need not be by Tarwater. But the story of the struggle to save Johnson, which ends so disastrously, is Sheppard's story, and the narration is overwhelmingly given from his point of view—again from both an inside view and an occasional observational stance.

Thus the change in story line is marked and, in the last analysis, is inseparable from some major changes in character. When you change what is done, the doers are no longer the same, and, conversely, different doers produce different doings. The conflict between Rayber and young Tarwater is, of course, the very core of *The Violent Bear It Away*. Why? Because Rayber's child is the "object" upon which is focused Tarwater's rebellion against his great-uncle's interpretation of God's will. He must fail in that first "mission" laid upon him by the old man—to baptize Bishop. Rayber himself functions in a secondary way. He confirms Tarwater's suspicions of him, planted by the old man, by making two mistakes which symbolize all his errors of "tone": he lets slip his intention to send the boy to school—and never having gone to school means "freedom" to the boy—and he tries to give Tarwater an intelligence test. Furthermore, Tarwater himself points out that Rayber could have saved him from the old man by coming back to Powderhead a second time with a gun. Clearly Rayber has failed to win Tarwater before even trying; Tarwater's "stranger's voice" has told him that the old man may have lied to him about many things. But in Rayber the boy sees no evidence of that, and in roaming the city his encounter with a child evangelist preacher makes clear that the old man's ideas are not totally absent in the city. The Rayber interlude in part 2 of the book is really Tarwater's search for a way of life outside of Powderhead and his failure to find it. In other words, his struggle against the "call" is not permitted to seem identical with an attraction to the secular values of the city as exemplified by his uncle—rational humanism, scientific psychology, education. Tarwater does not reject prophecy because he rejects the concept of an almighty God calling him to great deeds, but because he rejects the "bleeding stinking mad shadow of Jesus" (pp. 434–35).

Finally, Rayber articulates the old man's influence, and perhaps an innate, mysterious family trait, in a more sophisticated way than Tarwater does, and thus he gives a dimension to the boy's ultimate commitment that could not be achieved through inside views of the boy alone at his present age and stage of development. The kind of "grace" Rayber has rejected is expressed in terms of love rather than a call to prophecy. "The love that would overcome him was of a different order entirely. It was not the kind that could be used for the child's improvement or his own. It was love without reason, love for something futureless, love that appeared to exist only to be itself, imperious and all demanding, the kind that would cause him to make a fool of himself in an instant" (p. 372). To the extent that he shares "blood" and the old man's influence with Tarwater, the inside views of Rayber deepen and expand the meaning of and feeling for the significance of Tarwater's struggle and his eventual acceptance of the "call."

This brief review of *The Violent Bear It Away* brings into vivid relief the radical change in perspective represented by "The Lame Shall Enter

First." That story is Sheppard's, and the prophecy motif is gone. Rayber's plan to educate Tarwater never gets off the ground. Rayber relives his past bitterness against the old man, his guilt over his sister's child, but he never has a chance even to attempt to help Tarwater. Sheppard's contact with Johnson is in itself a function of rehabilitative, educative machinery. There is no common, shared kinship or past between them, and Sheppard consistently misunderstands and underestimates the depth of Johnson's beliefs as Rayber could not. On the other hand, Sheppard gets a chance to try to educate Johnson because Johnson has no sense of mission to complicate the task.[15]

Let me interrupt the "comparison and contrast" at this point to return to our initial assumption that O'Connor reworked the novel. First let me reformulate the novel's translative structure—human moral life as a constant, tense interplay between the inclinations of human nature and the imperatives imposed by the intervention of the supernatural in the form of grace, which confers both insight into true values and the strength to pursue them, a strength men naturally lack. Rayber rejects the grace clearly received—what else is the useless, overwhelming love if not a mode of Grace? Even if it is interpreted psychologically, it remains atypical and is therefore a structural and functional analogue to Grace as we are treating that term. Young Tarwater is not permitted to reject the Grace given him, and its form is interesting: unlike Rayber, he accepts intellectually, *believes* what old Tarwater told him. Then he says no, he doesn't like what it means, and he will refuse to live according to such an imperative. He flees and is pursued in various ways by the force against which he struggles. We don't have to interpret that force at the moment. It is enough to say that Tarwater flees a call to prophecy, but the sight of Bishop reminds and terrifies him, the unsatisfactory uncle narrows his options further, the child evangelist preaches an uncomfortable message. (Her phrases are painfully like the old man's "the word of God is a burning word to burn you clean." "Burning clean" is old Tarwater's constantly reiterated account of the prophet's fate in the hands of God.) Rayber as well as Tarwater is secretly listening outside, and each seems to feel her words addressed to himself, Rayber consciously experiencing a deep desire to save her from "exploitation," then:

> Suddenly she raised her arm and pointed toward his face. "Listen you people," she shrieked, "I see a damned soul before my eye! I see a dead man Jesus hasn't raised. His head is in the window but his ear is deaf to the Holy Word!"
> Rayber's head, as if it had been struck by an invisible bolt, dropped from the ledge.... Inside she continued to shriek. (p. 385)

When they leave on the trip during which Tarwater will drown Bishop:

> [Tarwater's] mind was entirely occupied with saving himself from the larger grander trap that he felt set all about him. Ever since his first night in the city when he had seen once and for all that the schoolteacher was of no significance—nothing but a piece of bait, an insult to his intelligence—his mind had been engaged in a continual struggle with the silence that confronted him, that demanded he baptize the child and begin at once the life the old man had prepared him for. . . .
>
> His fourth night in the city, after he had returned from listening to the child preach, he had sat up in the welfare-woman's bed and raising his folded hat as if he were threatening the silence, he had demanded an unmistakeable sign of the Lord. (pp. 398, 400)

We also learn earlier that since the breakfast at which the old man died, Tarwater has suffered a peculiar hunger, and the abundant city food given him by his uncle only "weakened him." Also, the many times he might have baptized Bishop, but refrained, he was able to refrain only because of "the wise voice that sustained him—the stranger who had kept him company while he dug his uncle's grave" (pp. 398–99).

The novel does indeed embody our formulation of its structure. Rayber rejects a more than mundane, natural love, at the price of constant vigilance and pain. At the end, he pays the price of terrible emptiness—even pain denied him. Tarwater who takes the call, the grace, for granted, who somehow always *knows* it is true that God calls people (even if he doubts his great-uncle's version of the call), doesn't *feel* the grace given as Rayber does; he begins to feel after the old man's death when he begins to run, and what he feels is purely physical—an odd hunger. At the end, when he sees the grave dug by Buford, he feels the hunger intensely and has the vision which explains it to him.

I have recapitulated these details to point out that to Rayber, who is educated and skeptical, Grace communicates unmistakably through a *nonnatural feeling* of love. Rayber feels grace because he can't believe, and he rejects the feeling as a kind of congenital madness, just as he rejected the ideas. But it is much harder to control the feeling, to reject it consciously and by means of the will, than to reject the idea of God and of Jesus Christ as redeemer of mankind. Tarwater's struggle, paradoxically if one attributes intellectual struggle to the educated only, is essentially intellectual. Thus an arguing, plausible stranger within must objectify his conflict; Rayber can't function as the opposing force, as antagonist, because he consistently misunderstands Tarwater's conflict. He thinks the boy feels guilty; Tarwater doesn't feel guilty even though he believes he burned his great-uncle. He *knows* the forces he's dealing with and believes that they are real, objective forces, and therefore he is afraid that burning the old man won't be a positive enough statement of rejection. And of course it isn't! He *didn't* in fact burn old Tarwater, and he *does* finally baptize Bishop. Rayber doesn't share Tarwater's structure of belief (or can't permit himself to do so consciously—it makes no difference which we suppose to be the case), and only someone who did might argue that God didn't call Tarwater to prophecy. Rayber is, rather, possessed by a structure of feeling commensurate with Tarwater's structure of belief. Tarwater, on the other hand, cannot feel until he has finally accepted the truth about his hunger.

If, as I believe, this view of the shape of O'Connor's novel is plausible, what did it *fail* to communicate, what meaning did it obliterate or exclude in order to embody the meaning we have organized for it? This seems a useful way of asking what the short story shows as missing in the novel, and, of course, the converse. Or, in other words, why did O'Connor rework the novel? We must bear in mind that this is not a substantive question framed to elicit a "true" answer. Rather, from the perspective of structure as communication, of structure as the thought of the whole, can the comparison of the two shed light on a dimension of meaning which might have emerged but did not in the novel? If the novel and story were not sufficiently similar, the question would be pointless, of course; it is just because they are so similar that the question arises. Let us first examine more carefully now, with the question in mind, some very marked differences between the two stories.

First of all, the question of "call," of "vocation" is absent from "The Lame Shall Enter First"; also, as we have seen, the story is focused on Sheppard. Whereas in the novel Tarwater's flight initiates the action, in the story Sheppard's gift of a house key to Johnson, his cultivating of Johnson, initiates the action. With respect to the agents, old Tarwater has not been replaced by some other historical link between Sheppard and Johnson; Sheppard, too, is a skeptic but lacks Rayber's bitterness toward a belief he once held. Johnson seems almost wholly evil; in behavior reported and in scenes with Sheppard and/or Norton, he is portrayed quite unsympathetically. His title to our sympathy stems from matter reported secondhand by Sheppard—mother in jail, grandfather beat him, is hungry and homeless. At no time are sympathy-evoking traits dramatized in the story except for the club foot, a silent physical trait which cannot negate the unpleasant impression conveyed by dramatized action and speech. Young Tarwater, on the other hand, is not especially likable, but the constant inside view of him inevitably communicates him as less reprehensible than Johnson, whose mind is known only in its expression in speech. We are permitted to understand young Tarwater's feelings, and these somehow mitigate his shortcomings. Finally, Norton is not a "hopeless case" as is Bishop; but, neither brilliant nor lovable, he has a normal intelligence capable of responding and changing.

With the novel and the story functioning as commonplaces, we can ask what one means in light of the other. One interesting result of that query is what we see in Rayber. Like all protagonists who are depicted as clearly suffering, he arouses sympathy. He is embittered by old Tarwater's failure to fight to keep him as a child, and old Tarwater's god who permits horrors like Bishop to be born and to thrive infuriates him; and Bishop is a terrible cross to bear together with his wife's treachery in deserting him and his own guilt over deserting young Tarwater. All of this—the suffering and its palpable causes—blinds us to Rayber's overwhelming self-absorption, his arrogant assumption that he can, all alone, without help, control his life. Then, too, a man of insight and learning, he presumes to judge his great-uncle mad and uses him without any thought for the old man's right to his dignity and privacy. His intelligence and insight ought to tell Rayber that his own bitterness might render his "scientific" judgments suspect, but they do not. Simple moral decency, a humanistic value without religious connotation, ought to prevent him from misleading the old man and using him for a learned article without his consent. Finally, Rayber knowingly permits Tarwater to relieve him of his burden by killing Bishop. Rayber's great suffering obscures the significance of what he has done throughout—to the old man; to Tarwater, deserting the child at the behest of the social worker he married who disliked and feared the infant Tarwater when she first saw him; to Bishop, whom he sends to an almost certain death which he can't himself inflict. It is sentimental not to judge him harshly.

But the suffering does elicit our sympathy; furthermore, he speaks the reader's language as the atypical Tarwaters, young and old, do not. It is Sheppard, treating a normal, grieving child shabbily, whom we can see with greater moral clarity. If we stop here, we can at least begin to answer the question. Rayber and Sheppard are middle-class educated skeptics; neither is depicted as a great or innovative scholar. Rayber is a schoolteacher and Sheppard a social psychologist of some kind as nearly as we can tell. They would seem to represent the kind of persons who hold master's degrees in education and social services. Each is unambiguously contemptuous of the ingenuous, unlettered, backwoods fundamentalist. Incidentally, it is both interesting and important that the beliefs of the fundamentalists are not treated in any great detail, or opposed by protagonists in any great detail. They believe that Jesus Christ was and is God in the flesh and mankind's redeemer. What flows from this varies. In the novel a prophet calls sinners to repent and *believe*; the belief is the object of Rayber's ambivalent contempt. In the story, belief in the devil also figures prominently[16] and Sheppard is contemptuous of that, too.

Thus far, then, I would suggest that Rayber's attitude toward his nephew and his son takes into account the fact that the one is defective and the other has been formed by the detestable teachings of old Tarwater. Rayber's two separate stances, then, determine courses of action he takes with respect to each and to the two together, the consequences of which might not be noticed if the complex relations of Rayber to Tarwater and Bishop are not taken into account. I have already discussed at length the effect of Rayber's relation to old Tarwater and the suffering it caused him. Also, if a child is as defective as Bishop, to feed and clothe him, protect him and refrain from mistreating him in any way, is sufficient. Thus, to judge Rayber as morally culpable is very difficult. In Sheppard, O'Connor removed the bitterness of background, the complex relation to young Tarwater which makes taking him in a matter of no choice for Rayber. Finally, she removed the retarded child only a monster could mistreat.

In Sheppard she depicted a man able to delude himself about his behavior toward his son because he didn't beat him or starve him! Yet Sheppard's cruelty to Norton is shocking. I have already quoted the relevant passages. His eating is criticized, his saving money, his continuing grief for his mother. With respect to Johnson, a habitual criminal whatever the reasons, Sheppard behaves irresponsibly, forcing him on a frightened and resentful Norton. Moreover, Sheppard is contemptuous of Johnson's beliefs and arrogantly convinced that he himself knows what to do for Johnson and why Johnson behaves as he does (ironically, indeed, since he admires Johnson for measurably extraordinary intelligence, yet he dismisses the reasonings of that mind out of hand).

In fact, Sheppard is arrogant and self-absorbed, and lacks respect for the privacy and dignity and opinions of others, specifically Johnson and Norton. In fact, as we have seen, these are Rayber's serious faults, too. And as Rayber puts Bishop in the power of a desperately obsessed boy, so Sheppard does the same to Norton. But Johnson is unequivocally a criminal as young Tarwater is not. What O'Connor has reworked then, first of all, is the kind of moral culpability characteristic of Rayber, but she has made those changes which make it less ambiguous, less obscured. Mitigating circumstances are gone. With the absence of an agonizing past, with a violent and destructive "Tarwater" and a "Bishop" who no longer seems less than human and without a future, the blind moral arrogance of Rayber becomes perfectly lucid in Sheppard.[17]

But if Rayber is illuminated by Sheppard, what does Rufus Johnson force us to see in Tarwater? As I have tried to point out, Johnson's unbridled speech and criminal behavior underline Sheppard's irresponsible arrogance: to try to help a delinquent boy is one thing; to remain blithely unaware that one has put one's child in danger in order to do so is quite another. Sheppard has a presumptuous faith in himself and his powers, and the presumption is vividly realized in his interaction with Johnson. But can Rufus Johnson show us something we have missed in Tarwater? It would be, as in the case of Rayber and Sheppard, a different illumination from the kind applicable to Sheppard in the story which contains them both.

Tarwater's story, like Tarwater himself, is atypical; indeed, the prophetic paradigm is atypical. I tried to emphasize, in comparing Tarwater's "call" and Rayber's "love" as instances of grace, that Tarwater's belief is never in question. He believes but doesn't like what he believes and wants to escape. Rayber only *feels* the intense love, and without a systematic way of life, a structure of belief with which to integrate that love, the love is terrifying, a form of madness to be fought and controlled.

Tarwater's struggle to evade his destiny tends to create the impression that he is struggling against belief in the universal power which has called him. The state of his mind, however, is much more fluid than his decisive actions would imply. At first he accepts his prophetic mission; then he is resentful because the old man's speeches about God's "trying" of the prophet and "burning him clean" sound grand at the beginning, but always end with Jesus multiplying loaves and fishes for all eternity, a final reward which horrifies and depresses the boy. Then, too, baptizing an "idiot," Tarwater's first mission according to his great-uncle, seems a paltry task beside that of Moses to whom God spoke through a burning bush. Still drunk, he sets fire to the house in which he supposes the body sits awaiting burial. That act and his subsequent behavior in the city are instigated by the stranger, the voice who repeatedly denies the accuracy of old Tarwater's beliefs.

Nevertheless, young Tarwater lacks throughout any cultural or intellectual resources that could sustain him in a serious rejection of his great-uncle's structure of belief. Rayber cannot reach him, as we have seen, and the city qua city, the urban milieu as opposed to the rural, fails to attract him sufficiently. The voice alone effectively counsels rejection, and always in a way that does not overtly deny God so much as it calls into question the old man's interpretation of God's will. The real issue for Tarwater is the prophetic life that he dreads, and not even the life, but the being caught up by it, hungering for it. Thus the idea of Jesus Christ as God and only source of redemption is muted in Tarwater by the complexities of the novel. Moreover, Tarwater is a fully realized protagonist, complex and ambiguous, morally and psychologically. His vision at the end may or may not be the delusion of a psychopath brought on by the severe traumas of killing Bishop and being raped. Is the stranger the devil or does Tarwater mistake an auditory hallucination for the devil when he sets fire to the surrounding shrubbery the last time he hears the voice? The text is open to either interpretation; consequently, Tarwater is never an unambiguous embodiment of Christian belief any more than Rayber is an unambiguous embodiment of its opposite.

In contrast to Tarwater, Rufus Johnson is not in conflict with himself or his beliefs. Thus Johnson set in opposition to Sheppard is an unambiguous criticism of Sheppard. Johnson is surely a monster—whether for the reasons Sheppard deduces early in the story, or for the reason he gives himself, that he is in the power of Satan; but his charges against Sheppard ring true. He is very intelligent, and he sees Sheppard's rationalizations and dogmatic pronouncements for what they are, egotistical and presumptuous. In "The Lame Shall Enter First" O'Connor cuts the symbiotic relations between Rayber and Tarwater and gives Johnson a catalytic function, shifting to Sheppard as protagonist. Then, with the dropping of the prophetic paradigm, a structure of ideas implicit in the novel can become explicit in the story.

The complex interplay between the irrational, overwhelming love *felt* by Rayber and the prophetic vocation *believed in* by young Tarwater, and the efforts of the one to defy the feeling of love and the other to defy the belief in vocation—these conflicts obscure a third implicit for both Rayber and Tarwater: is it true that Jesus Christ was God incarnate and mankind's redeemer? The answer to that question is overwhelmingly important once it is admitted as a question at all.[18] Rayber seems to deny it; however, his special functions vis-à-vis young Tarwater, and his consequent complexities as a character in this reading, reduce his capacity to function as a vehicle for the communication of that idea—affirmed or denied—as part of the intellectual structure of the whole. Tarwater, on the other hand, denies that he believes what the old man taught him—but the old man taught him that Jesus Christ was his savior as well as that he was to be a prophet. What he is denying is ambiguous, and when he listens to the skeptical "voice," even the voice doesn't deny God or Jesus. Toward the end of part 2, late in the novel, the voice says: "The Lord speaks to prophets personally and He's never spoke to you, never lifted a finger, never dropped a gesture. And as for that strangeness in your gut, that comes from you, not the Lord. When you were a child you had worms. As likely as not you have them again" (p. 399). Since the action is young Tarwater's, the prophetic paradigm dominates, and the existence of God and/or the divinity of Christ never emerge as clear structural principles of the novel.

In "The Lame Shall Enter First," Johnson, another fundamentalist, backwoods version of Tarwater, articulates the question clearly, for behind the vividly loveless self-absorption of Sheppard stands the arrogant belief that men can save themselves and one another, a belief given paradoxical evangelical fervor in Rayber yet softened in its boldness and obscured in its implications by his genuine grievances and agonized griefs. And Johnson, with no apparent ambivalence, presented only through his reported actions and quoted speech, is in unambiguous opposition to Sheppard. The story is Sheppard's, so that it communicates through him, and Johnson is known only in relation to Sheppard. Therefore, Johnson's inner life never obscures the clear view of Sheppard which Johnson's words and actions offer.

As fundamental, then, as the love-hate dichotomy in the story is that of truth and falsehood. Sheppard is blind to his selfish failure to love Norton precisely because the delusion that he has the power to save Johnson, and that he knows the truth about human beings and their motivations, makes him vulnerable to his weakness, his human need for self-esteem. The brilliant Johnson would be so much more exciting and gratifying to teach and mold and rescue from superstition and ignorance than the rather ordinary, average Norton who lacks even any interests his father could admire. In the absence of a belief in God is bred arrogance; no matter how benign Sheppard's motives with respect to Johnson seem, how sincerely he wants to help a terribly disadvantaged boy, because Sheppard "knows" the truth without God, he doesn't pay attention to Johnson at all, really, or recognize that his efforts are doomed to fail. He pays attention only to his own preconceived, conventional interpretations of behavior "like" Johnson's.

Sheppard's lack of love is not to be construed here as a lack of "feeling"; rather it is an intellectual matter, a question of deliberate choice. That is, Sheppard *behaves* unlovingly toward Norton. A man cannot help what he feels; even if he feels no warmth for his own child, sad as that is. But he can be faulted for treating that child as Sheppard treats Norton. And only a thoroughly, thoughtlessly arrogant man translates his lack of feeling into punitive behavior and moralistic judgments.

Sheppard, not burdened by a futureless child, then, expresses the arrogance of unbelief clearly, as the suffering Rayber does not. And Johnson's obvious "badness"—the theft and vandalism, the bullying, the lying and contempt for others—places Sheppard's blindness and moral irresponsibility in stark relief. Moreover, Johnson's unambiguous belief, uttered time and again in one form or another, renders a special sort of judgment on Sheppard's arrogance. One can judge Sheppard harshly from a humanistic point of view, and the text will support such a judgment. But Johnson's judgment goes beyond Sheppard's treatment of Norton—to which, to be sure, Johnson would seem to be cynically indifferent—and merges that treatment with Sheppard's benign intentions toward himself to produce a judgment, not against behavior but against the false beliefs which underlie it.

Rhetorical paradox is never resolved, however, and the terms of a translative dichotomy are not seen as substantive as are those of a dialectical dichotomy, but are rhetorical commonplaces and thus interchangeable. In other words, in both the novel and the story, good and evil, love and hate, knowledge and ignorance, truth and falsehood, the most important commonplaces we have been using, are composed, each of them, of interchangeable terms. For one thing, then, there is a sense in which the story is as much Johnson's as the novel is Tarwater's, for Johnson's unambivalent belief in what he perceives as truth makes him an active agent as the uncertain Tarwater cannot be. Johnson wants to leave Sheppard's home—he gets caught in a criminal act and achieves his desire. He believes in heaven and hell and tells Norton flatly that if his mother wasn't a whore, and believed in Jesus, she is in heaven. These consequences of his certainty generate movement. Johnson acts; Tarwater seems rather to react.

Conversely, the novel is as much Rayber's as the story is Sheppard's. Rayber doesn't share Tarwater's uncertainty, and Rayber's decision—presumptuously based on a mechanical use of psychology to conclude that Tarwater feels guilty—to drive Tarwater back to Powderhead to confront his impious act (of burning his great-uncle's corpse) places Bishop and Tarwater in the situation in which the murder of Bishop is inevitable; and the consequent baptism of Bishop seals Tarwater's fate.

The ambiguity in both novel and story is persistent, and in a comparative perspective each calls to our attention the ambiguities of the other. Johnson's delinquencies, his initial cruelties to Norton, the triumphant humiliating of Sheppard in the shoe shop—all of these are crowned by the brilliant symbol of the club foot. For in that foot are merged a psychological source of aberrant behavior, a diabolic symbol of unity with the cloven-footed Satan, and a Christian promise of a salvation into which the lame enter first. But the figure of Rufus Johnson *only seems* to embody evil unambiguously; for other than telling Norton about heaven and hell and committing crimes against property, he does nothing remotely as genuinely treacherous as burning the body of old Tarwater, the man who raised young Tarwater and believed in the resurrection of the body, or as truly wicked as drowning a helpless child.

If the intransigent ambiguity of this world of Flannery O'Connor is now evident, both a problem and its resolution should be emerging. A context for comparative analysis ought to be richly concrete, and in the course of trying to form a context, a "world" of Flannery O'Connor, I have been quite concrete. Furthermore, I have gone about the task of making a context for comparative analysis by *doing* comparative analysis. There is in fact no other way to achieve the concreteness we require. But in exhibiting the ambiguity of this world by concrete, detailed comparison of two texts, we risk losing the unity and coherence guaranteed by an organizational principle, and, even more unfortunate, we begin to see the exemplary particulars we have made for the sake of appreciating the richness of the texts as fixed interpretations of the texts' meanings. How do we regain coherence without sacrificing the rich specificity of our critical recreation of these two texts, and how do we recognize once more that there is an indefinite number of interpretations possible of each of the texts, and that the ones we have suggested are by no means meant to exclude the possibility of others?

We can solve these problems by returning to the commonplaces. First of all, we note that a translative organization gives us an englobing whole which is an instance of cosmic intelligibility. The world of Flannery O'Connor, then, is in effect a cosmos or the cosmos itself. Second, we remember that "cosmos," a stable, spatial, term, implies its unstable, moving contradictory, sequence, and of course, consequence. A translative organization too, because it is without beginning or end, isn't really given to "stories." Instead, the various works of Flannery O'Connor are simply aspects of the same world; instead of "story" and "theme," we look for slightly different instances of the same intellectual structure, and the various commonplaces, easily assimilated to the same intellectual structure, will nonetheless give us the different modes of instantiation of their world. For a translative organization is a rhetorical dialectic in which, because they are dialectical, dichotomous terms can be assimilated to one pair of terms, and because they are rhetorical, they are not obliterated but preserved. Thus we will be able to achieve a coherent, unified world as context for richly varied concrete instances of that world.

We have already established the context by examining two (we need at least two to accommodate diversity) texts. As soon as we free that context from the fixed particularity we gave it for the sake of the necessary concreteness, we will have a context of which the two texts themselves will be parts and which has already provided us with a number of commonplaces by means of which we can compare other manifestations of the world of Flannery O'Connor. At the same time we will also be able to see, *formally* rather than materially, "why" *The Violent Bear It Away* should have been reworked; in other words, what is "better" about "The Lame Shall Enter First."

To begin with the last point: both the novel and the story are aspects of the world of Flannery O'Connor, that world which constitutes all her works. Nonetheless, a choice can be made as to how to dramatize, tell about, aspects of this world, and one choice can be better in some respects than another. How do the commonplaces work in the novel? Tarwater believes in his mission and does not believe in it (and belief is a function of thought); he is in a state of precarious balance, a kind of teetering stasis. With respect to Bishop, who is retarded, there can be no moral emphasis to balance an intellectual aspect. In effect, in two principals a spring of action is lacking; the tension of commonplaces which leads to action is impeded by the absence of effective terms with respect to Bishop, and by the balance that paralyzes Tarwater because no effective alternative to belief presents itself to him in uncle or city. In this triangular structure, the father figure, Rayber, must function to initiate action; yet he does not know what he wants to do or how to do anything for Tarwater, and he perceives Bishop as no object for any effective action. Thus, he doesn't bring the two together, but rather lets what may, occur. When it does occur, his response is completely passive, and he disappears from the triangular figure. A deus ex machina is thus required, and it is present in the voice which moves Tarwater to drown Bishop.

The story is also structured triangularly. Now, however, what has disappeared is an inert Bishop who cannot act or be acted upon in normal interaction, and a Tarwater paralyzed by doubt. Rather, we have a Norton, not very bright, but morally guilty of no more than faults, bad manners, sins of etiquette. Johnson, on the other hand, guilty of major sins, the kind that can send him to jail, is very bright indeed. There is a balancing between them of the moral and intellectual. And, finally, whereas Rayber isn't sure of what to do with respect to the two boys in relation to each other or himself, Sheppard knows what he wants to do and does it.

Sheppard wants to educate Johnson; he doesn't really love Norton, but in a kind of substitute for love hopes to improve him "morally" through forcing him to share his home with Johnson! (The irony is a function of this structure.) Thus Sheppard, unlike Rayber, brings the two boys together. He fails to love Norton or to educate Johnson, but there are consequences of throwing the two together: Johnson, not paralyzed in the manner of Tarwater, does and says what he knows he wants to do and say—the interplay of great intelligence and moral idiocy guarantees that he will. Norton, possessed of a mind and feeling, kills himself—his mediocre intelligence and his need for the withheld love guarantee that he will after hearing Johnson on heaven and his mother. Sheppard is really the only agent, but the consequences of his acting to throw Johnson and Norton together lead to his own education and his final awakening to love. The price of the knowledge gained and the love realized is horrendous—or, if one prefers—the cost of grace is horrendous.[19]

What is important is that an altered working of the commonplaces has produced a more economical, more artistic structure. The third side of the triangle functions as agent with respect to the other two as patient, but simultaneously achieves significant consequence for himself as well, and a deus ex machina *is not required*. The devil, whether seen as operating in Sheppard or Johnson or both or neither, is integrated within the triangle and need not function externally as he (or a hallucination) does with Tarwater. And the third side of the triangle, Sheppard, need not disappear in an indeterminate way as Rayber does. In terms of this economy, of a clarity and harmony fully realized, one can say that "The Lame Shall Enter First" is a more perfect embodiment of the intelligible structure of O'Connor's cosmos than is *The Violent Bear It Away*.[20]

The formulation of a contextual "world of Flannery O'Connor" has evoked, among other things, some commonplaces which are suggestive for discovering ways of expressing the intellectual structure of that world, that is, its translative structure. Among these are love and hate, good and evil, knowledge and ignorance, truth and falsehood, nature and supernature, or grace. In addition, we have found that the structure of the two texts we united to form a context were really three-termed, triangular structures. We must be careful to avoid a reductive identification of the two terms of a commonplace with the several protagonists we identify in a text. The structures of the novel and story, triangular with respect to their critical agents, mitigated this reductive temptation; we could see that the "locations" of good and evil, for example, were always equivocal, never fixed, and complicated by the interplay of other commonplaces. Thus Johnson might be said to be good in *knowing truth*, evil in freely choosing to reject moral behavior despite his knowledge, and arrogantly assuming that he could predict the outcome of God's judgment, indeed manipulate it when he should choose.

Not all instances of "the world of Flannery O'Connor" are structured by means of three agents, however. Commonplaces will enable us to discover their intelligible structures regardless of the number of agents, and the same commonplaces we have used earlier will enable us also to compare stories that seem quite different on the surface. We should bear in mind, too, that whereas it would be inappropriate to refer to the "story" as "surface" or appearance only, in another kind of context, the story is only appearance or surface in a translative context; the reality is always the intelligible structure of the universe which that appearance implies and embodies.

"Parker's Back"[21] is one of Flannery O'Connor's most interesting stories, and it moves solely through the interaction between two agents. It is unlike *The Violent Bear It Away* and "The Lame Shall Enter First" in a number of ways; aside from the two-agent structure, the father and "sons" motif is absent, as is the concomitant educative motif. There is no overt devil issue such as characterizes both the novel and "The Lame Shall Enter First," nor is there a protagonist like young Tarwater, consciously wrestling with his ambivalence toward a religious vocation. Whether it can even be said that there are two protagonists is doubtful, for the function of one is solely instrumental.

The "surface" is simple. As we would expect when we attempt to make sense of a text translatively, the literal "beginning" is irrelevant. O. E. Parker is married; the first two words are "Parker's wife." The "story" is a structure of ideas and defies sequence, really; nevertheless, it does emerge sequentially in a first reading. Moreover, the mode of emergence allows for the maximal expression of idea, and the first noteworthy translative "fact" is that, after all, the story *does* begin at the middle because it is the marriage which will implement the full phenomenal emergence of that structure of ideas which will be seen to have been implicit throughout Parker's life; and we must bear in mind that Parker's life is an instance of the intelligibility of the cosmos—Flannery O'Connor's cosmos—rather than simply a text.

The O. E. Parker who is married knows that he married his wife because he could not "get her" any other way, "but he couldn't understand why he stayed with her now . . . . He was puzzled and ashamed of himself" (p. 510). Through appropriately placed flashbacks Parker's premarital history is given. Briefly, he was an ordinary child who was permanently affected by the sight of a tattooed man at a fair. "Until he saw the man at the fair, it did not enter his head that there was anything out of the ordinary about the fact that he existed. Even then it did not enter his head, but a peculiar unease settled in him. It was as if a blind boy had been turned so gently in a different direction that he did not know his destination had been changed" (p. 513).

Parker gets tattooed every time he feels ill at ease, dissatisfied. He leaves school at sixteen and works to pay for the tattoos. When his concerned mother tries to trick him into going to a revival with her, he flees and joins the navy. By the time he is dishonorably discharged for going AWOL five years later, his entire body is covered with tattoos except for his back, where he can't enjoy seeing them. However, Parker still suffers intermittent episodes of unease, for his own body never seems to him perfectly beautiful as did the man's at the fair.

Parker, now married, is working for an old lady on her farm driving her tractor; his wife is pregnant, and Parker is becoming increasingly tense and uncomfortable. He needs a new tattoo and will have it on his back. He wants to think of one to please Sarah Ruth, his wife, who, unlike other women, hates and despises his painted body. The daughter of a Straight Gospel preacher, Sarah Ruth thinks even churches are idolatrous and sin everywhere. She married him after learning that his name—a carefully guarded secret from everyone—is really Obadiah Elihue, biblical names which evidently please her. Parker cannot decide what sort of tattoo he ought to have, and the intensity of his felt need, coupled with indecision, affects him profoundly. He can't sleep, loses weight, and becomes more and more distracted. One day, while mowing a field in circles around an old tree his employer refuses to cut down, Parker apparently becomes dizzy from the hot, bright sun and the circular motion, and crashes into the tree, which seems to him to reach out and grab him. Parker is thrown from the tractor which bursts into flame igniting part of the tree and Parker's shoes which have somehow falled off him. In horror and awe, Parker flees the burning site and drives his own truck, past his and Sarah Ruth's shack, straight into the city where he seeks out a tattoo artist, chooses the head of a Byzantine Christ with compelling eyes from a folder of prints, and has it etched into his back. When he returns home and shows Sarah Ruth the picture of "God" on his back, she beats his sore, raw back mercilessly with a broom and throws him out of the house calling him an idolator and telling him that God is a spirit and has no face. The story ends with Parker, who, by now, has wanted desperately to please her, leaning against the single pecan tree in their yard, weeping.

Flannery O'Connor wrote within a complex tradition; behind her are Southern regionalists, American Gothic and English literature as well. These contexts would be relevant if one wished to compare her work with that of other writers. What is relevant for my purpose here, however, is the broad tradition of twentieth-century fiction which runs to an "objective" narrative point of view. On the whole, O'Connor preferred that narrative stance; and although "Parker's Back" deviates from time to time from what might be called—at one's peril—pure objectivity, the story is told by a narrator, with very little commentary, from Parker's point of view but in the narrator's vocabulary. I mention all this because if one may say that the artistic value of a story is a function of economy of means in relation to fullness of end—and I think one may—"Parker's Back" is a very good story and thus a very good instance of the intelligibility of its universe. Consequently, the functioning of the narrative point of view—third-person-limited, rather than first-person—deserves careful scrutiny.

My brief rundown of the story line has perhaps suggested some of the problems one may postulate as facing its author; the commonplace of knowledge and ignorance will help us to examine them. Parker and Sarah Ruth are limited protagonists in a very real sense, regardless of point of view. Both are uneducated, of limited experience and range of interest. Such characters are best explored in a short story rather than a novel; the two of them, as we have them, couldn't sustain interest in a novel. For the author to choose an objective rather than an omniscient narration, for example, was to deny herself many discursive resources for countering the intellectual and verbal limitations of the protagonists.[22] Indeed, O'Connor had to rely on the intensity generated by an inside view to lend greater interest than Parker might evoke otherwise. But that isn't enough. Parker has some sort of religious experience; he knows that, but he doesn't really understand it and believes Sarah Ruth will tell him what to do. She, on the other hand, is simply ignorant. She knows her father's version of God; but not only does she disapprove, because of it, of visual representations, she is ignorant of the fact that other versions of Christian belief do not. That is, she doesn't recognize the face on Parker's back at all. Without commentary, this two-agent structure lacks a means of intelligibility. Parker acts on feeling without knowledge; Sarah Ruth, without feeling, acts on a partial, distorted knowledge which bears no relation to Parker's actions and the reasons for them. What is required is a source of both action and intelligibility, or intelligible action. What moves Parker to act? We learn that he is never self-moving in a conscious, thinking way. The principal events or occasions which move Parker must be presented, then, and they must supply the intelligibility in themselves which Parker cannot supply and the narrator will not. In fact, it is at these points in the story that the narration deviates from strict objectivity to the extent of introducing explanatory comments about Parker's feelings which Parker himself would be unable to make, thus going beyond him not merely in form—the vocabulary—but in content as well. The occasions must, ideally, move the story forward in a manner consistent with the principals and their world, and at the same time embody the intelligibility of the whole—which is larger than and ultimately independent of Parker. To say that the occasions do serve all these functions admirably is to say that "Parker's Back" is in fact a very good story.

A translative structure has its being on two levels: as an instance of the cosmos of which it is part and thus identical with it and all other instances, and as uniquely particularized. Organizing translatively involves getting to the identity level from the particular. To do this we will use suggestive commonplaces to initiate and organize the action and examine the occasions which mark turning points in Parker's life. Two of these occasions are presented early: first we learn that Parker, at fourteen, is "turned" by a man at a fair. The description of the man is important: "The man's skin was patterned in what seemed from Parker's distance . . . a single intricate design of brilliant color. The man, who was small and sturdy, moved about on the platform, flexing his muscles so that the arabesque of men and beasts and flowers on his skin appeared to have a subtle motion of its own" (pp. 512–13).

Next, Parker runs when he sees the church to which his mother is taking him for a revival, and he joins the navy. Parker's actions in both cases stem from intuitive feeling. Feeling is evoked in Parker first by what is literally a vision of sensuous beauty, harmonious color embedded in living flesh and representative of living nature, men, beasts, and flowers. In effect, *appearance,* the phenomenally present, evokes in Parker a "wonder" which, it is implied by the *narrator's* explanation, intimates *reality:* "Until he saw the man at the fair, it did not enter his head that there was anything out of the ordinary about the fact that he existed" (p. 513). The change, however, announces itself with the "peculiar unease" which settles in him, and with the fact that the slight pain of being tattooed makes it "appear to Parker to be worth doing. This was peculiar too for before he had thought that only what did not hurt was worth doing" (ibid.). When, by his flight, Parker rejects the presumably antisensuous message of a revival, he joins the navy, intuitively choosing the one context in which tattooing is normal rather than deviant behavior. When Parker's "unease" can no longer be soothed with another tattoo because only his invisible back is free of designs, he goes AWOL, as if the navy had lost its only usefulness, i.e., as a way of life in which a man may get tattooed. Parker is not presented as *thinking* at all. "As the space on the front of him for tattoos decreased, his dissatisfaction grew and became general. After one of his furloughs, he didn't go back to the navy.... His dissatisfaction, from being chronic and latent, had suddenly become acute and raged in him" (p. 514).

Parker persists in acting in terms of appearance in a most literal way, then; and if appearance in the shape of the tattooed man first awakened him to the "extraordinary," appearance has consistently failed to satisfy, for the dissatisfaction becomes "chronic," and then "acute."

Parker's next impulse to change his life occurs after his discharge from the navy, when, in the course of selling apples in the country, he meets Sarah Ruth. Sarah Ruth is in herself, for Parker, totally deficient in sensuous appearance. She is too thin and bony for his taste and doesn't paint her face, and, above all, she insists that she despises his tattoos. He marries her nevertheless, but he does not understand why he remains with her: "he stayed as if she had him conjured. He was puzzled and ashamed of himself" (p. 510). She shuns the pleasures of appearances in every way, refusing to look at his body, and lecturing him about reality as she sees it: "At the judgement seat of God, Jesus is going to say to you, 'What you been doing all your life besides have pictures drawn all over you?'" (p. 519).

A discrepancy between appearance and reality governs yet another aspect of his life with Sarah Ruth. For whereas he works as farm hand for an old woman, he tells Sarah Ruth that his employer is a young, hefty blonde; the apparent sensuality of his situation in fact masks a cold, dry reality. Finally, Sarah Ruth's reality is radically different from any he knows; churches are idolatrous, and, he will discover, God is invisible, pure spirit.

Marriage "made Parker gloomier than ever." But something mysterious, inexplicable, ties Parker to Sarah Ruth: "Every morning he decided he had had enough and would not return that night; every night he returned" (p. 518). The unease intensifies. "Dissatisfaction began to grow so great in Parker that there was no containing it outside of a tattoo. It had to be his back. There was no help for it. A dim half-formed inspiration began to work in his mind. He visualized having a tattoo put there that Sarah Ruth would not be able to resist—a religious subject" (p. 519). The pressure of decision weighs upon Parker, and finally one day he runs the tractor into the tree. Insofar as appearance is concerned, Parker's accident is the result of preoccupation, exhaustion and dizziness induced by his circular motion around the tree. We must assume, however, that Parker interprets his experience in another way, since he does not respond to the physical shock appropriately by seeking medical help or even simple rest. What he does do suggests the strongly intuitive nature of his responses and the curious passivity implicated in any of his actions (we recall that he stays with Sarah Ruth "as if she had him conjured"). First there is the curious wording of this inside view of the accident: "All at once he saw the *tree reaching out to grasp* him. A ferocious thud propelled him into the air, and he *heard himself yelling* in an unbelievably loud voice, 'GOD ABOVE!'"[23] When Parker looks around, what he sees is highly suggestive. The description is offered as what Parker saw, so that his reaction, although not verbal, seems to indicate that he interprets what appears as a sign that he must get his back tattooed immediately, and with a religious subject.

> He landed on his back while the tractor crashed upside down into the tree and burst into flame. The first thing Parker saw were his shoes, quickly being eaten by the fire; one was caught under the tractor, the other was some distance away, burning by itself. He was not in them. He could feel the hot breath of the burning tree on his face. He scrambled backwards, still sitting, his eyes cavernous, and if he had known how to cross himself he would have done it. (p. 520)

Quite aside from Parker's state of mind, the passage in and of itself suggests an allusion to the passages in Exodus (3:2–5) in which Moses sees a burning bush which signals the presence of God, and is told to remove his shoes before approaching holy ground. I say suggest because there is no one-to-one likeness. Moses sees a bush, not a tree, and he removes his shoes himself when commanded to do so; nor do the shoes burn. Moreover, there is nothing in the story to support the notion that the prophetic paradigm is involved as it is, quite explicitly, in the novel in which burning trees and "burning" generally figure prominently. But the scene in Exodus involves not only the call to the reluctant prophet but also the phenomenal concomitants of the *presence* of God. It is the latter that is suggested by the biblical echoes. In the event, the experience does move Parker profoundly enough to send him straight to the tattoo artist in the city.

Parker's choice of a Byzantine head of Christ is also passive-intuitive. He asks to see pictures of God, and starts, for no apparent reason, at the back of the book where modern pictures are found. He recognizes some of them—"The Smiling Jesus," "Jesus the Physician's Friend"—but he keeps on.

> He kept turning rapidly backwards and the pictures became less and less reassuring. One showed a gaunt green dead face streaked with blood.... Parker's heart began to beat faster and faster.... He flipped the pages quickly, feeling that when he reached the one *ordained*, a sign would come.... On one of the pages a pair of eyes glanced at him swiftly. Parker sped on, then stopped.... It said as plainly as if silence were a language itself, GO BACK. Parker returned to the picture—the haloed head of a flat stern Byzantine Christ with all-demanding eyes.... his heart began slowly to beat again as if it were being brought to life by a subtle power.[24]

Parker's return is curious and terrible. First he visits a familiar pool-room where an old acquaintance slaps him on the back. He explains that his back is sore, and the men insist on seeing the new tattoo. They are shocked, but Parker's "uncertain grin" provokes good-natured teasing. They say he has "got religion," and he insists that he had the tattoo done for "laughs." When someone asks why he isn't laughing, Parker begins a fight which lasts until two men throw him out; "then a calm descended on the pool hall as nerve shattering as if the long barn-like room were the ship from which Jonah had been cast into the sea" (p. 527). He doesn't return home immediately.

> Parker sat for a long time on the ground in the alley behind the pool hall, examining his soul. He saw it as a spider web of facts and lies that was not at all important to him but which appeared to be necessary in spite of his opinion. The eyes that were now forever on his back were eyes to be obeyed. He was as certain of it as he had ever been of anything. Throughout his life, grumbling and sometimes cursing, often afraid, once in rapture, Parker had obeyed whatever instinct of this kind had come to him—in rapture... at the sight of the tattooed man... afraid when he had joined the navy, grumbling when he had married Sarah Ruth.
>
> The thought of her brought him slowly to his feet. She would know what he had to do. She would clear up the rest of it, and she would at least be pleased. (Ibid.)

During the night, after the artist's application of his preliminary sketch, Parker, lying on a cot in a local mission, had dreamed miserably of his accident and the eyes in the book. Then "he longed miserably for Sarah Ruth. Her sharp tongue and icepick eyes were the only comfort he could bring to mind . . . . Her eyes appeared soft and dilatory compared with the eyes in the book, for even though he could not summon up the exact look of those eyes, he could still feel their penetration" (p. 524).

Now Parker returns to find that Sarah Ruth is furious: the old woman wants Parker to pay for her tractor, and Sarah Ruth has discovered the reality behind his tale of the buxom blonde employer. But the Sarah Ruth to whom he has turned for comfort, who apparently knows all about the judgment day and God, doesn't begin to appreciate the reality of Parker's experience and his commitment. Parker has been brought to the eyes that demand obedience by an experience which Sarah Ruth, ironically the champion of austere spirituality, insists on interpreting on the level of appearance: careless Parker has irresponsibly ruined a tractor he must pay for; carnal Parker has lied about his employer in an offensive way. Indeed, the final events are starkly simple. When Parker returns from the city, Sarah Ruth will not open the door to him until, in response to her repeated "who's there?" he replies "Obadiah Elihue" instead of "O.E.," or "me." She confronts him with her discoveries about the old woman and the accident, and rejects his offering of the tattoo of "God":

> "God? God don't look like that!"
> "What do you know how he looks?" Parker moaned. "You ain't seen him."
> "He don't *look*," Sarah Ruth said. "He's a spirit. No man shall see his face."
> "Aw listen," Parker groaned, "this is just a picture of him."
> "Idolatry!" Sarah Ruth screamed . . . and she grabbed up the broom and began to thrash him across the shoulders with it.
> Parker was too stunned to resist. He sat there and let her beat him . . . and large welts had formed on the face of the tattooed Christ. Then he staggered up and made for the door. . . . Still gripping [the broom], she looked toward the pecan tree and her eyes hardened still more. There he was—who called himself Obadiah Elihue—leaning against the tree, crying like a baby.[25]

The story ends, then, in a fusion of appearance and reality which does justice to the temporality of O'Connor's discursive art, the eternity of the structure of idea that her discursive artifact instantiates, and finally, the profound ambiguity which, as we have seen, always characterizes a translative as opposed to a dialectical structure.

Temporally, a translative structure is an organization of a separate and unique discursive whole in terms of middle. As discursive whole, it "ends" when its phenomenal embodiment of the intelligible structure of the universe is adequate; that is to say, when whatever needs to be said in order to communicate that intelligible structure has been said. Parker has presumably acquired the tattoo he has been seeking all his life—he has substituted the overt, visible eyes belonging to God and demanding obedience, for the intuitions, covert and without identity, which have served to motivate his behavior in the past. Further, in a literal sense he has covered the last available part of his body with a picture. He has moved from ignorance to a kind of knowledge, including the knowledge that he is alone and that Sarah Ruth, a force which helped to move him to this state of being, cannot and will not understand him. Where he has been going since his first "turn," his first astonishment at being alive when he saw the tattooed man, is now clear—straight to a literal, physical, irrevocable relationship with God.

The eternity of a translative structure is found in the idea, the *logos*, the "intelligibility" it embodies, as its temporality is found in the *mythos*, the concrete events recounted. Since our experience of a work is phenomenal, on the level of appearances, of the variables of a "story," it is through our organization of those variables translatively that we find the idea. Thus, if it is only the concrete variables which can point to the idea, we must be attentive to them in a special way. We have already noted the "symbolic" values of the burning tractor, and all of Parker's driven behavior which preceded the tractor episode. Now the ending tells us "why" he stayed with Sarah Ruth—not because he wanted to (he didn't), but because she was the instrument for driving him to choose the numinous final tattoo, and because, having unconsciously functioned as such an instrument, she would be unable to offer him comfort or companionship once he made that choice. Her rejection of him is foreshadowed in the rejection of the friends who eject him from the pool hall as if he were a "Jonah." We recall that Jonah, who spent three days in the belly of a fish, is an Old Testament prototype of Christ in the tomb, then resurrected on the third day. Parker has "taken on" Christ, and in that identification is scourged and rejected as Christ was. Parker, clinging to a tree, his cross, weeps as Sarah Ruth looks on with "hardened" eyes.

The aspect of the intelligibility of the universe embodied in *The Violent Bear It Away* had to do with an eternally repeated conflict in which God's chosen messengers, each in his way consciously aware of his vocation, struggle to flee that vocation: old Tarwater agonizes in his youth; young Tarwater actively struggles against it, trying to burn the old man, drowning Bishop, only to succumb at last. In "The Lame Shall

Enter First" the savior Christ is affirmed by Johnson and ultimately revealed to Sheppard, who has denied him and imagined he could usurp his saving power. "Parker's Back" offers still a third aspect of that vision in the man who, indifferent to God, does not run away from him but runs toward him without knowing where he is going or why.

Translative structures are temporal and eternal; they are also ambiguous. This ambiguity is also perfectly realized in the ending of "Parker's Back." As was pointed out in chapter 5, the terms of a dialectical dichotomy are perceived as substantive, so that the universe of Flannery O'Connor which we have constructed would be taken to be a particularization of the intelligible structure of the universe. In dialectical criticism the structure of a literary work *is* the same as the intelligible structure of the universe itself.[26] The terms of a translative dichotomy are a rhetorical commonplace, empty until we structure a communication with them, and interchangeable. That is, as is the case in rhetoric, in debate we may argue either side of a question without prejudice, since we do not presuppose a conclusion that is merely waiting to be discovered; rather, we will make the conclusion through the process of debate.

Thus, the translative dichotomy our rhetorical criticism has formulated by means of a pair of stories, and confirmed with yet a third, remains ambiguous, its terms interchangeable. If we said that the *true* structure of the universe, according to O'Connor and as exemplified in O'Connor's world, is constituted by an interplay between nature and grace, the human world and God's periodic intervention in it, we would show how ambiguity and conflict are made intelligible by that structure, and that the principle will indicate how we must interpret the works which make up that discursive world. However, if we say that the *translative* structure of O'Connor's universe is constituted by the interplay between nature and grace, we are affirming the principle of nature and grace as one means of organizing that world, and we are affirming the persistent ambiguity of nature and grace because ambiguity and conflict *are* in fact the translative version of the intelligible structure of the universe.

This means that we cannot unambiguously locate the terms of any of the relevant commonplaces we have dealt with. At the end of "Parker's Back," Parker is alone, forever attached to the demanding image of God, the victim of eyes that will never leave off looking at him. Yet even this literal level is paradoxical, since Parker cannot see the compelling image. Sarah Ruth is clearly the instrument which has brought him from a frenetic, random search for unnatural (tattoos) sublime beauty to the particular, ultimate sublime supernatural beauty of the Byzantine Christ. Yet having united himself in the flesh to God has deprived him of his only source of knowledge of God's will! Is Sarah Ruth's rejection of Parker evil? Certainly she deprives him of instruction, of her knowledge of the Bible, just when he is willing to receive it; and she is curiously obtuse, curiously ignorant in her rejection—she says that God is a spirit, and no man shall see his face, but men did look on the face of Jesus. Thus Parker's stubborn, consistent search, always in terms of the sensuous, marks him as somehow more profoundly knowledgeable than she of the true incarnational essence of Christianity. But if Sarah Ruth is evil, if she hates when she should love, condemns when she should forgive, is her function not good insofar as it may be necessary? To reject Parker, after all, is to condemn him to live out the despised and rejected life of Christ.[27] Does grace, therefore, "harden"—the word is O'Connor's—Sarah Ruth to work God's mysterious will, or is her narrow rigidity, her austere self-righteousness the fault of her nature?

Ambiguity permeates the ending, finally, in the reiteration of Parker's full name. Earlier in the story he is forced to tell Sarah Ruth, reluctantly indeed, what O.E. stands for (p. 517), but attention is not called to his given name again until the end, when Sarah Ruth refuses to open the door to him until he pronounces the hated syllables Obadiah Elihue. Then the name is repeated in the final sentence of the story so that it stands out vividly, yet in a very curious way. The last line reads: "There he was—*who called himself* Obadiah Elihue—leaning against the tree, crying like a baby" (italics mine).

Does the "called himself" imply deception on his part? Or only that Sarah Ruth believes that he has deceived her about his name as he did about the old woman? Or does it mean that she questions his right to the biblical name she admires? The sentence represents the narrator's indirect account of Sarah Ruth's mind as she watches him from a window after beating him and throwing him out. Yet its position as the last sentence of the story gives it an insistent quality its source in the woman's mind might not otherwise warrant. Thus it is ambiguous on an initial, superficial reading. What does it mean for Sarah Ruth and for the story, and how are the meanings related?

First, Obadiah is one of the minor Old Testament prophets, and his message is short and uncomplicated. He tells the people of Edom, descendants of Esau, that God is angry with them for rejoicing in the downfall of Judah, since, after all, Esau was Jacob's brother. He says that they shall perish in their turn, and the house of Jacob and Joseph will triumph over Edom and all its other enemies.

Elihue seems more promising. He is the fourth human character, other than the chief protagonist, of the book of Job, and he is angry with Job and his three "comforters": with the latter because they condemn Job despite having themselves no answers to his complaint, and with Job because Job justifies himself rather than God. Elihue, who is young, doesn't speak until the others are finished, and the substance of his message is interesting: he argues that God cannot be sinful or unjust; God doesn't give an account of why he does what he does, and he need not; God hears submissive prayer and answers it; God is man's savior and his power is overwhelmingly great; and, finally, adversity is a kind of discipline. Job is wicked because "he addeth rebellion unto his sin, he clappeth his hands among us, and multiplieth his words against God" (Job 34:37). Elihue doesn't harp on Job's sinfulness as the other three do, but rather on rehearsing the glorious attributes of God, evident from one's experience of creation. He believes that Job is sinful, but in what seems to be a more generic way. Nevertheless, his emphasis is on God as always just in his judgments. The voice of God out of the whirlwind follows, and Job's three companions are condemned for their condemnation of the righteous Job, but Elihue's speech does not evoke any divine response, implying that his "justification" of God is more acceptable than the comforters' more oblique justification of God through admonishing Job.

It seems to me that the notorious ambiguity of the book of Job reinforces our initial impression, but the sources of the names at least suggest a more complex expansion of meaning. Of course Sarah Ruth's forcing Parker to utter the names and her own repetition of them at the end in a way that seems to deny the legitimacy of his claim to them, are plausible enough given her "nature" as it presents itself to us. How can a sinful idolator who has never acknowledged God's dominion bear the names of a chosen messenger of God and a man moved by the spirit to justify the judgment of God? The ambiguity of her reaction stems from its irony. Obadiah reproached Edom for rejoicing in the misfortune of Judah, its "brother"; Sarah Ruth who "owns" prophets as Parker does not, rejoices in his misfortune with the old woman's tractor when she ought to comfort him. Parker's raw, tender back is mercilessly beaten by one who ought to comfort him in his pain, as the sufferings of Job are exacerbated by the three comforters. Elihue alone of the four escapes God's wrath, but Sarah Ruth is incapable of pondering mysteries of that sort.

At the end, united with a Christ incarnate in his own flesh, Parker is transformed from O.E. to Obadiah Elihue, the hidden identity now fully overt, merging, too, Old Testament messenger and praiser of God with the New Testament word made flesh forever on his back. But this genuine communion, this close approximation of a truly real presence, remains ambiguous as the God of Job remains ambiguous. For the just God praised and magnified by Elihue, the God who recapitulates and expands Elihue's assertions and then restores the righteous Job to well-being, remains forever linked in uneasy, ambivalent ambiguity to the almost frivolous, cruel deity of the opening chapters of Job who destroys innocent children and visits upon this good man such terrible anguish for the sake of a wager with an unrighteous, fallen angel.[28]

It would seem that Parker in his plight and his belief in the demands of the terrible eyes is one with Elihue and the stricken Job in being hopelessly ignorant of what these demands are and why they are made. Like Obadiah, presumably, he may repeat a brief message one day— surely nothing very flashy since Obadiah was hardly one of the more glamorous prophets. But, like Elihue, he will never really understand that message whatever it might be. How, then, does "Parker's Back" take its place in the translative world of Flannery O'Connor?

First, all three stories obviously embody variant aspects of a universe of which the moving and sustaining principle is the Christian creator God, incarnated in Jesus Christ, and intimately involved in man's life so that his demands cannot be evaded except at terrible peril—witness Rayber; so that to deny him and to deny that his saving power is unique is devastating in its ultimate consequences—witness the death of Norton. And finally, to embrace him and affirm his power and submit to his will is to be rejected, confused, misunderstood, and alone.

We can formulate the principle as the interplay between nature and grace or appearance and reality—the terms will always be assimilatable to one another because the principle comprehends all experience including all speculation on the human condition. Consequently, the "nature" which "appears" to us initially is not as real or real in the sense in which grace is real because grace is the name for God's gift of "knowledge" to our "ignorance," truth to our falsehood, the path of good rather than our path which is evil; and God is eternal, as we in our phenomenal, mortal existence are not. In that sense, God and his gift of grace are real as our changing, phenomenal selves and works cannot be. Which pair of terms organizes a single work in O'Connor's discursive universe depends on the perspective that work instantiates. But the many perspectives are the many facets of a single, cosmic reality.

Further, with respect to these stories the ambiguity of the principle is at least threefold: as a rhetorical principle it derives from audience, is one of four ways in which we can organize separate discursive wholes to make them communicative. Consequently we are affirming of an instance of discourse that it is *formally* open to more than one interpretation—in fact, to a range of interpretations albeit a finite range. This approach implicitly denies a substantive status to the dichotomous translative principle. Thus, first, we *are not* asserting of O'Connor's world an analogy to the universe itself; and, second, we are not claiming that our view of what makes it a coherent universe states the only possible mode of coherence that universe could have. The third ambiguity derives from the interchangeability of the terms of the principle. For example, whereas the interplay of nature and grace organizes the O'Connor universe, as we have seen, for any given story it is hard to tell which event constitutes the working of nature and which grace. The role of Tarwater's "devil" as well as his identity is a perfect example.

It seems to me worth reiterating here the commitment of this approach to rhetorical criticism to the integrity of the text. All criticism must involve some notion of the interrelation of reader and text since to analyze a text, even to name it, is to imply a reader without whom a text *as experienced* does not exist. Some criticism may ignore the reader and some focus entirely on the reader,[29] but a reader's existence is implied once a text is discussed. The attitude expressed in this essay toward that relationship has been established in chapter 2, and I want only to emphasize here that it presupposes the critic-reader's activities within a range of formal possibilities with the text *alone* as the material with which those activities deal. Therefore, when I speak of an author I mean simply the agent who has furnished those materials as he is implied by their very existence, and I speak of author at all because to do so is often less awkward grammatically than to avoid doing so. Like the reader he is a necessary outsider, but in a sense he is even less necessary than the reader, for the text replaces him.

I have said this before, and I mention it now because I believe that a discussion of the world of Flannery O'Connor raises questions which must be acknowledged lest one seem deliberately disingenuous. More important, these questions offer an opportunity for making very clear the kind of relationship between reader and author that rhetorical criticism presupposes. The question or, better perhaps, the observation that may be evoked by the foregoing discussion is evoked because of the emphasis on ambiguity. Flannery O'Connor made no secret of her beliefs and their relation to her fiction. The recent publication of her letters offers additional evidence of her convictions and her intentions.[30] That she would have affirmed nature and grace as the *true* intelligible structure of the universe seems to me unquestionable, differences in vocabulary notwithstanding. I have said they are the ambiguous, translative principle of a universe of discourse only. I think, too, that she would have preferred Tarwater and Johnson to Rayber and Sheppard, as her readers and critics often do not, and because the former "know" the truth about God and Jesus Christ and the latter do not. Above all, I cannot be sure that she would have accepted my insistence on the ambiguity of the principle because belief was an important part of her artistic equipment, and she knew what she believed. Nevertheless, our critical response to the world of Flannery O'Connor must be evoked by the works that constitute that world, and we must recognize that the mind of an artist is not unambiguously reflected in the work. I have been concerned only with the Flannery O'Connor who emerges in the three stories treated in this essay.

It remains then to consider what can be said of that world as exemplified in those three stories. It is a world in which knowledge and ignorance, good and evil, are in constant tension and curiously intertwined. The evil Johnson knows about Jesus as savior and is ignorant of the rest of God's creation. The good and knowledgeable Sheppard and Rayber are ignorant of the truth because they refuse to know what good they *cannot* do; and their refusal is evil. Young Tarwater is surely evil; yet his rejection of God is not disbelief and denial but a result of being repelled by what he feels he knows! And evil or not in his actions, he is irrevocably "chosen"—just as, in a curious, inexplicable way, Parker is chosen. Parker "accepts"; but, concretely, what is he accepting? At the very least he is accepting the call to be prepared to do the bidding of the mysterious force represented by the demanding eyes. And it would seem, then, that the prophetic paradigm is suppressed in "Parker's Back," but there nonetheless; it is signaled by the imagery itself, the scenic allusions to Moses and his burning bush, and to Jonah cast out of the ship, and it is implicit in Parker's commitment.

If the grace of God intervening in nature holds this world together and makes sense of the events and persons that crowd it, and I believe it does, that grace is nonetheless ambiguous and mysterious. The stories seem to revolve around the offer of grace, always. Let us hypothesize one possibility for each story: Buford's burial of the old man, the discovery of which finally "turns" Tarwater, is a manifestation of the grace of God. Johnson's final act of vandalism and his speech before being taken away by the police are the grace offered Sheppard. The accident with the tractor which sends Parker to discover God in the flesh—the only way *he can*—is a manifestation of the grace of God.

The result is always a kind of self-knowledge or in any case a crucial knowledge. Tarwater knows his destiny; Sheppard realizes what he has been in the past; Parker knows that God demands obedience. Nature, furthermore, is never violated. Tarwater had been conditioned to prophecy as a vocation from infancy. Parker's knowledge doesn't suddenly transform him into a man of ideas about God and God's will; he remains as he has always been, a man of the senses, of feeling. Sheppard, a man of ideas, can articulate his insight, but his revelation cannot reverse the "natural" consequences of his actions throughout the story, i.e., Norton's suicide. Nor do the stories go beyond the immediate result of grace received and accepted. The drama of events which were climaxed by the intervention of grace is over. The world of Flannery O'Connor is a universe of discourse, not a theological tract; it never goes beyond what is artistically significant.[31] Beyond its theological drama lies the world in which it will be hard to tell whether grace—even if one accepts it as real—makes any difference or what difference it makes. The ambiguity is at the heart of the artistic enterprise as it is at the heart of the human enterprise.

Indeed, O'Connor's world is impressive because it does not sentimentalize God, who remains awesomely "other" in the stories, whose ways are inexplicable. Deniers like Rayber and latecomers like Sheppard suffer terribly. But Mason Tarwater's tales of being "burned clean" by the Lord are not reassuring about the fate of believers, and Parker's plight confirms our misgivings. The believer may perhaps be said to experience a genuine exhilaration when truth is revealed to him, at least Sheppard does toward the end of "The Lame Shall Enter First," before he discovers Norton's body. However, Tarwater's vision of loaves and fishes, and Parker's first sight of the Byzantine Christ seem awesome but painful. On the whole, despite some comic moments—when Parker courts Sarah Ruth, for example—and in stories we have not touched on, the world of Flannery O'Connor seems austere; and, beyond his unmistakable power, God remains mysterious. If he is benign, he has seldom manifested that aspect of his nature in the world of Flannery O'Connor.

It is best to end this discussion by pointing out that a fourth kind of ambiguity remains because we have not interpreted, focused on the essential temporality of, any of the three stories we have used to make the world of Flannery O'Connor. We simply constructed a context for comparative analysis by organizing two of the stories, then compared a third with the original two. The agents and events remain uninterpreted variables until thematic accounts are made by arranging those variables in expository, descriptive, narrative, or argumentative sequences. It seems to me proper to mention this, because readings in the various modes of discourse would reveal the rich particularity of O'Connor's work that is necessarily slighted on the level of organizing the discursive whole prior to and for analysis. Moreover, the translative organization of variables, with its focus on the transcendent, calls special attention to a kind of theological dimension in any work, and in O'Connor that dimension is dense enough to dominate the discussion. The stories, however, are not theology; the translative organization gives us a novel of ideas *and* feeling, and the true measure of that feeling emerges in the thematic variations of interpretation. In focusing on the world of Flannery O'Connor we have chosen to forego interpretations of the stories as separate wholes; therefore, we cannot claim to do justice to them as separate, unique works, but only as interrelated aspects of a single, artistic vision.

CONCLUSION

Let us return to the beginning of this essay from the fresh perspective of a completed inquiry. This inquiry was born, as much inquiry may be, in discomfort and puzzlement, in a personal, subjective response which must be attributed to some objective cause before serious inquiry can be undertaken. I began, therefore, to reflect on literary criticism and the novel with what seemed to me the unexceptionable conviction that the history of the novel and the history of criticism of the novel are in fact a single history, since what happens to the novel and what the novel is thought to be at any time are reflexively interdependent. Indeed, if one were to substitute "poetry" for "novel," the statement would surely seem a truism. The long history of criticism exemplifies such a truism again and again. To take the oldest, simplest, and clearest example, we have Aristotle determining what tragedy is and explaining how it works by observing the tragedies of ancient Greece; and on the basis of the *Poetics*, variously interpreted, later tragedies were written; their deviations from ancient tragedy led to new critical statements about the nature of tragedy, and so on. The novel has not quite so long a history, but the phenomenon is nonetheless the same once it is set into motion.

And, therefore, discomfort and puzzlement, but chiefly the latter, since the histories of the novel and criticism do not seem interdependent at all, truism notwithstanding. For many reasons, the long prose story does not emerge as a significant literary phenomenon until the eighteenth century,[1] and we can understand that criticism will not turn to contemplate it until its significance becomes obvious. Henry James's prefaces are a landmark which in turn inspire a serious critical work in Percy Lubbock's *The Craft of Fiction* in 1921. However, that work is partisan in its espousal of James's version of what a novel ought to be, and thus does not do for eighteenth- and nineteenth-century novels what Aristotle did for Greek tragedy. Moreover, it is too early to serve as a theoretical exposition of twentieth-century innovation.

In fact the novel rises and develops from its various sources without benefit of critique or theory, and the early twentieth-century innovators like Joyce, Lawrence, and Woolf make their own declarations of principle since there is no one to do it for them.[2] They repudiate their predecessors without having critical champions of nineteenth-century practices to repudiate as well. On the other hand, much of the inspiration of novelists like Joyce, Lawrence, and Woolf seems to have come from the same general ambience that produced the late nineteenth- and early twentieth-century movements in poetry. The innovations of Lawrence and Joyce with respect to subject matter are important obviously, but Lawrence was a poet, too, and his interest in and use of so-called poetic devices became very apparent when his subject matter no longer seemed shocking. Joyce's formal, linguistic experiments were always obvious since they made reading alone unusually difficult—one takes for granted an effort expended through a duration measured in lines, whereas it becomes formidable measured in hundreds of pages. Woolf's use of language, if a lesser obstacle than Joyce's, nonetheless announced its affinity with poetry early in her work.

The world that discovered the poetry of Hopkins and Dickinson, that produced the poetry of Yeats and Eliot and Pound, and the fiction of Joyce and Lawrence and Woolf, also produced the rich flowering of twentieth-century criticism; and the major work of critics during the first half of the twentieth century has been devoted to poetry. Two great seminal works of twentieth-century criticism, I. A. Richards's *Principles of Literary Criticism* and *Practical Criticism,* appeared in the twenties and inaugurated the "new criticism" which has dominated the field, in one version or another, ever since. The opposing "Chicago school" closed the first half of the century with *Critics and Criticism* in 1952. Certainly there was criticism of the novel during that time, but any list of major critics both in England and the United States will tell the same story: poetry predominates.[3]

The reason is probably obvious enough. Twentieth-century criticism has focused on the text as unique object to be addressed in itself regardless of its context, which includes author and audience. The text alone is considered a linguistic artifact and its nature and identity sought in its formal or linguistic structure. It is not hard to see that such a critical enterprise would be painfully difficult if not impossible with respect to literary works of any considerable length. Yet in such an intellectual milieu, to suggest, as Coleridge did, that a work of considerable length *should not be* all poetry, is to suggest that novels are unworthy of critical attention as well as intractable objects of it.[4] That combination is hard to overcome as an impediment to serious criticism of the novel.

We know, however, that since the mid-fifties critics have done serious work on the novel and have done justice to eighteenth- and nineteenth-century novels as linguistic artifacts as well as to the "poetry" influenced novels of the early twentieth century. But a principal dogma and its corollaries of twentieth-century criticism has never been seriously shaken: that the literary artifact is a work of art made of words, and *as a work of art* "a poem should not mean / But be" (as Archibald MacLeish's famous lines from "Ars Poetica" have it). Furthermore, the integrity of a text requires that we ignore author and audience as irrelevant to literary criticism, the only criticism relevant to literary works.

The puzzlement, then, could be resolved with some investigation and thought. Why is it that the novel at the beginning of the twentieth century seems to be molded by the same influences as is poetry, but twentieth-century critical theory ignores the novel for the most part for fifty years? This is a question to which I have contrived at least a plausible answer. The discomfort, however, remains, and it is less easy to articulate formally. But it is nonetheless persistent and demands to be taken seriously.

Even if one accepts MacLeish's statement at face value, qua statement and "line" it expresses a dilemma perfectly: only *because* that coda to the poem, "Ars Poetica" *means* can it emphatically deny that a poem ought to mean. Unfortunately that elementary insight cannot get one much farther unless one deduces from it that MacLeish is wrong, in which case one has achieved an easy victory. The next step is to see that MacLeish is both right and wrong, because a work of art may be taken to be more than one sort of thing. A second source of discomfort remains: to treat a literary work as embodying meaning is to treat it from a perspective outside of itself, since meaning is a function of interpretation, of experience, not of being. What becomes, then, of the integrity of the text, the preservation of which has come to be a sacred duty in the light of twentieth-century critical opinion?

It is at this point that inquiry begins. MacLeish's poem is a wonderful, brief exemplar of a very complex phenomenon of which we become acutely aware with twentieth-century fiction: in order to experience works of art at all, we must in some sense understand them, interpret them so that they convey meaning. We may do that badly or well, sensitively or obtusely, but we must do it. That on the level of theory early twentieth-century criticism turned so adamantly against "meaning" seems to me understandable since the temptation to treat linguistic artifacts as simple messages, seeking "morals" of stories, is very much greater than it is in response to nonlinguistic artifacts. In practice, literary criticism is discourse about discourse, and it is almost impossible to analyze poems, let alone novels, without implying meaning in some sense of the word.

Twentieth-century novels, as I said at the beginning of this essay, present, to greater or lesser degree, acute problems of meaning insofar

231

as they are linguistically experimental, and no tradition of critical distaste for discussions of meaning can change the need for addressing those problems. It seemed to me, too, that one could and should accept the approaches of the various "new critics" and "neo-Aristotelians" as given and not to be refuted, and that their strictures about the integrity of the text ought to be adhered to as a genuinely valid and valuable critical precept. Thus, if one could legitimately treat a text as a structure communicative of meaning, one needed to find a means of doing so that would not go beyond the text any more than did Aristotle or any devout "new critic." The only systematic treatment of texts as communicative structures of meaning occurs in treatises on rhetoric as theory of argument, and thus this inquiry began.

Two problems need to be resolved, concerning the object of criticism and the method of criticism. At the beginning it seems that the only real problem is methodological, but that is almost immediately seen to be false because how novels are treated depends on what one takes them to be, and no one definition has ever been universally accepted. The advantage of rhetorical criticism is considerable in this respect. Since its perspective is that of experience, we can grant the legitimacy of any definition of the novel, show what is done when in fact one does determine to treat a named text as a novel, without any commitment to a single, exclusive definition. In other words, we choose "argument" as the nature of the novel (as communicative structure) because an argument can be isolated and treated as a structure; we choose "rhetorical argument" because rhetorical arguments can be stated without commitment to or distortion by assumptions concerning the nature of thoughts, things, actions, or words extrinsic to the argument itself.

We began by recognizing that rhetorical arguments are "made" arguments, "fictive arguments," and that the scope of these is universal and all inclusive: there are arguments in what is thought, done, or experienced as well as in what is said; and the sequences and consequences of arguments can be detected and sketched in words, in actions, in thoughts, and in things. This complex interrelationship is recognized in the treatment given to four kinds of "discourse" in textbooks of composition, and we saw that the four modes—description, exposition, narration, argument—become kinds of entities difficult to identify in actual examples of discourse where they seem mixed, and proliferate in increasing combinations. However, if they are treated as "arguments" rather than discursive entities, dependent on extrinsic entities, it is possible to state their common structure and to differentiate their specific structures as *structures of argument*. The structure of argument is given in the hypothetical relation "if—then." The structure of an argument becomes a description when it is formulated in the existential-causal relation "as—so"; it becomes an exposition when it is formulated in the intellectual-holistic relation "because—therefore"; it becomes narration when it is formulated in the circumstantial-sequential relation, "before—after." Four kinds of fictive argument are differentiated by developing the consequences of four pairs of fictive arguments as structures for eight literary texts. If those texts were interpreted as entities, by reference to subject matters, they would be instances of highly divergent genres—history, drama, philosophy of science, psychology, political theory, novel, sociological treatise, political tract. The fictive arguments are not presented as interpretations drawn from the texts but as consequences constructed to open up meanings, to interpret the texts as argument, and it is recognized that each text can be formed and interpreted by each of the kinds of argument, not only by the one constructed for it. Each argument developed is interpreted as well in a positive and a negative sense, a normal and a tragic sequence, to try the argument "if—then" not only in its unimpeded mode but also its deviant modes: "if—then possibly, or accidentally, or sometimes, or not at all."

All things are and are made, expressed, and understood by fictive arguments. The third chapter makes the transition from the nature of fictive arguments to the making of fictive arguments. A made argument or *hypothesis* is, we have seen, the rhetorical mode that generates the others: we go from the "if—then" of argument to the "because—therefore" of exposition, which assimilates what is or is made in significant relations or *themes,* to the "as—so" of description, which defines *topics* within which things come to be, to the "before—after" of narration, which discriminates figures or *tropes* of speech, thought, and occurrence by which named things are classified in genres or kinds. Thus all literature comes to be as fictive argument in genres, themes, topics, and tropes. A made argument or hypothesis is a sequential argument or inference made by particularizing the variables of hypothetical arguments in constant meanings and fixed references. If particularity were to be sought in forms and matters external to the argument itself, we should seek the unity and scope of an argument endlessly. If we seek them within the argument itself, rhetorically, the form is no longer an abstract verbal proposition and the matter concrete realms of subject matter. Our search for meanings, data, processes, and terms continues to have no final end, but each argument does have a variety of rhetorical terminations in which the whole thought may be assimilated. The matter becomes particularizations of agents, problems, circumstances, and ideas in interplay. Structures of meaning—of significances and references—make fictive arguments which can be ordered according to themes and variations on themes.

When meanings are developed in inferences and their applications instead of in sequential themes and their variations, as they are in chapter 3, the subject matters of arguments are usually sought in things extrinsic to the arguments to which the meanings are applied. But when meanings are formed in fictive arguments, the content of the argument is broadened to include not only what is meant but what is thought, under what circumstance, and to what end; and the externalities of thought, matter, agent, and audience can be internalized into the argument. Further, if the determinants of arguments are internalized, the distinction between fact and fiction ceases to be the basis for distinguishing arguments according to meaning into true and fictitious, according to things into real and fictitious, according to intention into historical and fictitious. All arguments are fictive arguments, and fictive arguments make worlds of thoughts, of things, of agents, and of auditors, critics, or interpreters. Thus we are ready in the fourth chapter to turn to the problem of identifying the novel, the object of our literary criticism, since the novel cannot be interpreted by means of a plurality of fictive arguments until there is a novel to interpret. In other words, we have made fictive arguments qua sequence, and we must now make fictive arguments qua structured, organized *whole.*

Chapter 4 turns, then, from the universality of fictive argument to the universe of discourse, concentrating on verbal presentations of arguments rather than their presentations in ideas, things, or actions, and on verbal identifications by titles attached to texts, prior to giving texts meanings, references, or intentionalities by interpretative arguments. The problem encountered at this stage of our inquiry is a difficult one. The "modes of discourse" of contemporary rhetoric texts have been a useful tool in discovering the universe and the universe of discourse to be a realm of themes and variations; indeed, we have used named texts indiscriminately for that purpose, having found them in their *common place,* the universe of discourse. Now we must make wholes, distinct from other wholes, and make them novels as well.

It would have made perfectly good sense to go on in chapter 4 to show how to make discursive wholes, as opposed to sequences, and then address that most intransigent problem, What, why, or how is a novel? But if a novel, too, is some kind of discursive whole—and that seems an innocuous proposition—we could show how any wholes are constituted by constituting novels. Thus we turned in chapter 4 to the question of identifying a named text as a novel. We argued at the outset that the question is highly ambiguous, and citing selected named texts we were able to show that, in effect, *what we say a named text is is inextricably bound up with the kinds of questions we choose to ask of that text.* Since we are not interested in particular intentions but only in the range of intentionality which is possible with respect to naming texts, we required an exhaustive formal matrix that could enable us to discover kinds of texts possible and the characteristics which would be attributed to such kinds—among them the novel.

In search of our new matrix, we turned to classical rhetoric because rhetorical criticism, like the art of rhetoric, takes its start from audiences and internalizes the perspectives of divergent audiences to differentiate kinds of arguments, their meanings, intentionalities, and subject matters. Aristotle established the language of the art of rhetoric, which he distinguished as a universal art applicable to all subject matters, from the methods of scientific argument adapted to particular matters, theoretic, practical or poetic; and he treated rhetorical arguments in terms of places rather than contents. We found in Aristotle our matrix of intentionality because the *kinds* of speeches he identified—argument qua structured *whole* so to speak—are distinguished by one-term commonplaces taken from the common place of "time": *deliberative* arguments are oriented to the *future, forensic* to the *past, epideictic* to the *present; dialectical* arguments, counterparts of the rhetorical, are not time-determined at all, ergo we called them *timeless.* With respect to time this matrix is exhaustive and meets our needs. After exploring the characteristics that distinguish these kinds from one another, we discovered that the *epideictic* kind elicited a judgment from its audience radically different from that of the others. Forensic, deliberative, and dialectical arguments are judged with respect to what they are about; epideictic alone elicits, Aristotle tells us, a judgment of the skill of the speaker. We determined, then, that when questions are to be asked of a text relating to its characteristics as an instance of discourse rather than as communicative of truths of one kind or another, the text will be called a novel.

However, although Aristotle provided the exhaustive matrix we required, he did not provide the philosophic or intellectual validation for treating any named text as any one of the four rhetorical kinds. We turned then to Cicero, who generalized the uses of places to apply to all arguments or discourse. For Cicero, rhetoric as an art, a way of inventing arguments, was broadened to a universal method of discovering truths as well. Instead of distinguishing the art of rhetoric from scientific methods, he made rhetoric *the* method for all purposes, and instead distinguished general philosophic questions from practical, particular questions. Rhetoric as art or method employs *places;* when the uses of places are generalized to become fictive, made arguments, the substantive methods of sciences and the general questions of philosophy are particularized to the arguments of *texts* in which they are stated and interpreted. With Cicero, then, we validate our assimilation of the universe as a whole into the universe of discourse. Second, since Cicero removed the fixities of the three kinds of rhetoric and of dialectic, the methods of all four are identical and can be applied whether one is addressing an event in the past in judicial rhetoric, the future in deliberative, a general question for all time in dialectic, or the present in demonstrative. Thus, Cicero provides for us the methodological structure that permits us a range of free intentionality in giving us a world composed of named texts and a set of questions or single-term places, applicable to past, present, or future or to the timeless.

Aristotle gave us epideictic (or Cicero's demonstrative) rhetoric as the kind which is judged in terms of its own excellence as presentation, and Cicero gave us the freedom to treat any named text as a novel. It is worth remarking here that the novel as epideictic, the rhetorical modality of the present tense, is confirmed in our tradition, indeed our habit, of recounting the "story line" of any literary work in a historical present tense. We recognize that what is happening is always happening now. Finally, Cicero's four issues, the four one-term commonplaces applicable to all kinds of argument: the *conjectural*, the *definitive*, the *qualitative*, and the *translative*; these provided the places that would permit us to organize four kinds of novels, four genres, each of which internalizes the characteristics attributed to each kind of rhetoric, as the three kinds of rhetoric and dialectic each internalizes the characteristics attributed to each of the four modes of argument, which, in turn, correspond to the four kinds of literary criticism.

In chapter 5, the last chapter of part 1 of this essay, we turned to the final problem attendant on the invention of that complex argument we shall call rhetorical criticism: the making of discursive wholes. Making a discursive whole is something like changing a process into an entity, turning the temporal into the spatial—but only something like. Discourse is temporal, and a discursive whole is never *experienced* simultaneously in all its parts; but we can find a way analytically of specifying parts and discriminating a whole to be marked off as separate and distinct from any other instances of discourse. In order to do so we borrowed the boundaries Aristotle offered for identifying temporal wholes—beginning, middle, and end—and used them as commonplaces to make the wholes we would call novels. Why call them commonplaces? Because we used them not as terms of fixed meaning, designating substantive beginnings, middles, and ends, but rather as terms to enable us flexibly to invent four kinds of temporal whole, four *genres* of the novel.

Taking Cicero's four issues to enrich and illuminate the characteristics we attributed to each, and to name each genre, we discriminated first of all the conjectural novel, organized in terms of *beginning* and therefore to be characterized as generated and continuing in the arbitrary, unconditioned spontaneity of beginnings prior to which there is nothing. The conjectural issue, which gives it its name, is the issue that initiates communicative interchange, that asks whether anything has been, is being, or will be said or done. The conjectural novel is the novel of style and manners because it exists by virtue of an agent's inventiveness and communicates, as does an epideictic speech in Aristotle, itself as object to be appreciated. Its values, which it displays, are the values of discourse qua discourse.

The definitive novel is organized in terms of *beginning, middle,* and *end.* It is a composite of simple elements, full of beginnings, middles, and ends, and giving us a picture of the nature of the universe as it is, i.e., full of beginnings, middles, and ends. It can be seen as expanded to ultimate inclusiveness or contracted to *this* novel; but what gives it its coherence *in principle* is that potentially expandable inclusiveness. This is the novel which is a sequence of natural events, expandable at either terminus; the definitive novel of sequence which defines the universe qua natural.

The qualitative novel, organized in terms of *end,* is obviously a whole prior to its parts, logically, since in discourse the whole is reached at the end, and if end as such organizes the whole, end is logically prior, and the ordering is of parts as "actions-leading-up-to." Beginning is here defined in terms of end and no longer seen as spontaneous or arbitrary. Because end qualifies all the rest, the novel is experienced as actions leading to it, and we call it a qualitative novel of action.

The translative novel, organized in terms of *middle,* is perceived in terms of being, of an englobing, abiding presentness without beginning or end. Because that independence of boundary, of beginning or end, organizes the novel, its unity and coherence are seen as having been translated from the intelligibility of the universe to this one embodied instance of that intelligibility. The quantitative beginning and end of a novel so organized are given meaning as embodiments of the same principle of intelligibility. The structure is thus an intellectual structure and we call this the translative novel of ideas.

As we would expect in a rhetorical method, the means of operation are places. Of course, in a literal sense any novel must have a beginning, middle, and end in order to be recognized and experienced as a separate whole. We have used those boundaries as commonplaces in order to create genres organized in characteristically varied ways. Again, our matrix of commonplaces is exhaustive of ways of organizing discursive wholes in terms of boundaries. We begin to give content to the wholes organized when we designate a named text as a novel and proceed to organize it according to one of the terms of the matrix. We showed how it could be done using several named texts traditionally designated as novels, and emphasized the fact that any text organized as one of the genres could be organized as one of the others. Once the wholes are made, finally, they can be interpreted according to any or all of the four modes of argument, and the connections among variables characteristic of each mode will be validated by the principle of organization just as the variables of the organized whole will be particularized by the mode in which it is read or interpreted.

The final phase of this inquiry concerned the use of the method developed for the purpose for which it was developed: making particular wholes, novels, and interpreting them—by means of rhetorical criticism. Certainly what is implied in that statement is, in a sense, true. Part 1 was concerned with rhetorical criticism as theory. Part 2 would be concerned with the practice of rhetorical criticism. And yet such a formulation is misleading because, as this essay has made apparent, there is no genuine diremption in rhetoric between theory and practice. Throughout the first part of this essay it has been necessary to argue the case for the universality of fictive argument, for the relation between rhetorical arguments and the critical arts of grammar, poetic and dialectic, for the nature of genres, and so on, by showing them. It was necessary to explain what rhetoric does by doing what rhetoric does. With that granted, it can be said that the first part of the analysis is concerned with the *formation* of rhetorical literary criticism and the concomitant isolation of genres and of the novel as a genre. The second part is concerned with the *practice* of rhetorical literary criticism and the concomitant invention of short stories and novels and the discovery of their characteristic properties. Rhetorical theory is a mode of rhetorical practice; the two may be discriminated only in particular instances of application.

In part 1 we explored the continually varied themes, and the tropes or figures of words, things, thoughts, and actions that compose the universe and the universe of discourse. We examined topics of invention and invented the genres of discourse and of the novel, itself an invented genre of discourse. In part 2 we gathered together these devices of rhetorical criticism and brought them to bear upon particular named texts. There we tried to *do* rhetorical criticism.

We began with the conjectural novel of style and manners, the "novelist's novel," and the definitive novel of sequence, both of which suggest pluralities formally—of continuations in the case of the former, of the three commonplaces (beginning, middle, and end) in the latter. We chose first to organize Günter Grass's *Dog Years* as a conjectural novel; then we offered separate readings of it in all four modes of argument, showing how the spontaneous organizing principle of beginning gives its own special meaning to each of those four readings, meanings that would have differed had we chosen to organize *Dog Years* as any of the other three genres. We focused on multiple narrators as central and showed how their spontaneously generated accounts give three different descriptions of overlapping events. Our organization threw into prominence perspective and the genius of invention.

John Fowles's *The French Lieutenant's Woman* was organized as a definitive novel of events and consequences, and we emphasized three differing narrative accounts achieved by a single narrator, not in terms of spontaneity at all but as a mode of accommodating the multiple contingencies and necessities that are part of the nature of the world. The contingent and necessary elements that compose the world of the definitive novel validated the four separate arguments used to interpret it, and permitted us to discover significant meaning in a twentieth-century narrator creating a nineteenth-century world, meaning rooted in a conception of natural continuity that is brought to light in a definitive organization governed by an indefinitely expandable beginning, middle, and end.

In chapter 7 we turned to the qualitative novel of action and civility and used the principle of end to organize Robert Coover's *The Origin of the Brunists*. In this case we chose to take very seriously the title of the named text, and we made the interesting problem of an end—the Brunists as identifiable civility—our point of departure. What actions could be traced to lead up to that end? In fact we found multiple actions in organizing the novel; when we interpreted it in four modes, the interrelation between the organizing qualitative principle and each thematic account gave us a separate argument by means of which to explicate the origin of the Brunists.

In chapter 8 we turned, finally, to the translative novel of ideas and feelings, and organized one named text which could not be pointed to; rather, we not only made the text but named it as well, using a number of named instances of discourse for our purpose. No doubt that formulation strikes the reader as awkward; yet I trust he will be accustomed to such awkwardnesses at this point and will recognize them as my effort to reaffirm once more the commitment of this essay to a rhetorical stance that denies external entities having a fixed nature prior to being constituted as wholes and then interpreted and *given* meaning (i.e., a nature not seen as fixed, one hopes). Having illustrated the process of organizing a text, it seemed useful to conclude by showing a technique for using the translative organization to do comparative analysis, which is in itself a rhetorical enterprise, patently external to any given text and relevant only with respect to experience.

We chose the named texts of a single author, Flannery O'Connor, to create the least chaotic, the most easily encompassable discursive *place* for the exercise. We noted that a plurality of instances is required to make a context—else why compare at all?—and chose the smallest number, two. We made a translative whole of the two named texts, then made a third to relate to the named whole, "The World of Flannery O'Connor," which we had organized as context. Our task was to explore the way in which comparative analysis illuminates texts constituted and then related to one another, and permits us to evaluate them in light of that relation. We emerged with an exposition of multiple ideas interrelated in a context unified by the principle of middle, a structure of ideas expressing the intelligible structure of the universe.

In all of part 2 we have tried to show, as we had tried to tell in part 1, that the invented world of the conjectural novel is also a discovered, explicated, and evaluated world; that the discovered natural world of the definitive novel is also invented, explicated, and evaluated, and so on. Commonplaces like invention, discovery, explication, and evaluation are empty variables; depending upon our application of them, they take on meaning. But, indeed, they do not need to *mean*, but only to *be* an inexhaustible resource by means of which, in the practice of rhetorical criticism, we may give meaning to the inexhaustible variety of discourse.

NOTES

Chapter One

1. See Harry Levin, *James Joyce: A Critical Introduction* (Norfolk, Conn.: New Directions Books, 1941), pp. 18–20, 139.

2. (New York: Viking Press, 1956).

3. Many critics have commented on this aspect of twentieth-century fiction. Two critics have discussed it at great length. Cf., Wayne Booth, *The Rhetoric of Fiction* (Chicago: University of Chicago Press, 1961), Part 3, "Impersonal Narration," and Alan Friedman, *The Turn of the Novel* (New York: Oxford University Press, 1966).

4. Ian Watt, *The Rise of the Novel: Studies in Defoe, Richardson and Fielding* (London: Chatto and Windus, 1957), p. 134.

5. Dorothy Van Ghent, *The English Novel: Form and Function* (New York: Harper and Bros., Harper Torchbooks, 1953), p. 43.

6. *Republic* 10.607.

7. *Poetics*. They are, of course, not irrelevant in the context of the *Politics*.

8. Ibid. 4.1448b 5–20.

9. *Rhetoric* 1.2.1355b 26–36.

10. *Poetics* 1.1447a 15–30; 1447b 1–30.

11. Tzvetan Todorov, "Structural Analysis of Narrative," trans. Arnold Weinstein, *Novel* 3 (Fall 1969): 70–71.

12. Northrop Frye, *Anatomy of Criticism* (New York: Atheneum, 1968).

13. That rhetorical questions tend to be irrelevant in this kind of criticism is evidenced in Frye's rejection of judgment as part of the critical enterprise (p. 20). The relation of literature to the external world emerges in the interest in archetypes which are sometimes viewed as wider in scope than the realm of the literary.

14. *Poetics* 1.1447a 15–30; 1447b 1–30.

15. David Lodge, "Towards a Poetics of Fiction: An Approach through Language," *Novel* 1 (Winter 1968): 166.

16. David Lodge, *Language of Fiction: Essays in Criticism and Verbal Analysis of the English Novel* (London: Routledge and Kegan Paul, 1966), pp. 3–6.

17. Malcolm Bradbury, "Towards a Poetics of Fiction: An Approach through Structure," *Novel* 1 (Fall 1967): 52.

18. William K. Wimsatt, Jr., and Cleanth Brooks, *Literary Criticism: A Short History* (New York: Random House, Vintage Books, 1967), pp. 747–48.

19. I am convinced that Lodge is right, but not because Aristotle's philosophical assumptions have been undermined; at most they have gone out of fashion.

20. For the following discussion on language in Aristotle I have relied extensively on Richard McKeon, "Aristotle's Conception of Language and the Arts of Language," in *Critics and Criticism,* ed. R. S. Crane (Chicago: University of Chicago Press, 1952), pp. 174–231.

241

21. Ibid., p. 178.

22. R. S. Crane, "The Concept of Plot and the Plot of *Tom Jones*," in *Critics and Criticism*, pp. 616–47.

23. In the criticism of prose fiction there are two studies worth mentioning. J. Arthur Honeywell, "An Inquiry into the Nature of Plot in the Twentieth Century Novel" (Ph.D. dissertation, University of Chicago, 1963), and Paul Goodman, *The Structure of Literature* (Chicago: University of Chicago Press, 1954). Goodman's study comes closer to pure structural analysis than anything else I have read in criticism.

24. It seems to me that it would be almost impossible to produce an Aristotelian poetics at the present time even if Aristotle's problematic method were used instead of the topical, rhetorical method that Crane used. The prevalent philosophical orientation is toward an investigation of language and action, whereas Aristotle lived in a world of things, natural and artificial. A distinction between art and nature leads to the conclusion that artificial objects are imitations of nature, and this must be so in some sense for chairs as well as tragedies. That a modern critic simply doesn't think in terms of this distinction leads Crane to interpret the *Poetics* as dealing only with literary works that are imitations as opposed to works that are didactic, and none of his followers seems to have questioned it. A full exploration of the critical consequences of this distinction would take me further afield than the scope of this discussion warrants. However, it seems to me worth noting that one result of the mimetic-didactic distinction is that it seemed to lead Crane to feel that it is somehow wrong to examine the ideational structure of works he labeled mimetic. See R. S. Crane, *The Languages of Criticism and the Structure of Poetry* (Toronto: University of Toronto Press, 1953), p. 190.

25. Poetic has no conceptual apparatus for making comparative studies and evaluations; the beauties of apples and pears are incommensurate. But all literary works have ideas, and these are comparable. But we have had no *systematic* means of studying the structure of ideas in a single work. As a result, critics make comparisons anyway, and we are blessed with "great traditions" from which great works are excluded or we find ourselves back in the raft with Huck, honey, courtesy of extraliterary purveyors of useful criteria.

26. I. A. Richards, *Principles of Literary Criticism* (New York: Harcourt, Brace and World, [1925], especially chapter 13, for example.

27. Ernest Jones, *Hamlet and Oedipus: A Classic Study in the Psychoanalysis of Literature* (Garden City, New York: Doubleday and Co., Doubleday Anchor Books, 1954).

28. Kenneth Burke, *The Philosophy of Literary Form: Studies in Symbolic Action* 2d ed., rev. (New York: Random House, Vintage Books, 1957), pp. 3ff.

29. Arnold Kettle, *An Introduction to the English Novel*, 2 vols. (New York: Harper and Row, Harper Torchbooks, 1960).

30. In *The Rise of the Novel*.

31. *Rhetoric* 1.1.1354a 11–19. Of course Aristotle will deal with the matters treated by the handbooks on 'Arts of Speaking' as well.

32. *Rhetoric* 1.3.1358b 1–5. There has been some confusion about Aristotle's conception of epideictic oratory, the assumption being that the audience decides with respect to values: Is this kind of person or action good or bad, noble or base? But this is clearly not the case and seems so only by analogy to political and forensic oratory, in both of which a decision must be made concerning *what the speech is about.* The decision will depend on how persuasive the orator is, and thus his skill is relevant, but the decision involves action in a legislature or a courtroom. Epideictic, on this model, evokes a judgment about values. However, the text clearly distinguishes epideictic as evoking a judgment of the orator's skill, i.e., How good is the speech itself qua speech? This should not be surprising; what is surprising is that, the fact that the epideictic audience *alone* is referred to as "observers" rather than judges is overlooked. For Aristotle, we do not argue about ends; we discover what they must be in an appropriate science. Values are ends (and belong to

the *Ethics* and *Politics* as subject matter) and as such not debatable, not plausibly either this or that. For Aristotle we debate only about means. Values are implicit in all three kinds of rhetoric; but the legislator does not debate about what is desirable, only about how to achieve what everyone agrees is desirable, i.e., how to *act* in the future. The court doesn't debate on the desirability of a crime, only whether it was committed in the past. Epideictic, in displaying values in the present, cannot be evoking a judgment as to whether they are in fact values—not for Aristotle. Consequently, display oratory, eulogies and so on, are simply to be observed and enjoyed as more or less skillful performances.

Epideictic took on its characteristic pronouncements on values (as did the other two kinds of rhetoric) only after Cicero gave rhetoric a philosophic function by seeking to unite eloquence with wisdom.

33. See Richard McKeon, "Discourse, Demonstration, Verification, and Justification," *Entretiens de l'Institut International de Philosophie Liège, Septembre, 1967* (Louvain: Editions Nuwelaerts), pp. 37–55. Also, Richard McKeon, "The New Rhetoric as An Architectonic Art," *Center Magazine* 13 (March 1980): 41–53.

34. *Rhetoric* 2.1.1378a20–11.1388b30.

35. Dickens's *Nicholas Nickleby*, which attacked the Yorkshire schools, is a famous example, as is Mrs. Stowe's *Uncle Tom's Cabin*, of course.

36. I think it is worth recalling here that "going outside the work" has always been a thorny question in literary criticism. "Neo-Aristotelian" critics will look for documentary evidence to support a reading because they are especially concerned with an author's intention. See R. S. Crane, "The Houyhnhnms, the Yahoos, and the History of Ideas," in *The Idea of the Humanities and Other Essays Critical and Historical* (Chicago: University of Chicago Press, 1967), 2: 261–82. They will do this, however, only when there is no other way of making that intention clear from internal evidence. On the other hand, Kenneth Burke, interested in the work as expressive, sees no reason for eschewing any information that will help to illuminate it. See Burke, "The Problem of the Intrinsic (as reflected in the Neo-Aristotelian School)," in *A Grammar of Motives* (Englewood Cliffs, N.J.: Prentice-Hall, 1945), pp. 465–84. It seems to me, however, that Wayne Booth's approach was quite proper for his purposes. The only relevant author in a novel qua communicative structure is the author as he appears in the novel.

37. *Anatomy of Criticism*, pp. 303–14.

38. Sheldon Sacks, *Fiction and the Shape of Belief: A Study of Henry Fielding with Glances at Swift, Johnson and Richardson* (Berkeley: University of California Press, 1967), pp. 1–69.

39. Robert Scholes and Robert Kellogg, *The Nature of Narrative* (New York: Oxford University Press, 1966), p. 276.

40. Todorov, Frye, Lodge, Jones.

41. See *Philosophy of Literary Form*, pp. 16–31, for example.

42. Except for individual essays, no major work of Burke's is confined to a single literary genre or even to "imaginative" literature alone.

43. For example: "Could I reasonably expect Faulkner, say, or Joyce, to recognize my natural objects for what they *really* are, if I simply presented a fictional world to them with no clues as to how I viewed that world?" (*Rhetoric of Fiction*, p. 111. Italics in text.)

44. Ibid., p. 112. Italics mine.

45. Jean-Paul Sartre and Gabriel Marcel are two prominent examples.

Chapter Two

1. Jerome W. Archer and Joseph Schwartz, *A Reader for Writers: A Critical Anthology of Prose Readings*, 3d ed. (New York: McGraw-Hill, 1971), p. xv. Note the phrase "major forms"; it is curious, since formal systems can be made exhaustive, one of their chief attractions for us in the muddles we need them to help us cope with.

2. Cleanth Brooks and Robert Penn Warren, *Modern Rhetoric*, 2d ed. (New York: Harcourt, Brace and Co., 1958), pp. 38–39.

3. Robert W. Daniel, *A Contemporary Rhetoric* (Boston: Little, Brown and Co., 1967), p. 166.

4. New York: Simon and Schuster, 1963.

5. New York: Charles Scribner's Sons, 1960.

6. Trans. Crawley, with an Introduction by John H. Finley, Jr. (New York: Random House, Modern Library College Editions, 1951), p. 15.

7. This, it seems to me, is a good example of the way circumstance alters a structure of argument. We cannot help seeing the further implications of the argument whether or not the author could have seen them. We can see the implications of his text as not, in fact, tragic at all. Of course this is only one way of reading it in the altered circumstances.

8. *International Encyclopedia of Unified Science,* vol. 2, no. 2, 2d ed., enl. (Chicago: University of Chicago Press, 1970).

9. New York: Harcourt, Brace and World, A Harvest Book, 1970.

10. See Kuhn's discussion of why Newton's Laws cannot really be said to be "derived" from Einsteinian concepts, *Structure of Scientific Revolutions,* pp. 101–2.

11. Chicago: Swallow Press, 1927.

12. Aristotle, *Rhetoric* 1.2.1355b 37–44; 1357a 5–7.

13. New York: Random House, Vintage Books, 1963.

14. New York: Macmillan Co., 1962.

Chapter Three

1. New York: Harcourt, Brace and World, A Harvest Book, 1956 (first published 1929).

2. Frye considers genre theory rhetorical because "the basis of generic distinctions in literature appears to be the radical of presentation . . . determined by the conditions established between the poet and his public" (pp. 246–47). It is also worth noting here that rhetoric means ornamental language to Frye as it does to the grammatical critics I cited earlier. Either it is ornament for its own sake or the ornament is used to "reinforce the power of argument." That seems to be the sense in which rhetoric is an art of persuasion for Northrop Frye (see pp. 244–45).

3. Lodge, *Language of Fiction,* p. 86. Here Lodge is disagreeing with David Daiches about Virginia Woolf; he cites David Daiches, *Virginia Woolf* (1945), pp. 64–65 and 71–72. He believes that what Daiches sees is there, but for him, unlike Daiches, what's there isn't "good." Earlier he says that the value of tracing a "linguistic thread" "depends entirely upon whether it is a useful path, which conforms to the overall shape of the terrain, and affords the best view of it on all sides" (p. 79). Here and throughout he implies the possibility of multiple critical interpretations of a work, but he is very uncomfortable about it, it seems to me.

4. See R. S. Crane, *The Languages of Criticism and the Structure of Poetry,* pp. 166–67, and 182, for example.

5. I am calling attention here to the table of contents, which indicates a division into four kinds of criticism. I say "kinds of" advisedly. It becomes clear, of course, that archetypal criticism is the most important in what is a hierarchy rather than a pluralism of equals. In any case, rhetoric is one of the kinds; see Frye, chapter 3, n. 3 for an explanation of his reasons.

6. The final lecture in *The Languages of Criticism,* "Toward a More Adequate Criticism of Poetic Structure," pp. 140ff., discusses at length the superior attributes of a modified Aristotelian approach.

7. *Anatomy of Criticism,* p. 341.

8. Alan Friedman, *The Turn of the Novel: The Transition to Modern Fiction* (New York: Oxford University Press, 1970).

9. The eighth volume of the Pelican series on the history of England is entitled *England in the Nineteenth Century* with the addition in parenthesis of the dates (1815–1914); the reason seems obvious. Max Beloff discusses the twin horns of the dilemma of period-

theme as approaches to history in *The Age of Absolutism: 1660–1815* (New York: Harper and Row, Harper Torchbooks, 1962), pp. 11–12. Cf. J. H. Hexter, *Reappraisals in History* (New York: Harper and Row, Harper Torchbooks, 1963), chapters 2 and 8.

10. Kuhn, *Structure of Scientific Revolutions*, pp. 50–51, 92–93. An expository history would overlook the detail concerning the separation of "sciences" and stress the overall development of SCIENCE; either history can be quite validly derived from Kuhn's book.

11. See, for example, S. M. Scott, "Pride, Prejudice and Property," *Michigan Alumni Quarterly Review* 57 (1951): 172–99; D. W. Harding, "Regulated Hatred: An Aspect of the Work of Jane Austen," *Scrutiny* 8 (1940): 346–62; Samuel Kliger, "Jane Austen's *Pride and Prejudice* in the Eighteenth Century Mode," *University of Toronto Quarterly* 16 (1947): 357–70.

12. See Imre Lakatos and Alan Musgrave, eds., *Criticism and the Growth of Knowledge: Proceedings of the International Colloquium in the Philosophy of Science, London, 1965*, vol. 4 (Cambridge: Cambridge University Press, 1970). The papers in this volume offer a wide range of responses to Kuhn's book.

13. Joseph Frank, "Spatial Form in Modern Literature," in *Criticism: The Foundations of Modern Literary Judgement*, ed. Mark Schorer, Josephine Miles, and Gordon McKenzie (New York: Harcourt, Brace and Co., 1948), pp. 379–92.

14. See commonplaces of taste in *Kant's Critique of Judgement*, trans. J. H. Bernard (London: Macmillan and Co., 1914), pp. 230–31.

15. Archer and Schwartz, *A Reader for Writers*, p. 40.

Chapter Four

1. Frank Kermode, *The Sense of an Ending: Studies in the Theory of Fiction* (New York: Oxford University Press, 1967), p. 64.

2. Jorge Luis Borges, "Pierre Menard, Author of the Quixote," trans. J.E.I. [James E. Irby], in *Labyrinths: Selected Stories and Other Writings*, ed. Donald A. Yates and James E. Irby, with a preface by André Maurois (New York: New Directions Publishing Co., 1964).

3. For example, in Robert Penn Warren and Albert Erskine, eds., *Short Story Masterpieces* (New York: Dell Publishing Co., A Laurel Edition, 1954), pp. 538–42.

4. This is not to dismiss library classification systems out of hand. They are an eloquent, albeit oblique, testimony to the ways in which "audience" has persistently designated certain particular named texts. They indicate at least how the reading audience in general has classified such texts in a given culture; we shall see presently that more specialized audiences often ignore such designations from time to time. We need not be concerned, let me add, with the objection that librarians, not audiences, determine what books shall be preserved and what they shall be said to be; we can assume a reflexive interrelation between a culture and the human agents who are its products and its creators, and librarians and readers are subject to the same cultural influences.

5. Aristotle, *Rhetoric* 1.3.1358a 36–1358b 1–7.

6. Ibid., 2.22.1396b 5.

7. Ibid., 1.2.1357a 25–30.

8. A good test for the usefulness of a commonplace, I have found, is whether it can suggest replications of itself in terms of the most generalized pairs. For instance, time—timelessness or eternity: time is *many* (past, present, future), eternity is *one*. Time is like motion, eternity like rest. Time is thus becoming, eternity being. The problem is that some pairs of terms can't be sufficiently emptied of meaning, and thus they aren't really simply "places" for invention. On the other hand, the true empty places, like *one—many*, etc., are not always communicative for one's particular purposes. "Time" is useful in this inquiry because it gives the kinds of rhetoric an exhaustiveness we can experience, feel as exhaustive; *one* and *many*, applying to *one dialectic, many rhetorics*, would do as well technically, but it is a less emotionally persuasive topic. However, the ready transposition of time—eternity to many—one, which I was able to make, is the kind of operation that

reassures the rhetorical critic that his choice of commonplace is sound. Among other tests, it is a good one.

9. An excellent discussion of the relation between sciences and arts, and between rhetoric and dialectic in the context of the philosophy of Aristotle as a whole can be found in Richard McKeon, *Introduction to Aristotle*, 2d ed. rev. and enl. (Chicago: University of Chicago Press, 1973). See especially "General Introduction: 2. Science and Art in the Philosophy of Aristotle," pp. xvi–xxi.

10. Aristotle does use the term with respect to political oratory, although he names the "kind" political oratory. See, for example, *Rhetoric* 1.4.1359a 36.

11. Cicero, *Topica* 2.6.

12. Aristotle, *Rhetoric* 1.4.1359b 15.

13. Cicero, *De Inventione* 1.6.8.

14. Cicero, *Topica* 2.7.

15. Aristotle, *Rhetoric*, 1.1.1355b 15.

16. Cicero, *De Inventione* 1.6.8. Also see *Topica* 2.6.

17. McKeon, *Introduction to Aristotle*, p. xx.

18. It "embodies" those intentions accidentally—to use Aristotelian vocabulary—rather than essentially. Our knowledge of Disraeli's intentions is from a source external to the novel itself.

19. Robert Blake, *Disraeli* (New York: St. Martin's Press, 1967), pp. 193–94.

20. In the novel, Disraeli repeatedly refers to the rich and poor as "the two nations." See *Sybil* (London: Oxford University Press, 1926 [first published 1845]). Michael Harrington called the ninth chapter of *The Other America* (New York: Macmillan Co., 1962) "The Two Nations," and referred to Disraeli by name. Also see David Thomson, *England in the Nineteenth Century: 1815–1914*, The Pelican History of England (Harmondsworth, Middlesex, England: Penguin Books, 1950), pp. 38–39, where he quotes from the novel at length in order to explain the phenomenon of the "tommy-shop," what was called in the United States a company store. He cites the novel several times throughout.

Chapter Five

1. In *The English Novel*, pp. 125–38.

2. Günter Grass, *The Tin Drum*, trans. Ralph Manheim (New York: Random House, Vintage Books, 1962), pp. 17–18.

3. Jean-Paul Sartre, *The Reprieve*, trans. Eric Sutton (New York: Bantam Books, 1968).

4. James Joyce, *A Portrait of the Artist as a Young Man* (New York: Viking Press, 1964), p. 16.

5. Thomas Mann, "The Making of *The Magic Mountain*," in *The Magic Mountain*, trans. H. T. Lowe-Porter (New York: Alfred A. Knopf, 1952), pp. 720, 725.

6. *Classics of Modern Fiction: Ten Short Novels*, 2d ed., ed. Irving Howe (New York: Harcourt Brace Jovanovich, 1972), p. 339.

7. "The Making of *The Magic Mountain*," p. 722.

8. Nikos Kazantzakis, *The Greek Passion*, trans. Jonathan Griffin (New York: Simon and Schuster, 1954).

9. "Symbols, Myths, and Arguments," in *Symbols and Values (an Initial Study): Thirteenth Symposium on Science, Philosophy and Religion*, ed. Lyman Bryson et al. (New York: Harper and Bros., 1954), pp. 18–19.

10. *The Greek Passion*, pp. 9–10.

11. The mysterious power which makes coming too close to the "life" of the deity very dangerous in its consequences seems at odds with the benign aspects of Christianity. Of course Kazantzakis is by no means unambiguously orthodox in his use of Christian themes. There is an interesting parallel in Flannery O'Connor, whose Christianity was orthodox but not conventionally benign. See the discussion of "Parker's Back" in chapter 8 below.

12. Virginia Woolf, *Mrs. Dalloway* (London: Virginia and Leonard Woolf at Hogarth Press, 1925).

13. Erhard M. Friedrichsmeyer, "Aspects of Myth, Parody, and Obscenity in Grass' *Die Blechtrommel* and *Katz und Maus*," *The Germanic Review*, May 1965, pp. 241–43, citing Jung and Kerenyi, *Das göttliche Kind in mythologischer und psychologischer Beleuchtung* (Leipzig, 1940), pp. 67, 105, 110, 455.

14. Ibid., p. 244, discussing and citing Jung and Kerenyi, pp. 102–3, 109.

15. Let me repeat briefly the litany of my inquiry to forestall any misunderstanding. To point to a named text and say of it that "there is no communication," simply means it is being treated by some other mode of criticism than rhetoric. Qua communication we treat a text rhetorically as a structure of argument, which implies, given the nature of the commonplace, at least two possible opinions that might be attacked or defended. To say that a text is not a structure of communication is to say that one cannot discover the thought of the whole, or to deny that there is any. But that would be to treat a text as if it existed prior to being communicative, and it does not, obviously. Consequently, any text can be treated as communicative or in some other way; and as communicative, at least one of the four issues must apply.

Introduction to Part Two

1. Kenneth Burke, *A Grammar of Motives* (Englewood Cliffs, N.J.: Prentice-Hall, 1945), p. xv.

Chapter Six

1. In criticism not explicitly grounded in rhetorical theory, the "arbitrary," or the invention of the critic himself is brought in in other modes of expression. For example, R. S. Crane writes that there are "three independently variable factors which determine the character of any critical writing that goes beyond mere appreciation or the expression of emotional responses to literary works. Of these factors, *one is the critic himself*, as a man endowed with a certain set of interests, a certain intellectual capacity, a certain range of reading and information, a certain kind or degree of taste and sensibility" (*The Languages of Criticism*, p. 10; italics mine).

2. Günter Grass, *Dog Years*, trans. Ralph Manheim (Greenwich, Conn.: Fawcett Publications, 1965).

3. Needless to say, if we had organized the novel another way, we would interpret these passages differently, albeit in the mode of exposition.

4. John Fowles, *The French Lieutenant's Woman* (New York: New American Library, 1970).

5. Following Wayne Booth, we might call that agent the implied author. We are always interested in him because from his narrator we deduce our many versions of "the thought of the whole."

Chapter Seven

1. Robert Coover, *The Origin of the Brunists* (New York: G.P. Putnam's Sons, 1966). It won the William Faulkner Award for the best first novel of 1966; it was republished in 1978 as "A Richard Seaver Book," by the Viking Press in New York. All references are to the original, 1966 edition.

2. P. 391; italics in text.

3. P. 430; italics in text.

4. *A Portrait of the Artist*, p. 170.

5. Note that in a conjectural organization the explosion will look like the quintessential unconditioned, arbitrary beginning.

6. Pp. 139–40. Italics in text.

7. It is important to remember that no critical reading of a novel includes every detail;

each reading makes and highlights some particulars absent or slighted in other readings. However, every word of a text *can* be interpreted in a manner consistent with any thematic account of the text.

8. Note that in the narrative reading it is *lack of insight* which leads to his certainty that her "gonads" will help him communicate. Lack of insight is an incomplete discovery in a narrative reading, and it brings the agent's moral and intellectual shortcomings to attention. In the descriptive reading he is morally healthy to tell her the truth and emotionally healthy to try to win her and want to protect her from what he regards as dangerous folly. These are not separate and contradictory readings, although they are in a sense separate. They point rather to that ambiguity which is a mark of complexity in a novel and in the creation of its protagonists. The first (narrative) reading calls attention to his shock at her rejecting him out of hand. The second reading (descriptive) calls attention to his revulsion from subterfuge and to the fact that his love for her is more than simply physical.

9. That chastity is a value for Marcella is clear in the novel; indeed, her willingness to part with it is a measure of her deep feeling for Miller. However, the source of it as a value for her is never clearly indicated.

10. P. 431; italics mine.

11. Ibid.; italics in text.

12. Pp. 440–41; italics in text.

13. Pp. 435–36; italics in text.

14. Assimilation always means assimilation to one position in a dialectical sequence; but the mode of exposition is a rhetorical dialectic, and it accommodates multiple assimilations to multiple positions.

15. P. 430; italics in text.

16. It seems worth repeating here that "what is necessary" will be a function of the principle by means of which the text was organized, not the mode of discourse in which it is being read. Any descriptive reading will focus on the construction of natural "organisms"—individual persons, communities, the cosmos, etc. The elements out of which the organisms are constructed or for want of which they cannot be viably built, are construed in accordance with the genre by means of which the text as separate whole has been organized. As we have seen, in a qualitative novel action and civility provide what is "natural." For the detailed reading in the descriptive mode see earlier in this chapter.

17. P. 78; italics in text.

18. P. 98; italics and suspension points in text.

19. P. 107; italics in text.

20. P. 138; italics in text.

21. Pp. 201–2; italics in text.

22. P. 254; italics in text.

23. Miller's persistent wrongheadedness in attributing her devotion to the cult to a kind of curable naiveté seems less blind when we realize that he seems to be unaware of Marcella's long history of mystical experiences which have continued under Eleanor Norton's tutelage.

24. P. 390; italics in text. The words in roman type seem to serve two functions: Since the passage represents a kind of interior monolog—perhaps meant to be fully articulated, perhaps simply an impression of feeling—"God is here," etc., may be words spoken aloud. But these words in roman type do suggest, too, the external reality as opposed to Marcella's confused impressions. The reader knows that "it comes" refers to an automobile, whatever else it may mean in the economy of the novel and to Marcella herself. "God is here" may be taken as ironic or not—a question of interpretation—but it is certainly the case that the arrival of the automobile is in fact the arrival of the "ultimate" for Marcella. And "light," occurring twice, describes the reality of the scene externally as well as in Marcella's mind. Thus, the roman type, calling attention to itself, links Marcella's experience to the circumstances which precipitate and condition it. Coover uses every device available to him to create a remarkably subtle texture in this novel.

25. P. 332; italics in text. The circle is one of Eleanor Norton's occult symbols adopted by the group in addition, of course, to the cross.

26. See, for example, pp. 328–41, all of the seventh and last chapter of part 3; part 4, "The Mount," follows.

27. Pp. 239, 251, 350; italics in text. The suspension points with which each passage ends are also in the text.

Chapter Eight

1. See François Jost, *Introduction to Comparative Literature* (New York: Bobbs-Merrill Co., Pegasus, 1974). According to Jost, "Literary works should be studied together, whatever their national origins, as soon as they are ideationally or factually related, as soon as they belong to the same current or period of time, the same aesthetic category or genre, or as soon as they illustrate the same themes or motifs" (pp. 12–13). His series illustrates, of course, what can be meant by context.

2. See *The Rise of the Novel*. Watt's context for the rise of the novel is composed of social, religious, economic, psychological, and technological elements, all of which make possible the emergence of the novel as a major literary genre.

3. The context we assume and require for comparing stories by a single author is a whole called "The Works of . . ."

4. The first novel, *Wise Blood*, was first published in 1952, the second, *The Violent Bear It Away*, in 1960. The collection *A Good Man Is Hard to Find* appeared in 1955, and *Everything That Rises Must Converge* appeared posthumously in 1965. For references to *The Violent Bear It Away* I have used *Three by Flannery O'Connor* (New York: New American Library, 1962), which also contains *Wise Blood* and the stories collected in *A Good Man Is Hard to Find*.

5. Flannery O'Connor, *The Complete Stories* (New York: Farrar, Straus and Giroux, 1971).

6. See Robert Giroux's introduction to *The Complete Stories*, p. xvi, remarks attributed to Elizabeth Bishop.

7. The following six stories were submitted as an M.A. thesis: "The Geranium," "The Barber," "Wildcat," "The Crop," "The Turkey," "The Train." The last of these was among the four stories revised as part of *Wise Blood*; the other three were "The Peeler," "The Heart of the Park," and "Enoch and the Gorilla." "You Can't Be Any Poorer Than Dead" appeared as the first chapter of *The Violent Bear It Away*. Two previously unpublished stories, "The Partridge Festival," and "Why Do The Heathen Rage?" were written later than the first collection, but O'Connor did not include them among her choices for *Everything That Rises Must Converge*.

8. This story is part of *Everything That Rises Must Converge* and appears in *The Complete Stories*, pp. 445–82.

9. "The Violent Bear It Away," in *Three by Flannery O'Connor*, p. 305.

10. P. 442. It is worth recalling here that Tarwater's thoughts led to Jonah a little earlier. Now, amid burning shrubbery, the narrative voice alludes to Moses, of whom legend tells that when he was a small child Egyptian priests, wishing to test the intelligence of the Hebrew slave child adopted by Pharoah's daughter, lest he grow to be a dangerous adversary, offered him a plate of gold and one of hot coals. Naturally, the child was attracted to the shiny metal, but the Lord deflected his hand, he touched the coals and lifted the burned finger to his lips to cool it (the legend thus accounts for Moses' being "slow of speech," i.e., afflicted with an impediment). The priests decided that he was stupid and permitted him to live, one day to become the Lord's instrument. The burning coal that touched the lips of the prophet is referred to Tarwater's eyes; but the "burning" experience is archetypally prophetic in O'Connor.

11. P. 445. All the quotations which follow are from the same page and p. 446 until otherwise noted.

12. "The Lame Shall Enter First," in *The Complete Stories*, pp. 445–82. The passage quoted is found on page 445.

13. Ibid.; suspension points are in the text.

14. That she was aware of the parallels is not in dispute; she referred to Rufus Johnson as "one of Tarwater's terrible cousins" in a letter to John Hawkes. See Flannery O'Connor, *The Habit of Being*, Letters Edited and with an Introduction by Sally Fitzgerald (New York: Farrar, Straus, Giroux, 1979), p. 456. However, the hypothesis I will make, that the story was a reworking which implies an aim unachieved in the novel, cannot be documented in any materials now available. It goes without saying that such a working hypothesis is based on an acceptable notion of "unconscious intention" which doesn't require documentation in any case.

15. Johnson's sense of himself as under Satan's direction, so to speak, is a complication, of course, but not quite the same.

16. Of course the devil is implied in Tarwater's inner voice; however, the devil's existence and function as a matter of doctrine, as characterizing the relevant system of belief, emerge as prominent only in the short story.

17. And only in comparison does the additional irony emerge—that the criminal, "devil-possessed" Johnson kills only indirectly (if at all), whereas the "chosen" prophet, Tarwater, quite literally kills. And, too, it is Johnson's disinterest which points to Sheppard's guilt.

18. That the issue "lurks"—at the very least—in the novel is not surprising; O'Connor felt that it was "a matter of life and death." See Robert Giroux's introduction to *The Complete Stories*, p. xiii.

19. In Flannery O'Connor's work the experience which accompanies the intellectual and/or emotional recognition of the presence of God, or at least precedes it and makes it possible, is almost always physically or emotionally violent, and often involves behavior on the part of the protagonist which he himself perceives as unforgivable—behavior which makes him realize how desperately in need he is of a forgiveness which no one but God can give. In "Everything That Rises Must Converge," Julian publicly betrays and rejects his mother (like Sheppard's, Julian's are, from a secular point of view, good motives); Mr. Head betrays and rejects Nelson, his grandson, out of fear in "The Artificial Nigger." Sometimes the unforgivable behavior is simply a pattern of long standing, and the violence which precipitates insight is done to the protagonist as victim by someone else; this is closer to the structure of Sheppard's experience and is exemplified in "Revelation" by Mrs. Turpin. To be offered grace is profoundly disturbing, never warm, never "cozy." In O'Connor, God is, in the fullest sense of the word, awful.

20. I am convinced that "The Lame Shall Enter First," qua structure of ideas in a translative mode, is a structural improvement over *The Violent Bear It Away*; nevertheless, I think it can be cogently argued that the novel is often more moving, especially in some of its inside views of Rayber, and that the austere view of cosmic antecedent-consequent represented by Sheppard's conversion being too late to save Norton's life is almost unbearably brutal. It is certainly interesting to note that O'Connor herself did not like the story, and her reason seems to me wonderfully acute, for it hits precisely the impression the story conveys: "I don't know, don't sympathize, don't like Mr. Sheppard in the way that I know and like most of my other characters." Letter to Cecil Dawkins, 6 September 1962, in *Habit of Being*, p. 491. I would add, however, that whether or not one feels that the story works, the translative analysis does offer insight into a "structural motive" for the reworking and thereby illuminates both story and novel.

21. "Parker's Back," in *The Complete Stories*, pp. 510–30.

22. An interesting resolution of this kind of problem can be found in William Faulkner's "Barn Burning," in which the poignant suffering of a poor, unlettered twelve-year-old boy is rendered by a complex narrative stance of highly selective omniscience, intensive interior monolog in both the child's langauge and indirect discourse in the narrator's,

and, finally, a good deal of commentary. In the commentary, Faulkner goes beyond what is usual by commenting on the future of the child's descendants. See in *Short Story Masterpieces*, ed. Robert Penn Warren and Albert Erskine (New York: Dell Publishing Company, 1954), pp. 162–82. O'Connor's technique is similar with the exception of allusions to a remote future. However, she does go beyond the conventional range of omniscience in another way that also calls attention to the narrator as shaping intelligence. In describing Parker's thoughts and behavior after an accident, the narrator adds, "If he had known how to cross himself he would have done it" ("Parker's Back," p. 520).

23. P. 520; italics mine.

24. P. 522; italics mine.

25. Pp. 529–30; italics in text.

26. A few brief examples should suffice: "The destiny of art in our time is to transmit from the realm of reason to the realm of feeling the truth." Tolstoy's notion of what constituted truth is obviously not at issue. The passage cited is only one of many in a work devoted to a dialectical theory of art in which cosmic truth is reflected in the individual work of art. See *What Is Art? and Essays on Art*, trans. Aylmer Maude (London: Oxford University Press, 1930), p. 288. Coleridge insisted that poetry was produced by the creative imagination of the poet, that faculty of mind which perceives the truth about the structure of the universe. Poems exist phenomenally and may or may not contain poetry; poetry is always a structure of truth. See *Biographia Literaria*, especially chapters 12, 13, and 14. Herbert Read said that "all art originates in an act of intuition or vision. But such *intuition* or vision must be identified with *knowledge*." He argued that there is a coherence of thought in the poet "which is ever in accord with the universal." See *Form in Modern Poetry* (New York: Sheed & Ward, 1933), pp. 39 and 78; italics in text. Finally, I would note Northrop Frye in *Anatomy of Criticism*. Frye views the realm of literature as independent, literary works as embodying the structure of a universe of discourse, an "order of words." However, his careful analysis of myth and archetype reveals that these are somehow archetypes not simply of a separate literary cosmos, but of fundamental human experience. They assimilate all of the universe to themselves in typical dialectical fashion.

27. One is reminded in this connection that the *truth* about Judas is forever shrouded in mystery.

28. I can imagine O'Connor pointing out that what I've called ambiguity can be called mystery, thus making a very different ball game. And of course I would agree. Dialectically mystery would be the word.

29. I am thinking here particularly of Jacques Derrida and deconstruction.

30. See above, n. 20.

31. Needless to say this is so because we have chosen to treat it under the head of epideictic as a novel. If we discuss it as a theological tract, we see it quite differently, and of course it can be treated as concrete perspectives on Catholic theology interpreting a world peopled by non-Catholics. And so on.

Chapter Nine

1. See Watt, *Rise of the Novel*, for example. For the purposes of this discussion I will limit myself to the novel in English.

2. See Woolf's "Modern Fiction," *The Common Reader* (New York: Harcourt, Brace & World, 1925; Vintage Book, 1953), pp. 150–58.

3. There are twenty essays in *Critics and Criticism*, some on theories of criticism, some the theoretical statements of their authors, and some on literary works. Of *all* of these only *one*, R. S. Crane's "The Concept of Plot and the Plot of *Tom Jones*," is at all concerned with prose fiction. If one considers major theoretical works and their authors, the result is the same (leaving aside a genuine maverick like Kenneth Burke, who seems to me to defy classification in any case): L. C. Knights and William Empson in Britain, and Cleanth

Brooks, Northrop Frye, John Crowe Ransom, R. P. Blackmur in the United States, have all devoted themselves to poetry and poets. Edmund Wilson's work on novels had no great theoretical significance, and F. R. Leavis in *The Great Tradition* (New York: New York University Press, 1967 [first published by Chatto & Windus, n.d.]), ignores Woolf, dismisses Joyce with something like contempt, and approves Lawrence only (not on grounds of form) but does not discuss him at length.

4. See *Biographia Literaria,* chapter 14. Specifically, here is the relevant passage: "A poem of any length neither can be, or ought to be, all poetry." *Selected Poetry and Prose of Coleridge,* ed. Donald A. Stauffer (New York: Random House, Modern Library College Editions, 1951), p. 268. Since Coleridge himself was clearly Richards's critical inspiration, the statement has great import for the neglect of prose fiction by the innovative twentieth-century critics.

INDEX OF TERMS AND CONCEPTS

INDEX OF AUTHORS AND TITLES

Index of Authors and Titles